D0202724

Willa Cather and France

Willa Cather and France

In Search of the Lost Language

Robert J. Nelson

University of Illinois Press
Urbana and Chicago

PS
3505
.A73
Z745
1988

© 1988 by the Board of Trustees of the University of Illinois
Manufactured in the United States of America
C 5 4 3 2 1

This book is printed on acid-free paper.

Library of Congress Cataloging-in-Publication Data

Nelson, Robert James, 1925–
    Willa Cather and France: in search of the lost language/Robert
J. Nelson.
      p. cm.
    Bibliography: p.
    Includes index.
    ISBN 0-252-01502-9 (alk. paper)
    1. Cather, Willa, 1873–1947—Knowledge—France.   2. Cather, Willa,
1873–1947—Knowledge—Language and languages.   3. France in
literature.   4. Language and languages in literature. I. Title.
PS3505.A87Z745 1988
813'.52—dc19   87-24484
                                                               CIP

For
Gerald and Stan,
My Hoosier Hermeneuts
in
"Things French"
and
"Things American"

Contents

Acknowledgments

I acknowledge with pleasure and gratitude colleagues and friends whose assistance and advice enabled me to complete this book.

The Members of the Research Board at the University of Illinois at Urbana provided funds in the academic year 1980–1981 for the appointment of a research assistant, Mr. Mark Fee, to help me in the early stages of my research. In the summer of 1981 the Board provided funds to attend a meeting at Red Cloud, Nebraska ("Willa Cather and Nebraska: A National Conference," June 14–20, 1981) at which I gathered much valuable information and established useful perspectives and designs of investigation. I am grateful to the members of the Research Board, to Mr. Fee, and to many "Catherians" at the conference for their contributions to my project. The University of Illinois also granted me a sabbatical leave of one semester, Fall 1982, in which I hoped to continue work on the book. However, I became seriously ill while working on the book during that period in the South of France. Knowing I would be unable to complete the book, I requested that the university place me on sick-leave for the period and reassign my leave to the Spring 1983 semester. It is, therefore, with special gratitude that I acknowledge the granting of this request by Professor Carolyn Burrell, Assistant Vice-Chancellor for Academic Affairs of the University of Illinois at Urbana.

I wish also to thank Gerald Weales of Philadelphia, Pennsylvania, who "read along" as I completed portions of this book and who sent me criticisms, suggestions for emphasis (as well as deemphasis), and additional bases of support including some texts of Cather and other sources inaccessible to me in the South of France. While researching and writing the book in that part of France at various times during the past two years, I also had the good fortune to meet often with Professor Michel Gervaud of the Université de Provence at Aix-en-Provence, a savant Catherian whose writings on the novelist, like his penetrating reflections on her in many conversations we had throughout the period, illuminated not only Cather's "French markings" but her "American markings" as well. Again, friends in England—especially Felicity Baker, Richard Klein, Godelieve Mercken-Spas, and Ann Wordsworth—also provided invaluable insights in person throughout my year of residence (1981–1982) as Visiting Professor at the University of Reading as well as in extensive correspondence while I was doing the research and some writing for the book in France (1982–1983 and summer 1984). Their friendship was as helpful as their incisive reflections on transatlantic literary and cultural relations, psychoanalysis, French literature, contemporary literary theory, and criticism. My colleagues, Professors Zohreh Sullivan and George Hendrick of the Department of English at the University of Illinois at Urbana, also read an earlier stage of this book, providing insight and encouragement which enabled me to arrive at final formulations I trust they will find as cogent as those they first read. My colleague, Professor Stanley Gray of the Department of French at the University of Illinois, read me at all stages of this project, providing both American and French insights without which the project could not have emerged in this form. I am also grateful to Professor Armine Mortimer of the Department of French at the University of Illinois for superb suggestions at various stages of the project. May all these readers of me reading Cather take pride only in what will be considered of value by the wider readership of the book.

I also gratefully acknowledge the indispensable assistance of Brenda Masters for having made typographic sense of a handwrought draft in which she often risked losing her own sense of language.

Other individuals have offered help of a nonprofessional and non-academic nature. The encouragement of my children, Andrew and Alexandra, of my son-in-law, William Chin, and of many friends in the United States, England, and France, particularly during my illness in Fall 1982 and Spring 1983, was a constant source of support. In this connection, I wish in particular to thank my neighbors in the Village de Joucas (Vaucluse), Oscar, Christel, and Pascal Klunder, for their unforgettable practical assistance to me during my illness and for their warm friendship and generosity throughout the year I lived in Joucas. Themselves immigrants in France, the Klunders are bilingual and bicultural "prisms of France" vividly signifying what Willa Cather so long remembered: "Vive la différence!"

Urbana, Illinois

A Note on Annotation

For economy of reference for quotation, I have used the following abbreviations of Cather's works *after my first* quotation with full title:

AB	*Alexander's Bridge*
CF	*Collected Fiction*
DCA	*Death Comes for the Archbishop*
HP	*Hard Punishments*
KA	*The Kingdom of Art*
LG	*Lucy Gayheart*
LL	*A Lost Lady*
MA	*My Ántonia*
MME	*My Mortal Enemy*
NF	*Not Under Forty*
OB	*"The Old Beauty" and Others*
OD	*Obscure Destinies*
OO	*One of Ours*
OP	*O Pioneers!*
PH	*The Professor's House*
SL	*The Song of the Lark*
SR	*Shadows on the Rock*
SSG	*Sapphira and the Slave Girl*
UV	*"Uncle Valentine" and Other Stories*
WP	*The World and the Parish*

Other texts are identified by author and title, or by either author or title depending on the logic of my sentence. In the case of two or more texts by the same author, annotation is by author and title (or by either author or title depending on the logic of my sentence) and pagination. The majority of my footnotes are for pagination in citation of works by Cather and others. However, in order to assist the reader I have appended a lower-case "e" to those notes which are extensions of my discourse or that of others cited at that point.

Full information on publication of all works cited is given in my bibliography. Scholars of Cather will note that I have not been able to cite two book-length studies of the novelist because their publication was projected beyond my completion of this book: Sharon O'Brien, *Willa Cather: The Emerging Voice* (New York: Oxford University Press, 1986) and Susan J. Rosowski, *The Voyage Perilous: The Romanticism of Willa Cather* (Lincoln: University of Nebraska Press, 1986). However, as the reader will see, I have cited a number of articles by each of these scholars, addressing mutual concerns, especially spirituality and sexuality in the fictions, and drawing out similarities and differences of interpretation between us on views which I presume more fully inform their recent books.

Willa Cather and France

1

Soundings

Cather and Language

One day in 1935, Edith Lewis recalls, while she and Willa Cather were on a visit to the Papal Palace at Avignon, alone except for a guide,

> . . . this young fellow suddenly stopped still in one of the rooms and began to sing, with a beautiful voice. It echoed down the corridors and under the ceilings like a great bell sounding—but sounding from some remote past; its vibrations seemed laden with the passions of another age—cruelties, splendours, *lost and unimaginable to us in our time.*
>
> I have sometimes thought Willa Cather wished to make her story like this song.[1]

The "song" that would have been Cather's "story" is *Hard Punishments,* her unfinished novel about two boys in late fourteenth-century Avignon when that southern French city, dear to the novelist since her youth, was the site of the "exiled Papacy." In the story as we know it from Lewis and from a four-page fragment of manuscript, one of the boys, André, is speechless, his tongue having been cut out in "hard punishment" for blasphemy. The other, Pierre, has lost the use of his hands for having been hung by the thumbs in "hard punishment" for petty thievery. However fragmentary our knowledge of the novel, we might speculate that, as in so much Cather fiction, the novelist's voice and hand would have gainsaid the handicaps of her heroes, restoring speech and song to André and dexterity to Pierre.

Certainly, in Cather the primacy of doing over talking (especially over talking-about-doing), of song over speech, and of the unwritten over the written is familiar to her readers. Throughout her canon, the vehicle of artistic, erotic and, occasionally, of political power is the voice, often as a musical instrument. One thinks of the great actress in "Peter" (her first story, 1892), the singer at the funeral in *O Pioneers!* (1913), the operatic heroine of *The Song of the Lark* (1916), the voice of the gardener in the cloister in *One of Ours* (1922), the singers of *Mignon* at the beginning of *The Professor's House* (1925), Valentine's friend, the voice-teacher, in "Uncle Valentine" (1925), the great Modjeska in *My Mortal Enemy* (1926), Father Joseph in *Death Comes for the Archbishop* (1927).[2e] One remembers as well that Dillon and Trueman of "Two Friends" (in *Obscure Destinies,* 1931), get along so well and so please the narrator who tells their sad story because, in good part, they talk so well together—until their breakup over the issue of Dillon's support of William Jennings Bryan. The Populist "windbag" talks too much and too well for the little-spoken Trueman; in fact, for the latter, Dillon begins too much to follow Bryan's suit.

Generally, in Cather fiction, the letter is an ever-present danger to the spirit. For her, as critic as well as creator, the letter must be ever guarded against. As she wrote in 1922, in one of her rare theoretical pronouncements: "Whatever is felt upon the page, without being specifically named there—that, one might say, is created. It is the inexplicable presence of the thing not named, of the overtones divined by the ear but not heard by it, the verbal mood, the emotional aura of the fact or the thing or the deed, that gives high quality to the novel or the drama, as well as to poetry itself."[3] With the exception of some of the early stories, *The Song of the Lark* and, to a lesser extent, *One of Ours* and *Sapphira and the Slave Girl,* all of Cather's fiction can be said to attempt to reflect this theoretical ideal. Cather's text is, by the author's own desire, a countertext if not an antitext. Paradoxically, for this great writer so vaunted for her style, language must not call attention to itself. For her, in terms of Richard Poirier's thesis in *A World Elsewhere,* the writer attains to the "elsewhere" she seeks not by "writing up" and thus transcending the intractabilities of "this world," the world of the story in the ordinary-language sense of the term, but by "writing down."[4e] Cather would have her reader be ever aware of the lost world that the fiction seeks to recapture; she would remove as much furniture as the very idea of textuality would allow. The relation between the said and the unsaid, between written and spoken language, between text and voice, is, for Cather, an instance of a prior debate between human language in any grammatical expression and pre-human or nonhuman "language." In this perspective, human language comports both spoken and written form (verbal, pictorial, runic, etc.) as well as musical expression (vocally rendered in song or written in notation) and plastic rendition (painting, sculpture, architecture). Generally, Cather resolves this debate in favor of the unsaid, spoken language, voice. These modes of expression enact for her, as best the said-the textual-the written in her own text can, what all of her fictions rehearse: the sense of worlds "lost and unimaginable to us in our time."

In light of this pattern, Cather may well be seen as a continuing if somewhat delayed moment of the "American Renaissance" as studied in John T. Irwin's *American Hieroglyphics: The Image of the Egyptian Hieroglyphics in the American Renaissance.*[5e] Irwin does not include Cather among the array of authors he studies in light of Champollion's decipherings: Emerson, Thoreau, Poe, Hawthorne, Melville, and, more briefly, Twain. The critic considers speech and writing not as oppositional but appositional under what he terms the "phonetic" as the concept of verbal language, whether spoken or written. This, in turn, Irwin sees as related to a concept with which it *is* in opposition: the "pictographic" of non-verbal images. Now, for the skeptical tradition which Cather, in her own transcendentalism, resists in her conception of literary art and language, there is no first and founding model or image or voice, no lost language susceptible of recapture. As skeptical thinkers from Democritus to Derrida maintain, there is no founding reality which we can recover through the institutions of human thought—philosophical, religious, scientific, artistic. Human language is not a pale or fallen evidence of a transcendent origin to which literary art can at best point us. In terms of Derrida's thought, on which Irwin very largely bases his interpretations, there is no "outside (of the) text" (*"hors texte"*) on which to base a phoneticization of the pictographic; there is only *text*—human language in whatever form—however inadequate and undependable it be.

Cather notwithstanding, of course. For her, the pictographic not only *is* paratextual, it is *primary*. When profound doubt about this primacy does affect her, her artistic tongue is not in her cheek to the extent of Melville's, for example. For her, intimations of an utter absence of the real are but themselves signifiers of the distance human language has travelled from that real, evidences of the obstacles we have, blindly and perhaps unavoidably, thrown before our own original and clear-sighted perceptivity. Indeed, as in the Catholic current of the Christian faith to which she converted as a mature woman (Episcopalianism) and which she illustrated in what many consider her finest novel, *Death Comes for the Archbishop,* signifiers of the absence of the real may be seen as quasi-sacramental evidences of the real. Yet, in still other fictions—*The Professor's House, My Mortal Enemy, Sapphira and the Slave Girl,* for example—there lingers that haunting suspicion of the fundamental Protestantism in which she had been raised. For that current of the Christian tradition God and the language He had given human beings to know Him and themselves in faultless existence may be more than "Hidden" and "Lost and Unimaginable" to us "in our times." At best, there may be no human way of knowing and communicating with Him and of recovering the language we have "lost" in losing Him; at worst, He may not be there at all. The Anselmic argument notwithstanding, the very idea of Him may be a figment of our imagination.

Yet, the Cather project is precisely to recuperate through the imagination the reality of the sacred and of the language spoken under its aegis. The world in which these twin realities prevail, Lewis's formulation reminds us, is not only "lost," but it is also "unimaginable" to the times in which she and her sexagenarian companion lived. Not to all who lived then, however. Cather believed and wrote as if *she* would imagine those realities through her art. In imagining them the novelist validates the figured over the configured, the seen over the said, the image over the idea. Believing like her famous professor, Napoleon Godfrey St. Peter of *The Professor's House,* that art and religion come down to the same thing, she sought to restore to us that prelapsarian moment of language in which signifier and signified were one. In that Edenic state, *seeing* is not only *believing,* but it is, as the common root (OE *secgan*) indicates, also *saying.*

As little saying as possible, of course, is Cather's view. For her saying, whether in print or speech, communicates, at best, only a hint of the lost, Edenic language in which seeing is not only believing but also knowing. Thus, as her famous formulation about the "novel *démeublé*" indicates, the "lost language" is neither script nor utterance; it is perception. The faculty of perception is the imagination, aided not by the intellect but by the senses, sight and sound in particular. The seen and the sung, as many readers of Cather have noted, are especially telling in her work. They are moving in both the emotional and kinetic senses, creating pictographs of vital movement. Yet, this doubly moving movement is linked to the sense of touch only distantly. Touch itself is too close, too intimate, not appropriately distanced for the novelist from the transcendent in whose name she prescribes and, in many cases, proscribes the destinies of her characters. This link between the transcendent and the lost language is, as I shall bring out in close consideration of her fictions, especially significant for understanding sexuality and spirituality in the Cather canon.

Cather and France

In a writer as prolific and as diverse as Cather in her themes and settings, the interpretive paradigm of language obviously bids to a too-far ranging, catalogic consideration of the canon in its entirety. Again, a narrowly focused consideration of the writer's ideas on language, culled from her fiction as well as from her theoretical writings, might just as obviously involve the misprision of reading her more as critic than as artist. To be sure, there is a critical intent in every literary work of art, as critics from Aristotle to Harold Bloom and artists from Aristophanes to André Gide have taught us. Cather notwithstanding once again: her own dismay with theory is legendary, its earliest evidence being her mocking student essay on *Hamlet* giving short shrift to "the critic . . . and the intellectual students of literature."[6] However, this very hostility to the "critic and the intellectual" is of a piece with the problematic of language, which I trace in this book. It thus compels any interpreter focused on the problem of language in her work to confront her ideas on language with her fictions taken on the holistic terms in which she offers them.

Yet, the concept of language itself—or more precisely, of languages in the "ordinary-language" sense—points to the manageable focus the critic can adopt in an effort to understand the problematic of language with which her fictions wrestle. Cather had a lifelong interest in certain languages and their cultures: English, Latin, German, Spanish, and French. Thus, Cather scholars have long noted that Latin culture in general and Spain and Spanish culture in the New World can be said to represent a confluence of her own Anglo-Saxon roots and Latin culture rather than an influence of the Latin on the Anglo-Saxon in her fiction. Again, in more formally critical terms, Bernice Slote has shown the strong influence of romanticism in its English and German as well as French expression on the novelist's art.[7] Yet, the import of French language and culture for her thought and art is, I believe, the most enduring. As I shall show, from her first story, "Peter" (1892) to her last published novel, *Sapphira and the Slave Girl* (1940), the French mark upon her work is persistent and profound. It has, as far as I know, also been treated rather sparingly in itself or incidentally in connection with other paradigms. Only Kates, in his essay on *Hard Punishments,* has attempted a broad overview of the hold of France on the writer, and I shall draw on Kates's sensitive essay at appropriate points in this book.

Here, I would stress even more than he that the hold of the French language and *la francité* (Frenchness or things French) is more powerful than that of the other foreign languages and cultures in her work. It is striking to note that two of her novels have specifically French locales: the second half of *One of Ours* (1922) is set in the France of World War I, and the entire *Shadows on the Rock* (1931) is set in the New France of the French colony at "Kébec" in the late seventeenth and early eighteenth centuries. As I have noted, her unfinished last novel, *Hard Punishments,* is also situated in France; and what many readers consider her finest novel, *Death Comes for the Archbishop* (1927), is the story of two French Jesuits, Father Jean-Marie Latour and Father Joseph Vaillant, in their nineteenth-century mission in the American Southwest. Thus, one-quarter of Cather's published novels have specific French foci, in the literal or ordinary-language sense of the term.

These "French" fictions of Willa Cather, except perhaps *Shadows on the Rock,* are not about their obvious French subjects alone; they are also about that subject for which she has long been consecrated as a major novelist: the American experience. On the other hand, this French-American valence, which in its doubleness evinces many of the ambivalences I shall trace in the following pages, characterizes several other novels and stories to a significant extent both literally and figuratively. Thus, in *The Professor's House,* Napoleon Godfrey St. Peter of French ancestry seems personally as enthralled with the France in which he had studied as a young man (and where he had met his American wife) as he is professionally with the Spain on whose conquistadores in the New World he has written an eight-volume study. Furthermore, in Cather's last published novel, *Sapphira and the Slave Girl* (1940), the French-American nexus underlies the tensions between the Sapphira of English and Episcopalian ancestry and her husband, Henry Colbert, of Belgian-francophone and fundamentalist-Protestant ancestry, who worries so about his "bad French blood." Even in *O Pioneers!* (1913), where the novelist has seen herself as "hitting the home pasture"[8e] of the American experience, the French-American valence plays an important and, in fact, ominous part. It is at the picnic in "French Town" that Emil and Marie show their passion for one another and it is upon hearing the singer at his French friend Amédée's funeral in the French Church that Emil commits himself to her with a touching recklessness whose issue will be the encounter with Marie at which her husband slays both of them. Finally, a French setting, the swirling river in which the hero of *Alexander's Bridge* (1911) drowns, locked in the grasp of French-Canadian construction workers, provides an even earlier instance of the French-American valence in its ominous expression within the Cather canon.

Perhaps in these first two novels the writer was becoming disenchanted with a France with which she had thought herself too long entranced. Cather's early enchantment is perhaps no more poignantly expressed than in the following passage from the 1902 journal of her trip to Europe:

> Out of every wandering in which people and places come and go in long successions, there is always one place remembered above the rest because there the external or internal conditions were such that they most nearly produced happiness. I am sure that one place will always be Lavandou.
>
> Nothing else in England or France has given me anything like this sense of immeasurable possession and immeasurable content. I am sure I do not know why a wretched little fishing village with

nothing but green pines and blue sea and sky of porcelain should mean more than a dozen places I have wanted to see all my life. No books have ever been written about Lavandou, no music or pictures ever came from her, but I know well enough that I shall yearn for it long after I have forgotten London and Paris. One cannot divine nor forecast the conditions that will make happiness; one only stumbles upon them by chance in a lucky hour at the world's end somewhere, and holds fast to the days as to fortune or fame.[9]

In spite of her great love of the English and of English culture, particularly the literature, Cather seems to have loved France and French culture far more in this first experience of the two countries. Her journal contrasts the two with a decided advantage to France. From its early entries recording the diarist's arrival, first in England, then in France, to the last before her departure home, English "grimness . . . and disfigurement" is pivoted against the "fire and fervor" of her fellow passengers returning to their French homeland. The latter's shoreline brings out in them this "fire and fervor," makes them "erect and animated, rhetorical and jubilant," and in the "bond of brotherhood" finds them voicing "ardent murmurings and exclamations of felicity." The writer was particularly taken with "the voice of a little boy, crying with small convulsions of excitement: 'Is it France?' as he sees for the first time his native land in which he had not been born."[10] To be sure, in the first image of England there had been the "pretty voice" of the English to gainsay the general impression of grimness and disfigurement.[11] Yet that "English virtue" seems as nothing to the "convulsions of excitement" in the voice of the little French boy who has at last "returned" in fact to his home in France and in the "musical" voices of the "very porters" and "street boys" of Dieppe.[12]

In view of the diarist's own enthusiasm in this and so many other entries in the French portion of the journal, one senses that Willa Cather, too, has come home to a country where she was not born but which she had long loved. Since her childhood reading of *The Count of Monte Cristo* by Dumas *père* she had been an enthusiast of French literature. Her commitment to French literature in college is reported by her college-friend, Helen Seibel, in terms strikingly important for the lifelong involvement both creatively and critically with France: "Cather amazed and sometimes abashed some of her professors by caring more fiercely about their subjects than they did. *Especially French. There seemed to be a natural affinity between her mind and French forms of art.* During our undergraduate years, she made it a loving duty to read every French literary masterpiece she could lay her hands on."[13] Cather's francophilia was and would remain somewhat unusual, however. It is more southern than northern, and it is considerably less centered on Paris than is often the case with foreigners drawn to France, particularly Americans of any generation. For the traveler of 1902 Paris emerges as a very city of the dead. It is the cemeteries of Paris to which she devotes some of the most searing pages of the journal, particularly "Père La Chaise" with its great monument to the dead (the vast sculptural relief of the Last Judgment by Paul Albert Bartholomé) and the tombs of great writers, especially of Balzac. The great French novelist's "monument is conspicuously ugly and deserted. He lives in every street and quarter; one sees his people everywhere. The city of grey stone and stucco, interlaced by its clear green river and planted with sycamores and poplars, dominated by Notre Dame and the Invalides and the columns of victory, is no more a real city than the great city of thought which Honoré de Balzac piled and heaped together and left, a ruin of chaotic magnificence, beside the Seine."[14] This grim evocation of the French capital will reverberate three decades later in the novelist's depiction of the capital of New France, the "fortified cliff that was 'Kébec' " in *Shadows on the Rock*.

For the Cather of 1902 through the Cather of *Hard Punishments,* if any city was the capital of France, it was Avignon. Even as the best of France for her was that "Country of Daudet"—Provence—provoking some of the writer's finest if most melancholic prose:

> After one spends a day or two among the Roman remains in the museums here, the portrait busts and mosaics and beautifully sculptured tombs, it seems almost as if there may be some truth in the old story that the women of Arles owe their beauty to the vows they used to make to their pagan Venus in secret, and that their children come into the world with the fine, clear profiles that are cut on the old Roman tombs. In Italy itself one could scarcely feel (more) the presence of Rome, of the empire, and all it meant, of its self-devouring and suicidal vastness, than here where the richest and proudest of the colonies flourished. One sunny afternoon we were examining some broken columns and fragments of capitals tumbled beside a wall of turf and overgrown with white candytuft which makes the air sweet and keeps the bees coming and going. The finest thing we found was a section of cornice, perhaps six feet long, with a great eagle upon it, a garland at its beak. The eagle, the one and only eagle, here in the far corner of the earth where the shadow of his great wings falls, the one bird more terrible in history than all the rest of brute creatures put together. Yet they say that even the most remote of his descendants are doomed, that all who echo his

tongue and bear his blood must perish, and these fine, subtle, sensitive, beauty-making Latin races are rotten at heart and must wither before the cold wind from the north, as their mothers did long ago. Whoever is a reasonable being must believe it, and whoever believes it must regret it. A life so picturesque, an art so rich and divine, an intelligence so keen and flexible—and yet one knows that this people face toward the setting, not the rising sun.[15]

The nostalgic overtones of this final French entry of the journal are proleptic of the themes and mood of the densely French connections she will make in the second decade of her turn to the novel as her major form of artistic expression, especially in *One of Ours* (1922) and *Shadows on the Rock* (1931). A more joyous mood does, of course, inform Cather's most famous novel with dense French markings of this decade, *Death Comes for the Archbishop* (1927). Yet, the serenities and triumphs of that work are achieved in a setting which deliberately flees and denies the "cold wind from the north." Archbishop Latour, like Cather a lover of Provence, would build his great Cathedral in Rhone-like rock with the aid of French stonecutters in conscious rejection of the sterile churches he has seen in the northern and northeastern United States. Indeed, though less imbued with French connections, earlier and later novels present the American experience in French connections in which the nostalgia is more bittersweet than melancholy. I have already pointed to the ominous role of these connections in *O Pioneers!*, and I shall develop them more fully in my pages on that novel. Again, the Frenchness of the singer Clement Sebastian, the lover of the heroine of *Lucy Gayheart* (1936), is ominous not only for her but for him as well. Finally, in *Sapphira and the Slave Girl* (1940), Henry Colbert will be at odds not only with Sapphira and the slave girl Nancy but with himself because of what he regards as his "bad" French blood. I shall develop this French connection as well in later pages of this book.

When introducing "In the Country of Daudet," in *The World and The Parish*, the last of the reports on Cather's travels in England and France of 1902, Curtin shrewdly notes that the most "impressive section of the piece" is Cather's "comments on the conflict" between the south and north and that this "points to one of the two major themes of *The Troll Garden* (1905),"[16] the first collection of Cather's stories—among them "Flavia and Her Artists." Again, in his generally perceptive essay, "Willa Cather's Unfinished Avignon Story," Kates stresses the career-long import of the images of the Avignon region for the high points of the author's canon in settings non-French or French: "The setting exists for an almost familiar group of circumstances. Far from entering a past where the ills of life have been mitigated and struggle washed away, pressures have only become more literal, the pains and penalties of living more direct. Religion, in this papal setting, seems also neither more nor less present than it has been for some time. The title alone, *Hard Punishments*, affects a wonderful affiliation with past work."[17] The affiliation is with as well, I suggest, past readings—here, Dickens's *Hard Times*. Not in some specific sense of "direct influence" or intertextuality but in reference to that opposition between "Balzac . . . Dickens and Scott" and "the things which Flaubert stood for, to admire (*almost against one's will*) that peculiar integrity of language and vision, that coldness which, in him, is somehow noble."[18] I shall return to this passage in fuller context, but here I stress that it emerges from a journey to France the novelist made in 1930. That journey was primarily to northern and eastern sections of France (St. Malô, Paris, Aix-les-Bains and the nearby Alps) in connection with *Shadows on the Rock*, but it did include a return to Avignon and Marseille. E. K. Brown sets that visit against the background of Cather's concern for her mother, ill in a Pasadena, California, sanatorium: "The news from Pasadena was not disquieting, and Willa Cather decided to visit again the Provençal country, which always made her light of heart."[19] Brown also notes that "Old Mrs. Harris," one of Cather's finest stories, begun at Pasadena before the 1930 trip to France, was not finished until after that visit and published in 1931. It is, of course, an ironically grim northern French wind beneath the sunless sky of "French Canada" that blows in *Shadows on the Rock*.

Three decades after her notation about the defeat of the Latin races whose traces she so admired "in the country of Daudet" as a young writer, the old writer seems to convect her earlier insight with the grimmest historical reminder of that moment when the French sun of the South yielded to the English wind of the North. Yet, even as she was finishing *Shadows*, the writer also finished "Old Mrs. Harris" with its more positive reminder of "fine, subtle, sensitive, beauty-making Latin races." In that story, the friendship between Mrs. Harris, the little-read old lady of English ancestry from Virginia, and Mrs. Rosen, her Jewish neighbor, is intertextually revealing. In Mrs. Rosen's house one finds the Waverley novels translated into German and many German classics "done into English" and "many French books." Only that Latin language and its culture seems to be preserved in its integrity and one suspects that among the French classics are not only Dumas *père* (and *fils*) but also the Daudet of *L'Arlésienne* and other works. In the portraits of Mrs. Templeton (Mrs. Harris's daughter) and of Mrs. Harris herself one senses that "beauty . . . strangely Roman" noted by the young traveler:

The women of Arles alone might well account for the songful bent of their country. They are noted all over France for their beauty, which is of a rather Moorish type and now and then strangely Roman. Their clear cut features, olive skin, oval faces and fine, full eyes are well set off by their costume of velvet and lace, their fine fichus brought low about their bare brown throats, and their lace and ribbon caps on their blueblack hair. Their splendid, generous figures are an especial point of pride with them.[20]

In the "energetic step" of the "tall, handsome" daughter of "Old Mrs. Harris" as in the way that the mother holds her head with "the kind of nobility . . . that there is in a lion's" one finds Daudet's and Cather's "Arlésienne" of 1902. In the old woman's "warm, reddish brown"[21] eyes one finds the colors of the ochre hills of the Provence where imperial Rome left the traces noted by the young diarist of 1902. Indeed, to be found not only in the Harrises, *mère et fille,* whose "obscure destinies" Cather recounts in the collection of that title, but in another character more of northern than southern European stock, the Robert Emmet Dillon of "Two Friends," the third story in *Obscure Destinies.* Dillon's Irish extraction gives grounds for a French connection more Celtic than Roman, of course, but the blend of Celtic and Roman that goes to make the French is apparent in his "imperious head" so like old Mrs. Harris's and in his "bold Roman nose."[22]

The Franco-Roman nexus I have found here in the coherent French light directed on these many separated moments of the Cather canon suggests that the novel about medieval Avignon on which she was working when she died would have been her own answer to the question she poses in her Arles entry of the 1902 travel journal: "Why is it that neither Daudet nor Flaubert nor Gautier ever attempted to give us a study of the civilization of those proud old Roman colonies? In the south it seems quite as though the living tie between France and her mother country has never been cut."[23] Yet, along these lines, a finished *Hard Punishments* would have been but another in a long series of Cather novels and stories with a very pronounced French marking. Indeed, the French aura in so many of her fictions is so bright as to shed a particularly revealing light even on those in which French markings are barely visible—for example, *The Song of the Lark* and *My Mortal Enemy.*

The import of *la francité* for Willa Cather has been acknowledged as well by Willa Cather the critic. On a much later trip to France, in the summer of 1930, the fifty-seven-year-old American novelist made the acquaintance of a Frenchwoman, Madame Caroline Franklin-Grout *(née* Hamard), which she celebrated in a now-famous essay, "A Chance Meeting."

The Frenchwoman was the niece of Cather's long-admired Gustave Flaubert. "Caro," as Flaubert had called his niece in his correspondence, and Willa Cather had chatted a while before coming to self-introductions. When Madame Franklin-Grout, then eighty, identified herself as the niece of Flaubert, Cather reports:

> The meaning of her words came through to me slowly; so this must be the "Caro" of the *Lettres à sa nièce Caroline*. There was nothing to say, certainly. The room was absolutely quiet, but there was nothing to say to this disclosure. It was like being suddenly brought up against a mountain of memories. One could not see round it; one could only stupidly realize that in this mountain which the old lady had conjured up by a phrase and a name or two *lay most of one's mental past*. Some moments went by. There was no word with which one could greet such a revelation. I took one of her lovely hands and kissed it, in homage to a great period, to the names that made her voice tremble.[24]

My earlier indications of substantial French presence in nearly one-half of Cather's canon underscore the artistic significance Madame Franklin-Grout's disclosure must have had for her vis-à-vis in this "chance meeting." What is perhaps less evident for readers of Cather's fiction is the import of her formulation here: "one's mental past." Cather's intense preoccupation with French literature endured well beyond her child-hood reading of Dumas père and that first year as a university student awing her teachers and friends by her reading of every masterpiece of French literature. As a young journalist and editor, some of her most trenchant writings are about France, its language, its literature, its culture. Because of its obvious relevance to the paradigmatic concern with Cather's conception of language, the focus of my interpretation in this book, I quote at some length from one of these earliest Catherian reflections in an essay of March 1898 in the *Leader* comparing the English and French languages; her own article discusses a piece by Henry D. Sedgwick, Jr., in the March 1898 *Atlantic* comparing English and French literature.

> The French literature is not a language capable of high religious expression, of exalted spiritual fervor. It was born of a tongue in which faith was dead. The Latin colonists carried no ark of the covenant with them on their journey into Gaul. They took only the names of gods whose altars were already cold and the rituals of faith outworn. The French people from its earliest beginnings had no illusions, no childhood. It was the off-spring of a loveless union, of a father grown old and gray in the enervating excesses of decadent

Rome. The French people never had the highest privilege accorded a nation, that of groping after faith in darkness, of fashioning for itself and with its own hands its god, whether of marble, or wood, or mud. No gods ever sprang from the soil of France; no Druids ever chanted its forests, no nymphs bathed in its rivers. Over that land the spell of childish enchantment was never cast. Its people was born old, worldly-wise, critical, cynical.

When the intelligence no longer derives inspiration from the unseen, it employs itself wholly with the visible, leaves the speculation of alchemy for experimental chemistry. It confines itself either to analysis of, or enjoyment of the tangible. In short, it becomes critical.

The French language is primarily the language of sympathetic criticism; criticism of life, of manners and of art. No other language can so exactly describe, nay, almost reproduce, an artistic effect, a physical sensation, a natural phenomenon. *But it does no more than that.* The "over-soul" has not learned that facile tongue. It is a totally uninspired language, save for the personal inspiration of beauty which is perhaps the truest and most lasting inspiration of all, the sole one, at least, which has survived the death [of] nations and their creeds and the dissolution of gods. So flexible and exact is his tongue, that the Frenchman may say exactly and completely what he means, and, usually, to his reader, he means no more than he says. The epigram has no spiritual suggestiveness; it satisfies rather than incites the imagination. *The French language, like Andrea del Sarto's pictures, has the fatal attribute of perfection.*

The Anglo-Saxon, on the other hand, came without an inherited classical sense of fitness and proportion, into a language as dark and unexplored as his own forests, unwieldy as his own giant battle-ax matched with the French rapier. It has never been perfected. Every English author has known the continual torment and stimulus of writing an inexact tongue. The Anglo-Saxon could not make a literary language. Unable to build a pyramid or a Parthenon, in his titanic struggle, he cast up a mountain. Unable to fit his thoughts exactly to words, he made it the most spiritually suggestive language ever written. He made it the tongue of prophecy, he gave it reverence, that element of which French is as barren as a desert of dew. He learned to mean more than he said, and to make his reader feel it. He learned to write a language apart from words. You feel it in Emerson, when his sentences seem sometimes to stand dumb before the awful majesty of the force he contemplates; it is in the pages of Carlyle, when those great, chaotic sentences reach out and out and never attain, and through them and above them rings something that they never say, like an inarticulate cry. That is the cry of the over-soul, present to a greater or lesser degree in all the English masters.[25]

This is, of course, the Cather still strongly marked by the German and English Romantics (and, to some extent, by their American Transcendentalist counterpart Emerson) whose impact on the novelist Bernice Slote and others have stressed. Cather's complaint here is familiar to students of French literature. Indeed, as I have noted elsewhere, in no other Western literature except perhaps Italian, does a single moment of the tradition have the hold on the culture as that "high point" of the French tradition called "Le Classicisme Français."[26] The passage is not without its ironies for Cather as both critic and creator, of course. In *Death Comes for the Archbishop* she will, herself, create two great French "over-souls," the cultivated Jean Marie Latour and his rough-and-ready adjutant, Joseph Vaillant—with the cultivated Latour better by far expressing, in the French language they so often speak in their American setting, the spirituality of which the young Cather finds the French language so bereft here.

But even before this 1898 article, she had found within the French tradition an author and his book escaping from that "analytical" mode of fiction which "France will run . . . to death as it does everything else": the Dumas père of "that dear old book, *The Count of Monte Cristo.*" Reminded of Dumas's novel by Stanley Wyman's *The Man in Black,* itself "a story full of action and resounding with the ring of swords," Cather writes of *The Count:* "there never was a book that so held its readers and it will be a long time before the world sees another capital story teller as old Alexandre Dumas."[27] A year before this eulogy of Dumas, the young reviewer had written:

> Was Dumas ever more popular than he is now? The Three Guardsmen series are recognized classics and so long as there is youth and hope and imagination in the world, they will remain such. Dumas' influence has never ceased to be felt in England, as it has in France; and in a hundred years, Dumas, the elder, will be greater than Dumas the son, even in Paris. For France will run analytical fiction to death as it does everything else, and will go charging back to romance, singing a new Marseillaise. The possibilities of analytical fiction are limited; it can go on until it has lost all poetry, all beauty, until it reaches the ugly skeleton of things, there it must stop. The human mind refuses to be dragged further even in the name of art. We will all sicken of it some day and go back to romance, to romance whose possibilities are as high and limitless as beauty, as good, as hope.

Some fine day there will be a grand exodus from the prisons and
alleys, the hospitals and lazarettos whither realism has dragged us.
Then, in fiction at least, we shall have poetry and beauty and
gladness without end, bold deeds and fair women and all things that
are worth while.[28]

Nor is Dumas alone among the French novelists who had enthralled
the young Cather with the romance that she preferred to the analytical.
There was also Balzac. Reflecting on French literature in her essay
commemorating the chance meeting with Flaubert's niece, Cather writes:

Probably all those of us who had the good fortune to come upon
the French masters accidentally, and not under the chilling guidance of an instructor, went through very much the same experience.
We all began, of course, with Balzac. And to young people, for very
good reasons, he seems the final word. They read and reread him,
and live in his world; to inexperience, that world is neither over-
peopled nor overfurnished. When they begin to read Flaubert—
usually *Madame Bovary* is the introduction—they resent the change
in town; they miss the glow, the ardour, and temperament. (It is
scarcely exaggeration to say that if one is not a little mad about
Balzac at twenty, one will never live; and if one can still take
Rastignac and Lucien de Rubempré at Balzac's own estimate, one
has lived in vain.)[29]

Yet, for all the ironies that other moments of the Cather canon evoke
with respect to her 1898 reflections on the English and French languages,
those reflections offer enduring and fundamental concern with (1) phonetic
language as a means of communicating spirituality, what we might call
a beforeness and a beyondness of language and (2) the French language
in particular as it and its culture recur so insistently throughout her
long canon.

As I trust I have adequately suggested, the hold of France and its
culture on the novelist is so paramount among the foreign cultures to
which she was intensely drawn as to be rivaled by only the cultures of her
English-language ancestry, her Virginia-backcountry childhood, and her
Midwest formative years. France and particularly Provence seem to have
represented a symbolic conflation of at least two other Latin cultures of
profound significance for her: the Roman and the Spanish. The awareness
of this conflation of the French, the Latin, and Spanish prevents me from
overvalidating the French *per se* or from taking this specific language as
the lost language I believe is the shaping theme or subject of the novelist's
fiction. On the other hand, for her, as a specific "human language,"

French and French culture provide the framework for some of her most probing overtures towards and, paradoxically, denials of the recovery of the lost language so far as any specific human language can purport to recover it.

The French language and culture are, in a Thomistic sense, occasions of access or obstacle to the lost language. Given the writer's stress on the religious and spiritual, in the occasions of access the language and culture may be thought of as sacramental signifiers. By the same token, in the occasions of obstacle they may be thought of as misread sacraments if not, indeed, sacrilegious signifiers. Yet, as I shall show in close analysis of several fictions, in each occasion the pattern is never univocal. In serenely sacramental moments— *One of Ours* and *Death Comes for the Archbishop,* for example—one finds a subtext and, even at times, a text of doubt about French as an occasion of access to the lost language. In searingly sacrilegious moments— *My Mortal Enemy* and *Sapphira and the Slave Girl* —one finds a compensatory awareness of the salvific import of France and its culture as a possible access to the Kingdom of Art and Kingdom of Heaven. I stress possible because, in her French fictions, the Catherian text hints that the writer not only took *to* French but took *on* French precisely because of its "fatal attribute of perfection." From her youthful 1898 essay with its finally dismissive phrase until her 1922 essay, "The Novel *Démeublé,*" republished without corrective in *Not Under Forty* in 1936, the writer was drawn to a language anterior to words and grammars. In her French fictions she seemed determined to assert the superiority of the spiritual, the over-soul, the unseen, the unsaid, the pictographic over the phonetic at its best: French.

Interpretive Strategies

In taking on French with its analytical strain that she so deplored the novelist can be seen to be taking on as well an enduring philosophical approach to literature and to life which traditional Cather criticism regards as least Catherian: the skeptical. Yet, it is an approach to which the novelist shows signs of succumbing throughout her canon. The Edenic serenity of Archbishop Latour's Pascalian garden at the end of *Death Comes for the Archbishop* is perhaps the only moment in the canon in which God and reality as well as spiritual and social and sexual communion seem so transparently and unreservedly achieved. I say "seem," for, even in that sublime novel, there are signs of what I find throughout the canon: that God and Reality and communion are, ultimately, inaccessible, as hidden as Pascal's God.

Or, more appropriately for Cather, inaudible. My methodological framework is acoustic, rather than the visual one of "point of view" familiar in the theory and criticism of fiction. I adopt an acoustic framework because of Cather's general preoccupation with language and particularly with voices, divine as well as human and animal, as would-be users of the lost language. For her, it is the longing for an originary language spoken by an originary presence that shapes her fictions in each of the modes of my acoustic framework. In her faith in the recuperability of this originary voice she stands far apart from that skeptical French tradition from Montaigne to Derrida on which I concentrate in these pages; she stands, rather, somewhat subversively with Pascal and more fully with her contemporary of the *élan vital,* Henri Bergson. In a more obviously literary connection, she stands as well with Rousseau to a certain extent and, to a far greater extent, with her great contemporary whom she so admired, Marcel Proust. Undoubtedly, it will be obvious to readers of both Proust and Cather that the "kingdom of art" to which language gave entry for the great French novelist is scriptural rather than vocal. As I shall show more fully later in my study, it is, in sum, a text from and of the kingdom that Proust offers his readers; it is a call to the kingdom that Cather offers hers.

This call is reflected in the concepts under which I explore the Catherian troping towards France as a prime instance of her search for the lost language. I interpret her French-marked fictions in two sets: (1) those in which the spiritual, psychological, and social or sociopolitical concerns of the fiction present a *consonance* (*Collins Dictionary of the English Language:* "agreement, harmony, or accord") of the two terms of the French-American valence; (2) those in which the same concerns present a *dissonance* (*Collins:* "discordant; cacophonous") between the terms of that valence. Within each set there emerges still another distinction, even more technically musical than the main categories under which I arrange the fictions: *crescendo* (*Collins:* "a gradual increase in loudness or the musical direction or symbol indicating this") and *diminuendo* (*Collins:* "a gradual decrease in loudness or the musical direction indicating this"). In the fictions of consonance as in those of dissonance in the mode of diminuendo, the French markings serve, in more familiar literary and musical categories, as a minor theme to the main theme, as a subtext to the major or main text. As a rule, this minor or subtextual French theme is at odds with the major or main text. Thus, in "Flavia and Her Artists" (1905), for example, a fiction of consonance in diminuendo, the French subtext states a set of harmonies (the young American returned from France) and cacophonies (the supercilious French art critic, Roux) shedding light on the main text with its own consonances of intergenerational friendship, marital loyalty, artistic pleasure, and joyful lesbianism. In the dénouement, however, the harmonies of the French subtext, joined with those of the main text, gainsay both the French cacaphonies of the subtext and the American cacaphonies of the main text. On the other hand, in "Uncle Valentine" (1925), a fiction of dissonance in diminuendo, in the subtext about France the harmonies of the lost language resonate as beautifully as they do in *Death Comes for the Archbishop* (1927), a fiction of consonance in crescendo. However, in the end, those harmonies confront the cacaphonies of the main text at best nostalgically and at worst bitterly; they seem themselves relegated to a past ever more irrecuperable. An exception to these patterns is *My Mortal Enemy* (1926), which I briefly consider. There, the notation of the French subtext is ambiguous, a mixture of consonance and dissonance that is not resolved.

As the table of contents shows, I do not discuss the French-marked fictions of Cather in chronological order. Because the canon of some writers is a prolonged internal dialogue, and their development is synchronic as well as diachronic, their canons are a series of turns and returns to obsessive concerns. I have already explored this pattern in my *Pascal: Adversary and Advocate,* a study of that great French writer with whom Cather was overtly concerned in *Death Comes for the Archbishop* (and, implicitly so, I believe, in *My Mortal Enemy* the year before the appearance of *Death Comes*). The preoccupation with France as well as with language itself in her great novel about the two French missionaries in the American Southwest is pervasive in her work. This francotropism strikes me as one of her principal ways of considering the nature and use of language as well as the problem of signification in general. More cogently, as with Pascal, her canon shows a phasic pattern of affirmation and negation, of faith and doubt, of hope and despair. The Cather canon is an envelopment with as much as a development of concern about any human form of signification as a revelation of or access to the transcendent. It is, then, in this perception of the writer's art that I adopt an a-chronological pattern in considering her canon in this book.

I would stress both the concepts of envelopment and development. I have already pointed to the ironies her later canon poses for her 1898 denial that the French language is capable of expressing the "over-soul." More personal as well as artistic evidence of this irony emerges in a further reflection on the chance meeting with Flaubert's niece in the summer of 1930, an irony which bears on my a-chronological consideration of the canon. The old woman asked Cather which of her uncle's novels she preferred. "I told her," Cather writes, "that a few years ago I had reread *L'Education sentimentale,* and felt that I had never risen to its greatness before."[30] Cather's long-time favorite had been the French novelist's *Salammbô;* one suspects it had been her favorite because, like

Wyman's *The Man in Black* which had reminded her of *The Count of Monte Cristo,* it, too, can be considered "a story full of action and resounding with the ring of swords." *L'Education sentimentale* is, of course, not without its "ring of swords," but it is hardly one of the romances the young Cather had preferred to the analytical and realistic fiction which had so provoked her (and others in the same vein) in her 1898 article.

Yet, Cather continued to love both *Salammbô* and *L'Education sentimentale,* for beneath the floridity of the former as beneath the asceticism of the latter she sensed that concern of the great French writer that had for almost a decade now been even more insistent in her own thought than when she had been a young writer: a disenchantment with the modern world. Her "Prefatory Note" to *Not Under Forty* (1936), the collection of her essays about literature opening with "A Chance Meeting," reads:

> The title of this book is meant to be "arresting" only in the literal sense, like the signs put up for motorists: "ROAD UNDER REPAIR," etc. It means that the book will have little interest for people under forty years of age. The world broke in two in 1922 or thereabouts, and the persons and prejudices recalled in these sketches slid back into yesterday's seven thousand years. Thomas Mann, to be sure, belongs immensely to the forward-goers, and they are concerned only with his forwardness. But he also goes back a long way, and his backwardness is more gratifying to the backward. It is for the backward, and by one of their number, that these sketches were written.[31]

"1922 or thereabouts," was the publication time of *One of Ours,* written in the "thereabouts" since *My Antonia* (1918). The 1922 novel is the story of Claude Wheeler, a Nebraska farm boy who, lost in the prairie setting of America, finds himself only in the France in which he heroically dies near the end of the "Great War." Through the coherent light of France that Cather sheds on his experience, Claude leaves the anglophone roots of his last name, with its overtones of the "wheeling/dealing" of his entrepreneurial father, to discover his true roots in the soil of his very French first name Claude (fr. Latin *claudus,* cripple). On the American prairie, he is a "crippled clod" in the eyes of others and himself. Not surprisingly in Cather's onomastics, some of his neighbors pronounce his name as "Clod"; it is not until he walks in the clods of French soil that he feels sure-footed. Claude also has overtones of Latin *claustrum,* enclosure whence cloister. Thus, it is not until he is in the cloister of France that he feels, paradoxically, at home. Become French, Claude is an American Wheeler who is no longer one of ours but one of theirs.

I anticipate in these reflections on *One of Ours* certain aspects of my study which, so far as I know Cather scholarship, are somewhat unusual in their emphases if not, indeed, in their nature. It will, for example, be perhaps somewhat surprising to readers who think of Cather as the literary patron saint of the American prairie that one of her most sympathetic prairie heroes, Claude, should find himself more — indeed, only — at home in France. For Americans of every generation France may, to be sure, have been our oldest ally, the military savior of our Revolution and the donor of our Statue of Liberty. However, France is also the emblem of that high culture, an aristocratic and foppish fanciness and elegant *savoir-faire,* against which the American democracy in its pragmatism pits its rough-and-ready, democratic know-how. It is also, like other Latin countries, a little too taken with the erotic in its extra-artistic as well as artistic expression. Culturally and politically, the United States has had a long love-hate affair with France, and Cather herself is one of the most passionate partners in this affair. Indeed, as we shall see, for all the at-homeness that the alienated Nebraskan Claude Wheeler finally finds in France he is not at home in that country's language.

In connection with that language, my exploration of the etymology of Claude's first name calls attention to an interpretive strategy that I use frequently in this book: personification through names. On this, I follow the novelist herself. At the end of the last fiction published in her lifetime, *Sapphira and the Slave Girl,* Cather added the following note:

> In this story I have called several of the characters by Frederick County surnames, but in no case have I used the name of a person whom I knew or saw. My father and mother, when they came home from Winchester or Capon Springs, often talked about acquaintances whom they had met. The names of those unknown persons sometimes had a lively fascination for me, merely as names: Mr. Haymaker, Mr. Bywaters, Mr. Householder, Mr. Tidball, Miss Snap. For some reason I found the name of Mr. Pertleball especially delightful, though I never saw the man who bore it, and to this day I don't know how to spell it.[32]

Within the novel itself the narrator points to the "queer things" others could do with names — in the instance, with "Lawndis" who had been christened "Leonidas." In my later commentary on this novel I draw what I believe is the "queer" thing Cather has in mind in her characters' names. The writer often puns onomastically. I follow her suit, warranted as much by the novelist as by the evident importance of names for an interpretive strategy relying as much as mine on theology, psychoanalysis and linguistic philosophy. Perhaps by what the French call "professional deformation," foreign-language teachers are frequently drawn in their literary study to the personifying signification of an author's choice of names for characters and sites. In this connection, I am reminded that Cather herself was a foreign-language teacher: she taught Latin in the first semester of her appointment as a teacher at Central High School in Pittsburgh, 1901–1902; she also taught English there and, subsequently, at Allegheny High School. I would like to believe, therefore, that Cather herself would find my etymological probing of the names she gives to her characters cogent. As a novelist, she uses names, it seems to me, as but one of the many pictographic devices in language to get to that something before and beyond language that was so important to her as an artist.

Finally, since I read Cather's French fictions as paradigms of her overarching search for the lost language, I shall also briefly consider what might be called a number of non-French fictions of the canon. However little marked by French motifs, these novels and stories are, obviously, "Cather-marked"; and, as such, they are instances of the problematic of language which I trace primarily through the prism of the "French" novels. Though some of these non-French fictions do bear interesting French markings, those markings alone do not lead me to comment on them. It is rather their import for an understanding of Cather's intense concern with language I find so much more readily accessible in the French fictions.

With its "fatal attribute" of phonetic "perfection," French seemed incapable of expressing the ideals and values Cather sought to express in her own ambiguous situation as a deeply spiritual offspring of the Virginia gentry transported to the harsh plains of the Midwest, as a woman artist with a cosmopolitan outlook, and as a lesbian. Yet, it is my conviction that it is precisely through the equally ambiguous francophilia that we can probe more deeply aspects of her art and thought only recently beginning to emerge in Cather criticism. The writer's ambiguous stance towards French language and culture is an instance of the larger tension she felt in enacting through language, the medium of her art, thoughts and feelings on religion, sexuality, politics, and art itself. Perhaps the most neglected of these domains in traditional Cather criticism has been that of sexuality, and, like recent Cather critics, I address this domain to considerable extent in this book. However, I foreground sexuality as such with less paramountcy than recent critics (for example, Sharon O'Brien, Susan J. Rosowski, Blanche Gelfant and, in more gingerly fashion, Phyllis Robinson) to whose work I shall turn at appropriate points. I explore sexuality in Cather's fiction as I do other domains, particularly politics and religion: as a communicative system through which the writer sought to recapture the lost language. Nevertheless, I am grateful to these critics for the often convincing and always heuristic perspectives to which their work has led me in my research of Cather's search for that language.

2

Consonance: Crescendo

One of Ours (1922)

There were few days in the year when Wheeler did not drive off somewhere; to an auction sale, or a political convention, or a meeting of the Farmer's Telephone director; — to see how his neighbors were getting on with their work, if there was nothing else to look after. He preferred his buckboard to a car because it was light, went easily over heavy or rough roads, and was so rickety that he never felt he must suggest his wife's accompanying him. Besides he could see the country better when he didn't have to keep his mind on the road. He had come to this part of Nebraska when the Indians and the buffalo were still about, remembered the grasshopper year and the big cyclone, had watched the farms emerge one by one from the great rolling page where once only the wind wrote its story. He had encouraged new settlers to take up homesteads, urged on courtships, loaned young fellows the money to marry on, seen families grow and prosper; until he felt a little as if all this were his own enterprise.[1]

Cather here introduces Nat Wheeler, father of Claude, the one of ours of the novel's title. Nat came from Maine. From his New England heritage he had brought Yankee know-how and enterprise. Throughout the first half of the novel, in which he figures prominently, he is often off somewhere, seldom at home with his wife and sons. Cather says of him in this profile, "the French saying, 'Joy of the street, sorrow of the home,' was exemplified in Mr. Wheeler, though not at all in the French way."[2]

Nothing is "exemplified . . . in the French way" in Wheeler père. He shows none of the French ways of the Mainers he very likely knew as neighbors there: citizens, given that state's location and history, of French descendance. In his indifference to surroundings except as the site of his "wheeling-dealing," he is very different from his middle son, Claude. However, right and wrong pronunciations of Claude's name point him and us towards the soil of France. Sacrificing his life there near the end of the war, he will become a very clod, "cloistered" in that soil, at home.[3e]

He is not at home in Nebraska, the setting for the first three of the five books of the novel, slightly more than half of the narration. Claude's alienation in and from his native soil is in the pictograph of his physique as in that of his name: "His eyebrows and long lashes were a pale corn-colour—made his blue eyes seem lighter than they were, and, he thought, gave a look of shyness and weakness to the upper part of his face. He was exactly the sort of looking boy he didn't want to be. He especially hated his head—so big that he had trouble in buying hats, and uncompromisingly square in shape; a perfect blockhead. His name was another source of humiliation. Claude: it was a 'chump' name, like Elmer and Roy; a hayseed name trying to be fine."[4] In Claude's chump, hayseed name we sense that he is at one with that "wind" which "wrote its story" across fields whose natural productions Claude's father mistakenly sees as the products of his own enterprise.

Claude has a truer sense of the land and the creatures upon it. The novel opens with his tender treatment of a faithful old mare mistreated by one of his father's farmhands. Claude feels the hand should have been discharged for his handling of the poor animal. Throughout the Nebraska sequence of the novel, alone among the Wheeler men Claude has this feel for the land and its natural inhabitants. His older brother Bayliss is certainly Nat Wheeler's son; he lives in town as a businessman, running a general store, writing and bookkeeping in an indifference to the lovely creek (the title of "Book One") on which the Wheeler land sits. The youngest son, Ralph, does live on Lovely Creek but more in the spirit of his father and Bayliss. He is mad about automobiles, farm machinery, and modern mechanical "labor saving" devices: " 'Now, Mother,' said Ralph good-humouredly, as he emptied the syrup pitcher over his cakes, 'you're prejudiced. No body ever thinks of skimming milk now-a-days. Every up-to-date farmer uses a separator.' " Nobody, of course, but Claude, who tells his brother: " 'there's no point to trying to make machinists of Mahailey and mother.' "[5]

Mahailey, the old woman helper from Virginia, and Mrs. Wheeler are the only members of the family with whom Claude gets along. Like him, they are ill-at-ease in the bustling mechanics of business and modern farming imposed by Nat on Lovely Creek and on land in far off Colorado, where Nat Wheeler acquired some property through the default of another pioneer as inept as Claude in modern farm management. Claude's closest relation is with his mother. Ever since he was a small child, she had protected her middle son against the ridicule of his father toward the boy who "squirmed before he was hit; saw it coming, invited it." For Nat

Wheeler, this "trait" in the "little chap" was "false pride." The ridicule was intended to harden his son, "as he had hardened Claude's mother, who though "still more or less bewildered, . . . had long ago got over any fear of him and any dread of living with him . . . accepted everything about her husband as part of his rugged masculinity, and of that she was proud, in her quiet way."[6] Claude does not become hardened.

In his young manhood he remains the "little chap" who has never forgotten and "never quite forgiven his father for some of his practical jokes." The most telling of these occurred when he was "a boisterous little boy of five, playing in and out of the house." He heard his mother entreat her husband to go down to the orchard to pick the cherries from an overloaded tree. The father was annoyed as usual at his wife's physical weaknesses. He went out and soon came back to tell her that she would no longer have to worry about the cherries. Mother and child went down to the orchard, only to discover that Mr. Wheeler had cut down the tree. On seeing the felled tree, "with one scream Claude became a little demon . . . until his mother was much more concerned for him than for the tree." His mother remonstrates:

> "Son, son," she cried, "it's your father's tree. He has a perfect right to cut it down if he wants to. He's often said the trees were too thick in here. Maybe it will be better for the others."
>
> "Taint so! He's a damn fool, damn fool," Claude bellowed, still hopping and kicking, almost choking with rage and hate.
>
> His mother dropped on her knees beside him. "Claude, stop! I'd rather have the whole orchard cut down than hear you say such things."[7]

In the father's "rugged masculinity," the son's "invitation" of paternal outrage, the mother's "pride" in the father, the son's persistent "rage and hate," we have classic elements of the oedipal challenge and the castration complex.[8e]

In the incident of the cherry tree that Claude "never quite" forgets, Claude remains fixed in the phallic phase of psychic life. "Cherries" are a familiar slang signifier of the hymen — obviously, in this oedipal context, Mrs. Wheeler's. One can well imagine that the image had figured in "the talk of the disreputable men his father kept about the place at home." Such talk, "instead of corrupting [Claude] had given him a sharp disgust for sensuality." In a wide-ranging consideration of anemic sexuality in normative heterosexual terms throughout Cather's work, John J. Murphy has also noted Claude's disgust with sensuality. The critic sets the fright the hero feels in the light of Claude's typical reticence before its expression in women.[9] That the "disgust" is linked to this "primal scene" seems to me cogent to an understanding of Claude's sexuality. When Nat Wheeler cuts down the cherry tree ("your father's tree," as Mrs. Wheeler puts it to the boy), he is symbolically castrating the oedipally rebellious son whom he knows to be his wife's favorite; he thus warns the boy to choose another sexual object. And, in defending the father's "right" to cut down the tree, the mother indicates her own psychic complicity with the father.

But Claude does not learn the lesson. In the psychosexual realm he is what his young contemporaries on the plains see in his name, a "chump." In his relations with other young men of his time and place who do "destroy" their oedipal complex, he is also, in a characterization he himself provides, a "sissy." He uses the term in a conversation among himself, his fellow-officer David Gerhardt, and their hostess, Mme. Joubert, during the war:

> She called David by his first name, pronouncing it in the French way, and when Claude said he hoped she would do the same for him, she said, Oh, yes, that his was a very good French name, *"mais un peu, un peu . . . romanesque,"* at which he blushed, not knowing quite whether she were making fun of him or not.
> "It is rather so in English, isn't it?" David asked.
> "Well, it's a sissy name, if you mean that;"
> "Yes, it is a little," David admitted candidly.[10]

"Claude" is romanesque, is a sissy, but is not a chump—not in France, not for Mme. Joubert, not for David in particular. David himself would be a sissy to the Nat, Bayliss, Ralph Wheelers of the America Claude has left behind: he is a classical violinist, an elegantly cultivated Easterner whose excellent command of the French language would be too much of a piece with his Jewishness and foreignness for Claude's father and brothers. Their rugged masculinity is no more David's than it is Claude's; they would find the two young officers and their friendship suspiciously "sissy" (that is, an effeminate, weak, or cowardly boy or man, according to the dictionary). However, it is not Cather's definition in her portrayal of the two young officers. Neither is weak or cowardly; each will die heroically.

In this narrative moment, as in her novel's preoccupation with Claude's name, Cather gives the lie to such prairie simplifications as sissy to designate a boy or man who does not fit the conventional signifiers of rugged masculinity. Her preoccupation with this particular signifier echoes her earlier preoccupation with its gender counterpart, "tomboy," in "Tommy, the Unsentimental" (1896), in Thea Kronberg of the "prairie" portions of *The Song of the Lark* (1915), and in characters of other stories and novels. This Catherian preoccupation does give the devil his due. Claude back in Nebraska gets along best with women: his mother, Mahailey,

Mrs. Erlich (the mother of university classmates during his brief time as a student). Again, like Tommy in her "romantic" relation to the bank clerk, Harper, so Claude with his wife, Enid: the respectively "sissyish/tomboyish" components of their characters make for a poor marital relationship. Yet, "Tommy" saves the day for the inept Harper and for the conventionally feminine "Jessica," whom Tommy tomboyishly calls "Jess" and to whom she yields Harper "romantically." Similarly, the "sissies" Claude and David save the day of battle, at the cost of their lives and thus, like Tommy, at the cost of any further possible romantic relationships.

Except their own, of course. The relationship between Claude and David is homoerotic; they are happier in each other's company than in the company of women. Their separate histories provide the ground for this relationship. In terms of the chopped-down cherry tree of Claude's childhood, the American reader cannot but remember the legend of George Washington, the "Father of Our Country," cutting down the cherry tree and then dutifully reporting the deed to *his* father. Claude, the sissy for his compatriots back home, and David, the dude for his compatriots who serve under him, are "American sons" who do not cut down the cherry tree. Rather, they cultivate and cherish it throughout their short lives.

I speculate about David. The narrative provides little explicit background on his life before his friendship with Claude. We do learn, that, like Claude, he is particularly attached to his mother and that when home he does not feel "at home." At the beginning of the war he had left Europe where he had been studying violin "to see my mother" and during his stay over a couple of seasons " 'I was getting more nervous at the time; I was only half there.' "[11] For Claude, David is a mythic figure. He is David, son of Jesse, friend of Jonathan, appeaser of Saul (King of Israel) through his music, slayer of Goliath, future King of Israel himself. He is also "Gerhardt," German *Ger,* javelin or spear (signifier of David Gerhardt's soldiery virtues). However, he is also German *hard,* "hard, firm, solid" in his steeliness or purpose and, at times, in his heart. Claude will note this later when the two of them consider the relation between a slain German officer and the picture of a young man they find on the German's body: "Claude observed that when David had an interesting idea, or a strong twinge of recollection, it made him, for the moment, rather *heartless.*"[12] Finally, Gerhardt is also, possibly, German *herd* ("hearth, foyer") and German *herz* ("heart"). These last two possible overtones conflate in the narrative and symbolic structure to depict David Gerhardt as the heart in which Claude-Jonathan finds a hearth, a home.

If David is a mythic figure through the narrator, he is also one for himself in his own "self-narration." Puzzled about the American role

in the War, the very reasons they are in it, Claude asks why David is
fighting. David replies:

> "Because in 1917 I was twenty-four years old, and able to bear
> arms. The war was put up to our generation. I don't know what for;
> the sins of our fathers, probably. Certainly not to make the world
> safe for Democracy, or any rhetoric of that sort. When I was doing
> stretcher work, I had to tell myself over and over that nothing would
> come of it, but that it had to be. Sometimes, though, I think some-
> thing must . . . Nothing we expect, but something unforeseen." He
> paused and shut his eyes. "You remember in the old mythology tales
> how, when the sons of the gods were born, the mothers always died
> in agony? Maybe it's only Semêle I'm thinking of. At any rate, I've
> sometimes wondered whether the young men of our time had to die
> to bring a new idea into the world . . . something Olympian. I'd like
> to know. I think I shall know. Since I've been over here this time,
> I've come to believe in immortality. Do you?"[13]

Semêle is the daughter of Cadmos (Founder of Thebes) and Harmony
(daughter of Aries and Aphrodite) who, being loved by Zeus (the father
of the gods and of men), becomes the victim of Zeus's wife, Hera. When
Semêle obliges her divine lover to keep his promise to come to her in all
his glory, the jealous Hera causes her to be struck by lightning. However,
Zeus draws from his dying mistress's womb their son, Dionysos, the god
of wine and ecstasy who will later descend into hell to withdraw his
mother into the heavens. In this "self-mythifying" David obviously sees
himself as Semêle, the mistress of the father of Gods and men who will
give birth to "a new idea in the world." Generalizing this self-mythification
as a woman for his comrade-in-arms, David obviously sees Claude also as
Semêle, as mistress, as mother, as woman. Psychically, he is describing and
accepting himself and Claude as sissies, that is, effeminate.

With respect to the usual behavior of "men at war," when they come in
contact with women, neither David nor Claude conform. When the unit
takes a French town from the Germans and billets there over a day or two,
the "men" (military and other sense here) indulge in normal manly
behavior. Claude and David just look on, though not disapprovingly.
When one of the men, "skinning rabbits before the door of his billet,"
tells Claude " 'Bunny casualties are heavy in town this week,' " Claude
does not express disgust at the obvious and familiar sexual innuendo.
David asks him if he is going to put a stop to the excursions into the forest
after mushrooms by the men and the townswomen. Claude says no, only
if the " 'girls, or their people, interfere;' " To this David replies: " 'Oh,
the girls-' " and laughs softly. " 'Well, it's something to acquire a taste for

mushrooms. They don't get them at home, do they?' "[14] David and Claude are beyond sexuality of that kind.

In psychoanalytic terms, they are *before* that sexuality: "short of castration, that is, short of something which says no to the phallic function, man has no chance of enjoying the body of the woman, in other words, of making love."[15] It is the negation of this "no to the phallic function" in David's dismissive "Oh, the girls-" here. It is the same *negation* that we have known in Claude's lifelong rage and hate of his father for having cut down the cherry tree. The phallic function is signified by the mother toward whom each continues to trope, refusing the castration warning of the father, remaining on the hither side of it in the cathexes of the phallic stage. Each is a "Momma's boy," although we get biographic evidences only in Claude's case. As Murphy has noted, Claude is frightened by the erotic heterosexual energy of women he has known back home: Peachy Millmore and Gladys Farmer. Yet, there is even more to Claude's choice of Enid Royce as wife than the similarity Murphy sees between Enid and Claude's mother: "semi-fanatic, evangelistic, strongly influenced by Preacher Weldon and worried about Claude's salvation."[16] Psychosexually, in their pejoration, these similarities are signifiers of the "phallic mother" whom the "little chap" of the cherry tree incident so passionately desired. In marrying Enid, Claude pleases his mother to displease her. He confirms the psychic rejection of her that ensued upon her rejection of him in the name of the father on the occasion of that incident. The irony of his wife's locking Claude out on their wedding night is an irony that, in his unconscious, Claude welcomes and seeks.

While Claude is no more than any man incapable of loving women in certain fashions, Claude is not incapable of relating to women with love. Back home, he loves his mother, Gladys Farmer, and even Enid (in the ironic sense I have indicated). In France he loves the young woman whom he espies caring for her wounded lover near the Church of St. Ouen at Rouen; he also loves Mme. Joubert, Claire de Fleury, and, most of all, Olive de Courcy.[17e] In her gentle wisdom, her solicitude for the land about her, her love of all living things, Claude finds in the young Frenchwoman his mother with whom he learned about France by reading to her from history books and looking at maps in the years just before the United States entered the war. Mlle. Olive's enthusiasm for the American soldier as a "new kind of man" is the counterpart of Mrs. Wheeler's enthusiasm for the French. In the younger Frenchwoman as in his mother Claude finds the openness, the respect, and the love of difference so missing in most of his compatriots in Nebraska. However, Claude feels no erotic pulsion towards Olive.

That pulsion goes to someone else in her ambiance: to Louis, the one-armed young man who helps her at the old cloister that has been converted into a Red Cross station. In the fifteen-page chapter of this interlude, where Claude finds so many resonances of the Nebraska that could have been, the dominant attraction for Claude is not Mlle. Olive. It is Louis:

> In the far distance the big guns were booming at intervals. Down in the garden Louis was singing. Again he wished he knew the words of Louis' songs. The airs were rather melancholy, but they were sung cheerfully. There was something open and warm about the boy's voice, as there was about his face—something blond, too. It was distinctly a blond voice, like summer wheat field, ripe and waving. Claude sat alone for half an hour or more, tasting a new kind of happiness, a new kind of sadness. Ruin and new birth; the shudder of ugly things in the past, the trembling image of beautiful ones on the horizon; finding and losing; that was life, he saw.[18]

This is an erotic reverie, bathed in yellow and its variants, a signifier of the erotic throughout Cather's canon. Here it serves as cathexis for the erotic fulfillments Claude had not known in the Nebraska wheat fields to which he compares the voice. He fulfills those erotic wishes denied by the phallic mother and the castrating father who had turned him in rage and hate toward both. Not saying "no to the phallic function," Claude finds no heterosexual objects for his erotic pulsions, neither in his erotically anemic wife nor in the erotically energetic Gladys Farmer; but he does find them in men, in Louis and in David.

In his refusal of normal erotic calls Claude relates to the magnetism of Mrs. Erlich as he does to the more homebred but not unsophisticated eroticism of Gladys Farmer: with love but not with sex. In his university days, short as they are, Claude prefers the less worldly magnetism of his course in European history and more particularly the scholarly cloister he chooses for himself: "a criticism of the testimony of Jeanne d'Arc in her nine private examinations and the trial in the ordinary."[19] The thesis impassions him, and it is relevant to Claude's sexuality as well as to his fate in France that it studies this French heroine. Among the principal charges brought against Jeanne is that she wore men's clothes and took on a man's job if ever there were one—the generalship of armies. Jeanne d'Arc was a tomboy. Like the heroine on whom he writes a good thesis, according to his professor, he will lead men into battle while being, like her, psychically at odds with his biological destiny.

He leads them in battle in defense of the homeland of Jeanne d'Arc— and of his. France becomes in the last two books of *One of Ours* what it promised to be in the readings about it that he and his mother made in the middle years of the First World War. "Paris . . . the capital, not of France, but of the world!";[20] "he had never seen anything that looked so strong, so self-sufficient, so fixed from the first foundation, as the coast that rose before him. It was like a pillar of eternity";[21] "flowery France . . . fields of wheat, fields of oats, fields of rye; all the low hills and rolling uplands clad with harvest."[22] In France he will at last fulfill himself both as a manly man in leadership of other manly men in armed conflict and as an unmanly man in his reveries of Louis and his attachment to David.

Not literally, of course. There is seldom in any Cather fiction an acknowledgment, or explicit treatment, of sexual love of any kind. Unto his very death Claude remains as naïve about sex as he ever was. When he and David open the necklace locket of a slain German officer, they find not, as Bert the noncom hoped, the painting "of a beautiful woman but of a young man, pale as snow, with blurred forget-me-not eyes." Claude compares it to a poet and supposes it's "probably a kid brother, killed at the beginning of the war," but "Gerhardt took it and glanced at it with a disdainful expression. 'Probably. There, let him keep it, Bert.' "[23] The mythic David is more worldly than the earthy Claude in recognizing the German officer's male lover in the painting. David's disdain is not for the relation between the dead officer and his lover; in telling Bert to leave it on the body, he is respecting that relationship. His disdain is more for Claude's naïveté. The sophisticated Gerhardt—musician, Easterner, fluent speaker of French, self-mythified womb of Dionysos— might well shake his head at the hayseed simplicity of his comrade. David undoubtedly knows their relationship to be the same in every respect except *les derniers faits.*

They will lie together only in death, David's body "blown to pieces" by the German barrages, Claude's riddled with enemy fire as he rallies his wavering troops to withhold the German advance. Their remains lie in a soil that tolerates differences better than the American soil from which they were sprung. In death they are one and at one, each with himself and with each other, for they are at one with "France."

He was having his youth in France. He knew that nothing like this would ever come again; the fields and woods would never again be laced over with this hazy enchantment. As he came up the village street in the purple evening, the smell of wood from the chimneys went to his head like a narcotic, opened the pores of his skin, and sometimes made the tears come to his eyes. Life had after all turned out well for him, and everything had noble significance. The nervous tension in which he had lived for years now seemed incredible to him . . . absurd and childish, when he thought of it at all. He did not torture himself with recollections. He was beginning over again.[24]

Claude's France is not the France of high culture, of art, of fashion; in fact, it is not the France of the French language. In high culture, in manners, and in the French language Claude feels ill at ease. By dint of having to deal with French people on behalf of his even less linguistically gifted men, Lieutenant Wheeler does manage to communicate in the language, rapidly improving his earlier bookish learning of it. But in general and especially in the presence of the fluent David, Claude feels the bumbler he was in so many other things back home in Nebraska. "Clearly his new fellow officer spoke Mme. Joubert's perplexing language as readily as she did herself, and he felt irritated and grudging as he listened." Later, "he wished he could talk to her as Gerhardt did. He admired the way she roused herself and tried to interest them, speaking her language with such spirit and precision. It was a language that couldn't be mumbled; that had to be spoken with energy and fire, or not spoken at all. Merely speaking that exacting tongue would help to rally a broken spirit, he thought."[25] But Claude never achieves this "spirit and precision" of French.

This would be true despite the time he spent in France prior to his death for France. That country's language is lost to him by virtue of the very concept of language that he has and that he represents: the language of the land, of the wind, of the flowers, of the stars, of the spoken rather than the written, of the grammar and rhetoric of nature. The grammar and rhetoric of the French spoken so well by David and Mme. Joubert is but a poor medium of translation of this other language.[26e] The language of nature had been lost to Claude back home in Nebraska, its voice stilled by the noise of the motor cars and modern farm machinery and labor-saving household devices of his father and brothers. He finds it again, experientially, in France, especially in Louis. It is appropriate that Louis should be crippled; he lost an arm in the war saving his master, Olive de Courcy's brother—a homoerotic motif in keeping with others I have traced in the novel. Appropriate, too, that, in hearing Louis's blond voice sing the melancholy lyrics very cheerfully, Claude should not know the words of Louis's songs. Claude is a linguistic cripple, semantically and rhetorically, in French even as he is in English; however, words and grammar are not the signifiers of the lost language. It may help to know them so long as they do not get in the way of the song or of song itself. As for Whitman, so for Cather: singing is signing. On the other hand, it is significant that in France Claude does recover the lost language. There he even overcomes his sense of awkwardness in the face of French *politesse* and his general fear of the French. He fears the French even more than the Germans, as he admits to David.[27] The French language as well as the conventional view of France as the most civilized country of the West proves to be not a medium but an obstacle to his discovery of the lost language. Louis's French song and Olive de Courcy's welcome in the French cloister garden "lying flattened in the sun; the three stone arches, the dahlias and marigolds, the glistening boxwood and all"—these pictographs overcome the obstacle of phonetic French to the lost language in the land of Jeanne d'Arc.[28] And yet the crescendo of Claude's life and death yields to the final frame in diminuendo of his mother's life.

"He died believing his own country better than it is, and France better than any country can ever be . . . "[29]—so Cather sets Mrs. Wheeler's mourning for her "splendid son" of whose sight her "old eyes cheat her"[30] as he leaves for the "Voyage of the Anchises," the ship that will take him, another Aeneas, son of Anchises, to the death she knows awaits him in France. Mrs. Wheeler knows and accepts in such a way as to indicate that Cather is not so naïve as the hero-son in believing that France or any country can restore the lost language. When Mrs. Wheeler hears of the suicides of so many "heroes of that war, the men of dazzling soldiership . . . she feels as if God had saved him from some terrible suffering, some horrible end. For as she reads, she thinks those slayers of themselves were all so like him; they were the ones who had hoped so extravagantly,—who in order to do what they did had to hope extravagantly, and to believe passionately. And they had hoped and believed too much. But one she knew, who could ill bear illusion . . . safe, safe."[31] Of course, there is Mrs. Wheeler's faith in God; she "always feels that God is near." Yet, Mrs. Wheeler's religious faith seems the self-consolation of which the self-consoler least of all is duped. In the face of her intense disillusionment, she testifies to the loss of hope and belief. She seems to have lost hope in the power of the lost language that Claude had found in France and that David/Semêle thought would be the language of the "new idea . . . something Olympian" shaping the postwar world. Neither Claude nor David shares Mrs. Wheeler's "faith in God." In Claude's rejection of it we see still another instance of his oedipal rejection of both father and mother, of God the Father and of the Phallic Woman who would deny the son "In the Name of the Father." But in Mrs. Wheeler's disillusionment we might see as well more than the rejection of Claude's belief in some "Other world" of values. In psychoanalytical terms she now knows the "Other" to be "Øther," inaccessible to human languages, lost or found.

Mrs. Wheeler consigns her son to a "generation happily lost" to postwar Americans of the 1920s. Claude Wheeler's creator is not considered a member of the Lost Generation of American writers of that decade; yet, as much as many of those writers, she rejects the wheeler-dealer values of an America whose business is business. Indeed, in some ways her rejection of *that* America is more direct and pointed. The novel mocks modern plumbing, for example. Again, the beginnings of agribusiness on the plains and modern marketing brought by the American Expeditionary Forces to the heart of France confront "business America" and "la belle France" with a starkness that is rare in the Hemingway of *A Farewell to Arms* and *The Sun Also Rises* or the Fitzgerald of *The Beautiful and Damned.* However, Cather evokes more *la belle France* of the countryside, of cloisters, of the land, and of landed gentry. It is not the France of the Latin Quarter and the Riviera, of the all-night binges, the night-and-day scrapes and escapades of physically and morally disfigured ex-soldiers who consider themselves ex-Americans willingly lost to their home country. The lost generation of Cather's Claude and David look not away, but back. As Mrs. Wheeler thinks of how fortunate her son has been to have died in France, she looks back to an America of countryside and gentleness as lost as the language of sight and sound her beloved son spoke so well.

In the diminuendo of the closing paragraphs of *One of Ours* there resounds more the melancholy of the setting than the cheer of Louis's songs as "the long shadows were falling in the garden." It is the melancholy of nightshade, of moonlight evoked earlier in the novel.

In his own mother the imprisoned spirit was almost more present to people than her corporeal self. He had so often felt it when he sat with her on summer nights like this. Mahailey, too, had one, though the walls of her prison were so thick—and Gladys Farmer. Oh yes, how much Gladys must have to tell this perfect confidant! The people whose hearts were set high needed such intercourse—whose wish was so beautiful that there were no experiences in this world to satisfy it. And these children of the moon, with their unappeased longings and futile dreams, were a finer race than the children of the sun. This conception flooded the boy's heart like a second moonrise, flowed through him indefinite and strong, while he lay deathly still for fear of losing it.[32]

Death Comes for the Archbishop (1927)

Father Latour's recreation was his garden. He grew such fruit as was hardly to be found even in the old orchard of California; cherries and apricots, apples and quinces, and the peerless pears of France—even the most delicate varieties. He urged the new priests to plant fruit trees wherever they went, and to encourage the Mexicans to add fruit to their starchy diet. Whenever there was a French priest, there should be a garden of fruit trees and vegetables and flowers. He often quoted to his students that passage from their fellow Auvergnat, Pascal: that Man was lost and saved in a garden.[33]

. . . .

Beautiful surroundings, the society of learned men, the charm of noble women, the graces of art, could not make up to him for the loss of those lighthearted mornings of the desert, for that wind that made one a boy again. He had noticed that this peculiar quality in the air of new countries vanished after they were tamed by man and made to bear harvests. Parts of Texas and Kansas that he had first known as open range had since been made into rich farming districts, and the air had quite lost that lightness, that dry aromatic odour. The moisture of ploughed land, the heaviness of labour and growth and grain-bearing, utterly destroyed it; one could breathe that only on the bright edges of the world, on the great plains or the sagebrush desert.

That air would disappear from the whole earth in time, perhaps; but long after his day. He did not know just when it had become so necessary to him, but he had come back to die in exile for the sake of it. Something soft and wild and free, that whispered to the ear on the pillow, lightened the heart, softly, softly picked the lock, slid the bolts, and released the prisoned spirit of man into the wind, into the blue and gold, into the morning, into the morning![34]

This morning sunshine of the soul shines on the dying Archbishop Jean Marie Latour, the hero of *Death Comes for the Archbishop.* Throughout his life, Father Latour is as much a child of the day and the sun as Claude Wheeler is a child of the night and of the moon; he is a child of God as Claude is not.

The cloister to which the aged Archbishop of New Mexico retires after a life of rich meaning and purpose is not the hillside cloister in northern France where Claude Wheeler at last discovers his sense of purpose; it is rather the garden of the small house Latour had purchased many years before, beginning then this garden that retrieves the loss of "a garden in the south of France where he used to visit young cousins."[35] The retired Archbishop's garden in the American Southwest is modelled on the garden of his young cousins in the south of France. It is but one of many gardens evoked in the novel. Gardens provide a parabolic structure for the narrative: from the first opulent hanging gardens at Rome of the Cardinal Garcia Maria de Allende, who appoints Latour to the Vicarate of New Mexico (prologue), through the opulent gardens of the simoniacal Father Baltazar Montoya, onto the dying Latour's simple Pascalian retreat. The play between opulence and simplicity in these gardens signifies the play between the loss and salvation of man in Latour's recollection of Pascal — between the Garden of Paradise and the Garden of Gethsemane.

Of all the legendary sites in Cather's fiction before the novel, the one in "The Namesake" (1907),[36] the sculptor Lyon Hartwell's father's homestead, the garden with "Uncle Lyon's tree," sheds the most revealing light on the gardens of the 1927 novel about New Mexico but especially on the dying Archbishop's garden retreat. Unlike the garden in "The Garden Lodge," the first story in *The Troll Garden* (1905), neither the Hartwell garden nor the Bishop's garden is a mausoleum. In the "Garden Lodge," it is the "lodge" and not the "garden" which symbolizes for the heroine, Caroline, the memory of Raymond d'Esquerré, the dead French singer who used to work at the lodge during his stays at her house on Long Island Sound. Caroline retreats to the lodge, not the garden — to a man-made monument to the dead past.[37] In "The Namesake" the monument is a living thing, Lynn's tree. In *Death Comes for the Archbishop*, Latour's garden is not a monument at all but a continuation in the American Southwest of the gardens he had known in his youth in the south of France. Like the sculptor, an American living in Paris at the time of the story, Father Latour finds in his garden as he does in all of his experience the feeling of "union with some great force, of purpose and security, of being glad that we have lived."[38]

In the novel, the great force is the sacred, of course, not the transcendentally sacred alone nor the immanently sacred alone, but both in the sacramental theology that informs the novel theologically and aesthetically. Thus, upon being named to the Vicarate of New Mexico by Cardinal de Allende, Father Latour is consecrated by his choice at the same time as "Bishop of Agathonica *in partibus.*" Agathon was the seventy-ninth Pope (678–681); his papacy is best remembered for its having condemned Monotheletism (mono = one + *thelema* = will) at the Council of Constantinople (680–681). Though admitting the two natures of Christ, the divine and the human, the heresy attributed only one will to Him, the divine. Theologically and humanly, Latour is faithful to his episcopal "namesake." He moderates when he does not refute the transcendentalizing tendencies of his adjutant, Father Joseph Vaillant. He also doctrinally refutes the paganistic sanctification of the things of this and the other world by Padre Martinez, the pastor of Santa Fé. Joseph, for example, is carried away by the miraculous portrait of the Blessed Virgin commemorating a miraculous visitation by her to the uninstructed people: " 'Doctrine is well enough for the wise, Jean; but the miracle is something we can hold in our hands and love.' " Latour's thaumaturgy is less apocalyptic: " 'The Miracles of the Church seem to me to rest not so much upon faces or voices or healing power coming suddenly near to us from afar off but upon our perceptions being made finer, so that for a moment our eyes can see and our ears can hear what is there about us always.' "[39] Years later, the Bishop recalls Joseph home in a manner that reminds Joseph of a still-earlier recall whose apparent necessity proved wrong and thereby due to a "miracle." The Bishop replies: " 'I sent for you because I felt the need of your companionship. I used my authority as Bishop to gratify my personal wish. That was selfish, if you will, but surely natural enough. We are countrymen, and are bound by early memories. And that two friends, having come together, should part and go their separate ways—that is natural, too. No, I don't think we need any miracle to explain all this.' "[40]

Though Latour does not go so far as his fellow Auvergnat, Blaise Pascal, there is in his view of the miraculous and the ordinary the sentiment that miracles do not convince and that they are far from converting. For the Jesuit Latour "human vision corrected by divine love" and the "natural" in almost all of its manifestations are sacramental in character. They are signifiers of the divine, sacralized by participation in the transubstantiative relation between natural and supernatural of which the Eucharist is the supreme sacrament. Throughout his long vicarate he will not be appalled by such things as the "parrot skull of great antiquity" cherished by Father Jesus of Isleta. The latter "fondly believed that it was a portrait, done from life, of one of those rare birds that in ancient times were carried up alive, all the long trail from the tropics."[41] We remember the live parrots (*"perroquets"*) which Charley Bentley bequeaths to Lyon Hartwell in "The Namesake." One cannot but believe that Hartwell with his respect for historic things will take as good care of Bentley's live parrots as Father Jesus of his wooden one. More cogently, live or in effigy, the parrot is a bird "speaking" human language. The voice Hartwell will hear from Bentley's parrots will be that of his dead uncle-hero. The voices which Father Jesus hears in his wooden parrot are those of the rare birds whom the pre-Christian peoples had brought into North America from the American tropics "in ancient times." Bishop Latour does not reproach this reverence on the part of the old priest of Isleta. The sacramental validity of pre-Christian things and images is not compromised by their pagan association and once idolatrous ritual function.

This incorporation of the pre-Christian and the Christian emerges in another debate with Joseph. The latter tells him of the "remarkable bell" found in the basement of the church at old San Miguel. Joseph admires

its alloy of base metal and the " 'plate and silver and gold ornaments' "
contributed by the pious citizens of the Spanish town in which it was cast
back in 1356, during the wars between Moor and Spaniard. Latour
reflects that Spanish silver was really Moorish, the Spaniards knowing
" 'nothing about working silver except as they learned it from the Moors.' "

> " 'What are you doing, Jean? Trying to make my bell out an infidel?'
> Father Joseph asked impatiently. The Bishop smiled. 'I am trying to
> account for the fact that when I heard it this morning it struck me at·
> once as something Oriental. A learned Scotch Jesuit in Montreal
> told me that our first bells, and the introduction of the bell in the
> service all over Europe, originally came from the East. He said the
> Templars brought the Angelus back from the Crusades, and it is
> really an adaptation of a Moslem custom.' "

Joseph is not satisfied and reflects that "scholars always manage to dig
out something belittling." Latour maintains that he, glad there is Moorish
silver in the bell, is doing the reverse. He reminds Joseph that the one
good workman they found upon arriving years ago was a silversmith.
" 'The Spaniards handed on their skills to the Mexicans, and the Mexicans
have taught the Navajos to work silver; but it all came from the Moors.' "[42]
In the peal of Joseph's bell which he has not literally heard as in the
voice of Father Jesus's wooden parrot which he cannot literally hear,
Latour hears the unity of all throughout the universe. Everything in
creation validates the Catholicism he and Joseph represent and re-present.
The things of this world testify to the ever-present things of the other
world. Sounds and effigies are figures of the eternal for Latour. Thus,
when he admits to Joseph that there is something selfish in his second
recall of him from other duties because he himself was lonely, he has
faith that God regards human motives as a "base metal" alloyed with a
divine one. "Surely natural enough" human friendship is also a sacramental sign of the surely eternal enough friendship of God for Man, as
the Jesuit Latour sees it.

On the other hand, Latour's sacramentalism does not incorporate evil
itself. It does, however, give him a sure footing in both recognizing and
confronting it in human and nonhuman form. Accompanied by an Indian
guide, young Jacinto, he makes a trip into the Indian country to visit
outlying parts of his jurisdiction. On the way they are caught in a terrible
snowstorm and must take refuge in an old cave known to the young guide.
This turns out to be the site of one of the many "dark legends"[43] of the
Pecos, the "altar" of snake worshippers, "shaped somewhat like a Gothic
chapel." Latour is uneasy as he is "struck by a reluctance, an extreme
distaste for the place. The air in the cave was glacial, penetrated to the

very bones, and he detected at once a fetid odour, not very strong but highly disagreeable. Some twenty feet or so above his head the open mouth let in gray daylight like a high transom." The setting is infernal, Dantesque in its evocation of the cold of the last circle of hell. The weary priest asks the guide to build a fire, but the guide is uneasy in spite of having found shelter; he tells Latour, " 'I do not know if it was right to bring you here. This place is used by my people for ceremonies and is known only to us. When you go out from here, you must forget.' " Jacinto builds the fire, but not before taking some small stones used to fence the ashes of a previous fire they find and carrying them to the back of the cave where he fits them into a hole in the wall high above his head, plastering up the hole with earth and wet snow. A little later, their rest around the foul-smelling fire is disturbed by "an extraordinary vibration in this cavern; it hummed like a hive of bees, like a heavy roll of distant drums." The puzzled priest looks at his guide who, for answer, silently leads him back deep into the cave to a spot where he bends over a fissure in the earth. He picks at it with his knife, puts his ear to the fissure. At Jacinto's bidding, Latour does the same, "listening to one of the oldest voices of the earth. What he heard was the sound of a great underground river, far below, perhaps as deep as the foot of the mountain, a floor moving in utter blackness under ribs of antediluvian rock. It was not a rushing noise, but the sound of a great flood moving with majesty and power. 'It is terrible,' he said at last, and rose."

Priest and guide shut up the power of darkness, the voice of the devil, leaving it to roar its eternal plaint of divinely imprisoned majesty and power. Latour "made Jacinto repeat a *Pater Noster,* as he always did on their night camps," and they sleep. During the night, however, Latour awakens to espy his guide "against the wall . . . listening with supersensual ear, it seemed, and he looked to be supported against the rock by the intensity of his solicitude." Latour does nothing, turns back to sleep soundlessly "and wondered why he had supposed he could catch his guide asleep."[44] Latour knows that the "supersensual" ear of Jacinto hears the unnatural voice of evil. Latour turns away from this evidence of the unnatural even as "he turns away" from Joseph's thaumaturgic Catholicism. He would not deny the truth of the miraculous and of the diabolical. However, in *his* Catholicism, one misunderstands the relation between the transcendent and the immanent by overreading either the natural of Joseph's temptation or the unnatural of Jacinto's temptation. He will gently refute Joseph's excesses, and he will make Jacinto repeat the Lord's Prayer. Beyond this, he will leave them to heaven. That, too, is heaven's will.

However, he will not leave to heaven the immanentist excesses of Padre

Martinez, the sacrilegious pastor of Taos. In combatting those excesses Latour is, by his very charge as priest and as ecclesiastical authority, the instrument of heaven's will. In portraying Martinez, Cather re-evokes the infernal imagery of the snake-worshipper's cave as well as the suffusive garden image in "The Legend of Fray Balthazar." That priest's cultivation of a lush private garden for his own visual and culinary delight leads to his execution by the Indians of his remote parish after he has killed one of his Indian servants for having spilled a "hare *jardinière*" on one of his simoniacal guests. Martinez's garden is the entire district of his parish. His Luciferian voice is heard not rumbling from the depths of the Pecos but from the pulpit of his church.

> The Bishop had never heard the Mass more beautifully sung than by Father Martinez. The man had a beautiful baritone voice, and he drew from some deep well of emotional power. Nothing in the service was slighted, every phrase and gesture had its full value. At the moment of the Elevation the dark priest seemed to give his whole force, his swarthy body and all its blood, to the lifting-up. Rightly guided, the Bishop reflected, "this Mexican might have been a great man. He had an altogether compelling personality, a disturbing, mysterious, magnetic power."[45]

The "deep well of emotional power" on which the voice draws and the "disturbing, mysterious, magnetic power" are one with "the sound of a great flood moving with majesty and power" that Father Latour heard in the fissure of the earth in the snake-worshippers' cavern. Although Martinez is Lucifer reincarnate, it is in the name of another son of heaven incarnate that Latour must resist his magnetism. Linguistically speaking, this, too, is sacramental. Martinez's voice, personality, high intelligence (as in his debates with Latour about the impossibility of forbidding the "dark things . . . part of the Indian religion"),[46] his great physical strength used to endure "more scourging than anyone" in the rites of Holy Week[47] — these are all things of this world figuring those of the other world.

But, theologically speaking, Martinez's traits are signifiers of the descent of Lucifer into hell. The logic of sacramentalism is not that of Manicheanism. The darkness, represented by the infernal and Luciferian images of the underground river and Father Martinez, is not the Manichean "Dark" in opposition to the Manichean "Light." Rather, in sacramental theology the darkness of the diabolical is utter immanence, thingness itself in the "things of this world." Lucifer is supernatural not in being beyond the natural but in being supremely, utterly natural, the *"bête"* opposed to *"ange"* in Pascal's famous definition of Man as *"ni ange ni bête."* In the very middle ground that the

human occupies lies the theological and ontological ground of sacramentalism.

This is the ground occupied by Pascal's fellow Auvergnat, Bishop
Latour. " 'You cannot introduce French fashions here,' " Martinez tells
him. These, however, were the very fashions Cardinal de Allende had in
mind in appointing Latour to the Vicarate of New Mexico. The French,
the Cardinal told his fellow Eminences on that occasion, " 'are the
great organizers.' " When his Venetian colleague asks " 'Better than the
Germans?' " de Allende answers " 'Oh, the Germans classify, but the
French arrange! The French missionaries have a sense of proportion and
rational adjustment. They are always trying to discover the logical relation of things. It is a passion with them.' "[48] But Father Joseph shows it is
not a passion of all the French missionaries. Latour tells him that " 'for the
present I shall be blind to what I do not like there' " — Martinez's militaris-
tic panoply of power, his whoring, his materialistic exploitation of his
parishioners. Joseph is scandalized and tells of still another new abuse by
Martinez he has just learned. A young girl had managed to preserve her
virginity during many years of captivity by the Indians only to be
debauched by Martinez and married off to one of his peons after her
rescue from the Indians. As usual in his debates with Joseph, Latour
remains calm. In keeping with that "sense of proportion and rational
adjustment" de Allende thought so French, he tells Joseph that he knew
of the story already, " 'but Padre Martinez is getting too old to play the
part of Don Juan much longer. I do not wish to lose the parish of Taos in
order to punish its priest, my friend.' "[49] Latour's judgment wins out in
the long run. Martinez sets up a schismatic church, but it withers away
when he and his fellow simoniac, Father Lucero "The Miser," die shortly
thereafter.

In the passing of Padre Martinez we have the passing of the Spanish
Dominion in its most puissant expression in the novel. The Spanish
Dominion was that of the conquistadores. If, as de Allende reminds us, it
could count many Spanish Jesuit martyrs, it also counted, as Tzvetan
Todorov has reminded us in his *La Conquête de l'Amérique: La Question de
l'autre* (1982), the decimation of the indigenous populations conquered
by Cortez and his fellow Spaniards. In Cather's fiction the passing of
Spanish Dominion is evoked before *Death Comes for the Archbishop:* in
"The Enchanted Bluff" (1909), the story of prairie boys who dream of a
"cliff city" visited by the uncle of one of them in a story; in "Tom Outland's
Story," later published separately but figuring more importantly as the
centerpiece of *The Professor's House* (1925) which itself signifies through
Tom's friend, the Belgian (French) priest Father Duchêne, the passing
of the Spanish Dominion to a French presence; in *The Song of the Lark*

(1915) in Thea's visit to a cliff city in the American Southwest; in *My Antonia* (1918).

In the novel of 1918, the image of the plough "exactly contained within the circle of the disk" has become so famous that it has overshadowed the image of the Spanish sword evoked only a page earlier. Yet, the sword is as powerful an image in the "legend of Antonia" as the more famous one of the plow. The plough/disk figure replaces and overcomes the image of the sword: Spanish dominion yields to American dominion; in terms of the familiar pacifist ideal, the "sword is turned into a ploughshare." The American dominion celebrated by Cather is not that of the "American Century" pronounced by Cather's contemporary, the entrepreneur-journalist Henry R. Luce. "American" for Cather comports the respect for and love of differences, of ethnic diversity, and cosmopolitanism celebrated in her 1923 essay on Nebraska.[50] In theological terms, this is a secular orientation, but the linguistic relation between signifier and signified is that of sacramental theology in its religious terms. The Spanish sword had putatively been the "arm" of a Christianizing entry into the heathen New World, but it had been deviated for a materialistic pursuit of the "Seven Golden Cities." The plough/disk restores the spiritual significance of newcomers to the New World (Jim and the hired girls in the immediate instance). It is the signifier of a purpose beyond them, a hieroglyph of a transcendent real of supreme meaning; it signals the passing of the Spanish dominion. The transcendent impact of the ploughshare "displacing" the sword has psychoanalytical overtones as well. In that famous image, the sun dominates by its very containment of the ploughshare. The phallocentric yields to the vaginocentric, ploughshare/sword to disc.

The passing of the Spanish dominion in *Death Comes for the Archbishop* is signified by the visit of the two priests to an isolated hill in the Rio Grande Valley "exposing a rugged wall of rock—not green like the surrounding hills, but yellow, a strong golden ochre, very much like the gold of the sunlight that was now beating upon it. Picks and crowbars lay about, and fragments of stone, broken off." Latour tells Joseph that he had been looking for just such a hill over many a long trip through the region, for " 'That hill, Blanchet, is my Cathedral.' " Blanchet (Father Joseph's nickname) wonders if the stone is hard enough, although he *is* impressed with the color — " 'something like the colonnade of St. Peter's.' " Not only the color but also the architectural evocations are impressive. "The Bishop smoothed the piece of rock within his thumb; 'It is more like something near home—I mean nearer Clermont. When I look up at this rock I can almost feel the Rhône behind me.' 'Ah, you mean the old Palace of the Popes, at Avignon! Yes, you are right, it is very like. At this hour, it is like this.' " The Rhône will oversee the Rio Grande. French

Romanesque will witness the passing of Spanish Baroque as well as of the "red-brick English coachhouse" churches, "horrible structures they are putting up in the Ohio cities." As Latour tells Vaillant: " 'Our own Midi Romanesque is the right style for this country.' "[51]

The meaning of "Midi Romanesque" for Latour and for Cather can be sensed from my earlier citation of passages from Cather's 1902 travel journal: it is a syncretic, Catholic, incorporative style, blending Roman and Gallic. "This country" for which it is the "right style" is not only the country around the Diocese of New Mexico. It is also the country of the United States and of the New World. In Latour's sacramental vision of time and place, these are but the continuation of the Old World. The "gold" of Latour's rock cathedral will stand as a more enduring sacramental figure of his mission, of God's presence in this New–Old World, than the excessively immanentist precious metal of the "Gold under Pike's Peak" (the title of the chapter containing this episode). The architect from Toulouse whom Latour will engage and the "good French stone cutters" of the architect will leave not "picks and crowbars . . . and fragments of stone" lying about. Instead, they will leave a hill of God that will dominate the mountain in whose bowels the Bishop had heard "the sound of a great flood moving with majesty and power"—the sound of hell.

Before his cathedral can be built, Latour will have to listen once more to a "sound of Hell" that threatens to prevent its construction. That sound is the insidious whisperings of the devil into the ear of the vain Dona Isabella, widow of the wealthy Don Olivares, Latour's patron in so many episcopal enterprises. Unfortunately, upon Olivares's death, it is discovered that he had never added to his will the codicil in favor of the cathedral fund. His brothers contest the will which leaves the bulk of his estate to his widow and his daughter, Inez. They seek to render the will invalid by claiming that Dona Isabella could not be the mother of Inez, who was really the daughter of one of the promiscuous Olivares's many mistresses, as could be proven by her age. If Isabella was, as she claimed to be, in her early forties, she would have been between six and eight years old at the time of Inez's birth. Isabella's claim is a signifier of the vanity whispered to her by the devil, and she persists in it when the two priests come to reason with her about its terrible effects for all concerned: " 'I can't help it about Inez,' she pleaded. 'Inez means to go into the convent anyway. And I don't care about the money. *Ah mon père, je voudrais mieux être jeune et mendiante, que n'être que vieille et riche, certes, oui.*' "[52] Isabella falls into French quite naturally. An American born in Kentucky where no birth records were kept, Isabella, educated in a French convent, often entertained guests by singing French songs.

Vaillant is not only piously scandalized by Isabella's vanity, but he is also concerned about Jean's dream of the cathedral. However, the adjutant's blustering does not succeed with her. Latour's French Jesuit "sense of proportion and rational judgment" does:

> Father Latour glanced sternly at his Vicar. "Assez," he said quietly. He took the little hand Father Joseph had released and bent over it, kissing it respectfully. "We must not press this any further. We must leave this to Madame Olivares and her own conscience. I believe, my daughter, you will come to realize that this sacrifice of your vanity would be for your soul's peace. Looking merely at the temporal aspect of this case, you would find poverty hard to bear. You would have to live upon the Olivares' charity, would you not? I do not wish to see this come about. I have a selfish interest; I wish you to be always your charming self and to make a little *poésie* in life for us here. We have not much of that."[53]

Isabella yields to this subtle appeal to her vanity in still another of its outlets. She asks what is the oldest she will have to declare herself before the Court in order to forfend the threats to the estate; the young lawyer handling the case says "fifty-two." She agrees but, once the suit is resolved in their favor, not without telling her priest friends that she can never forgive them for " 'the awful lie you made me tell in court about my age!' "[54] Like Latour's own "selfishness" in recalling Vaillant from other duties, Isabella's vanity is used by God through Latour's French "sense of proportion and rational judgment," to achieve His ends. Sin itself, "venial" as in Isabella's vanity or "mortal" as in Padre Martinez's utter immanentism, is gainsaid in the divine plan of which the two French priests are the instrument.

The *two* French priests. The relation between Father Joseph Vaillant and Father Jean Marie Latour is a signifier of the sacramental compact which governs "this world" in its relation to "the other." Their very names show it. Joseph, Latour's Vicar, is a valiant husband and helpmeet to the "Marie" in the Bishop. Joseph is the "things of this world" in both his temperament and bodily presence. He is direct, practical, and basically unreflective, and his appetite for hard work is matched only by his appetite for good food—which, in this novel as in so much of Cather's fiction, is synonymous with French cuisine. Latour is at once the "things of this world" *and* of the "other." In the terms of his fellow Auvergnat, Pascal, of the "three orders" he is more of the order of mind (*esprit*) than of flesh (*chair*) even as in Joseph the relation is reversed still more extremely. With respect to the highest order, charity (*charité*), Latour feels that he is, himself, not so much of it as Joseph: "During their Seminary years he had easily surpassed his friend in scholarship, but he always realized that Joseph excelled him in the fervour of his faith," with little "vanity about grammar refinement of phrase."[55] Joseph learns to speak English and Spanish far better than Latour. In Joseph's unreflective linguistic access to the peons he gives evidence of the close link Pascal sees between the orders of charity and of flesh represented by the people.

Pascal emphasizes this link in special caution against the arrogance of the order of mind to which his fellow Auvergnat, Latour, sees himself as primarily belonging. Yet, when one considers the signifier of the Bishop's entire name, one sees that he is at once of all three orders. Jean Marie Latour: as "Jean Marie" he is at once the beloved disciple of Jesus, John, whose gospel announces that "the word was made flesh," and Mary, the flesh of the only human being "immaculately conceived" without the stain of original sin. Mary thus escapes the heritage of the Fall into the immanent creation from the Garden where Man "lost" an existence in which the immanent and the transcendent were one. It is thus appropriate that, of the two mules that Joseph wangles from the Mexican rancher, he should ride "Contento" and Jean Marie "Angelica," for Jean Marie is of the order of the angels, the order of charity. The Bishop is also Latour: the tower which reaches from "this world" into the "other world," his "sense of proportion and rational judgment" marking him in the order of mind as a very tower and pillar of strength.

If the union of Jean Marie and Latour is theologically significant in the novel, it is psychoanalytically significant as well. In his religious double forename the Bishop is an androgynous figure, in his family name a phallic figure (Latour = the tower). He thus harks back to the heroine of *The Song of the Lark:* Thea's union with Kronberg becomes the juncture of the divine with crown of the mountain; this is an etymological personification with special psychosexual significance for the image of Thea seen by Fred Ottenburg atop the cliff city in another southwestern setting of Cather fiction.

Thea would seem to manifest the androgynous voice Robinson hears in Cather's depiction of male and female roles.[56] I suggest that in its leitmotiv of secrecy the text provides a different understanding of Thea's sexuality. The secret which Ray Kennedy cannot understand is not the one Thea shared with her music teacher, Dr. Wunsch. The latter tells Thea about the secret of art itself in what I have called the voice of the lost language. There *is* a connection between this secret and the secret she knows but Ray Kennedy will never understand, though it might be half-intuited by Dr. Archie. In the familiar role in Cather of the gentle, erotically ineffective father figure, Archie lives in a dream of an erotically neutral narcissistic object: Thea as a young girl without visible erotic pulsions of her own. Thea's pulsions—her secret—are lesbian.

However, since there are no other characters as occasions for the heroine to realize her choice of the female body as the subject of her secret, she must choose herself. Beyond the homologous solitude of her life in Panther Canyon, she can know only "anxiety and exaltation and chagrin" which are relieved on stage alone. In her art, she returns to the autosexual phallocentrism of her psychic life. For Thea, singing is her signature. Fred tells her that she " 'gets effects and not only with your voice. That's where you have it over all the rest of them; you're as much at home on the stage as you were down in Panther Canyon—as if you'd just been let out of a cage. Didn't you get some of your ideas down there.' " Thea replies: " 'Oh, yes! For *heroic* parts, at least. Out of the rocks, *out of the dead people.* You mean the idea of *standing up* under things, don't you mean *catastrophe?* No fussiness. Seems to me they must have a reserved, somber people, with only a *muscular language,* all their movements for a purpose; simple, *strong,* as if they were dealing with fate *"bare* handed' " [my emphasis].

These are signifiers of the autophallism of Thea as the "stag/eagle" in the episode of the Cliff City peak. Here, however, they are set in that moment in psychic life when the subject is threatened with castration—in the text here, catastrophe or downturning (Gr. *kata* = down + *strephein* = turn). After the episode in Panther Canyon, Thea went back into the world of "living people." There, her secret of autosexuality is constantly under the threat of castration, of her destruction as a phallus sufficient unto herself. Fred's proposal to marry her as their walk comes to an end represents such a threat. She declines, but not without an affectionate "you can send me your spear," a playful allusion to the role she projects for him in her work. Fred is the only man with whom she has ever slept— on their trip to Mexico after leaving Panther Canyon. Fred thus betrayed Thea, for he was already married. However, his first betrayal is that he is a man. Appropriately, then, he is cast in the role of the naïve Ray Kennedy and the passive Dr. Archie: patrons to the solitary goddess of the mountain crown. Castrated or self-castrated, Thea's men are "spear carriers"—not spear users—in attendance like the dessicated accompanist, Landry. Though she eventually does marry Fred, their marriage seems very much to be one in which he is spear-carrier rather than spear-user. Thus, even Fred Ottenburg, one of the rare powerful heterosexual males of the canon, is finally cast in the role of subservient or defeated male like so many other men in the canon.

This outcome suggests that the gender relations in the heroine's name are to be viewed in a less subtle and more straightforward fashion than those in the name of the hero of *Death Comes for the Archbishop.* Thea Kronberg's life story suggests that the two parts of her name show her going from female to male identity: the first wholly female form Thea leads to a second name in which the mountain top on which she stands in erectile sublimity is, symbolically, not the round of a woman's breast but the linear and upright form of the male phallus. Thea *is* the "phallic mother" of classic psychoanalytic discourse and as such shows Cather inscribed in phallocratic discourse, Robinson's thesis of androgyny and O'Brien's of nonphallocentric lesbianism notwithstanding. In the Archbishop's name, the gender relations are worked out more subtly and more fully within this inscription: the male (Jean) seeks the female (Marie) who seeks the phallus (Latour).

The story of Joseph and Jean-Marie works out these psychoanalytic personifications narratively and theologically. When they were young students at the seminary it was the earthy, manly Joseph who turned to Jean-*Marie*, to the "Mother" Herself. The frightened baker's son Joseph found in the Jean Marie "of an old family of scholars and professional men"[57] someone to lean on. When they decide to become missionaries rather than simple curates in France, Latour must again be a tower of strength as Joseph's vow "made to Heaven" falters before the effect of his departure on his father. " 'Allons!' said Jean lightly. '*L'Invitation au voyage!* You will accompany me to Paris. Once we are there, if your father is not reconciled, we will get Bishop F— to absolve you from your promise, and you can return to Riom. It is very simple."[58] Joseph goes and "he always said that if Jean Latour had not supported him in that hour of torment, he would have been a parish priest in the Puy-de-Dôme for the rest of his life." They go to the New World as "brides of Christ" to set up a parish and a household. This couple, Joseph and Jean Marie, resembles the couple, Claude and David, of *One of Ours*. The earthy and earthly Claude turns to the musical, scholarly professional man David. In his sissiness of name Claude was not so obviously the husband of the self-mythified androgynous David-Semêle; however, Claude is like Joseph in the relationship in other respects. Most notably, Claude becomes commanding officer of their unit and thus David's "superior" in the "things of this world," much as it is Joseph who runs the "things of the Vicarate" even if Jean is, administratively, his superior. Moreover, as Joseph depends on Jean for guidance in the way the other world relates to this, so Claude depends on David for guidance on such things as the reasons for fighting the war.

In this ultimate dependence of flesh on the order of charity an ironic light is shed on those who would see in Cather the American superpatriot of the prairie. In his quicker adaptation to the New World and especially in his rapid linguistic immersion into it, Joseph proves a better immigrant than Jean. He becomes an American to an extent that

Jean never does, especially when Joseph is named to his own bishopric in Colorado. There, his episcopal and public career resembles that of Dr. Archie when he leaves Thea Kronberg and his own nagging, erotically anemic wife dies. Yet, in their practical business efficiency and *bonhomie*, Archie, Claude, Joseph and, in *Death Comes*, the priests' great friend, the legendary Kit Carson, are portrayed as adjutants both narratively and intrinsically. Even in these most sympathetic American characters of her fiction in relation to equally sympathetic European and especially French characters, the novelist shows Americans chiefly as catalysts to the dreams and ideals of others. American bodies clear forests, chop wood, shed blood, and proselytize desert tribes so that the divine spirit, usually represented in a European or a Europeanized American, can become manifest. In this ironic relation of American order of flesh to French order of charity, the lost language of nonspeaking beings in Cather's fiction often stands in an equivocal relation to that of speaking beings. The pictographic language of landscape and uncultivated humans prevails uneasily over the phonetic language of continental tongues, over great art and cultivated human beings. Now the lost language is transcendent but without specifically Christian reference, now both transcendent and Christian. Moreover, in its non-Christian reference, the transcendence becomes an antireligious or a paganistically erotic power. It seems to point, philosophically, to a pure secularism if not to the utter immanentism represented by Padre Martinez.

In *Death Comes for the Archbishop* this equivocation seems to be dissolved by Latour's sacramental theology of consonances. In fact, the equivocation is psychologically dissolved between Joseph and Latour by their complementary makeups; it is dissolved temporally and geographically, between Old World and New World, through the rock of his Midi Romanesque Cathedral; it is dissolved morally, between good and evil, through God's use of evil to advance the good as in the cave incident and Dona Isabella's vanity. The narrative itself shapes this message of consonance. Its legendary nonchronological recounting sets moments of danger or crisis or even evil itself in a pattern of eschatological emergence. Good frames bad throughout the novel. On the very first page of the novel proper, we meet Latour, lost and thirsty "somewhere in central New Mexico." However, his hope is restored by the "cruciform tree." Again, the Bishop realizes the dream of his cathedral in spite of the machinations of Olivares's brothers and the vanity of Isabella. As in fairy tale and legend, time does not unfold, it radiates, suffusing the vision of the Eternal through all events of which the narrative components are but signifiers. And yet, there are unresolved equivocations in the novel. As with Claude in relation to his mother, they emerge in Jean Marie Latour's

relation to the Mother and woman in general. Of the various crises of the
spirit Latour undergoes the most crucial is in his relation with "The
Woman" as represented for him in Sada in the "December Night" chapter of the seventh part of the novel, "The Great Diocese."

"Father Vaillant had been absent in Arizona since mid-summer, and it
was now December. Bishop Latour had been going through one of those
periods of coldness and doubt which, from his boyhood, had occasionally settled down upon his spirit and made him feel an alien." It is about
three weeks before Christmas, and one night the crisis is particularly
keen as Latour lies abed

> unable to sleep, with the sense of failure clutching at his heart. His
> prayers were empty words and brought him no refreshment. His
> soul had become a barren field. He had nothing within himself to
> give his priests of his people. His work seemed superficial, a house
> built upon the sands. His gray diocese was still a heathen country.
> The Indians travelled their old road of fear and darkness, battling
> with evil omens and ancient shadows. The Mexicans were children
> who played with their religion.[59]

The incident of the cave in the mountain may be seen as Latour's
"temptation on the mount." This December night is Latour's night of
Gethsemane-*cum*-cry to heaven upon the cross: *"Eli, Eli, lama sabacthani!"*
Rising, the soul-weary priest looks out his window to be surprised by
falling snow. He feels a longing to go into his church, but lies down
again, realizing he does not want to face the cold of the church. In
self-doubt, he gets up again, puts on his cloak and goes out into the
moonlit, snowcovered courtyard. From there he espies in the doorway of
the church an old Mexican woman, Sada, weeping bitterly. He raises up
the distraught woman, leads her into the sacristy. Servant to an American Protestant family who dislikes Catholics, Sada has slipped out of
their house in the middle of a wintry night to go to the church only to
find all entries closed. She has satisfied herself with being close to it in
the court in spite of the slight protection her cast-off shoes and frayed
clothing provide. Latour slips his cloak about her and tells her they will
now go into the church to pray. There, Sada falls to her knees, kisses the
floor and the feet of the statue of "the Holy Mother," telling the priest
through her "tears of ecstasy" that it has been nineteen years since she
has seen "the holy things of the altar." Latour tells her that it is all over
now and leads her in prayer, " 'O Holy Mary, Queen of Virgins.' "[60]
Latour knows the persecution Sada suffers from the Protestant family. He
tells her he is glad she remembers her prayers so well; she tells him she
says her " 'Rosary to my Holy Mother every night, no matter where I

sleep!' "[61] The deeply moved priest assures her he will remember her in his prayers in the coming year.

Never, as he afterward told Father Vaillant, had it been permitted him to behold such deep experience of the holy joy of religion as on that pale December night. He was able to feel, kneeling beside her, the preciousness of the things of the altar to her who was without possessions; the tapers, the image of the Virgin, the figures of the Saints, the Cross that took away indignity from suffering and made pain and poverty a means of fellowship with Christ. Kneeling beside the bond-woman, he experienced those holy mysteries as he had done in his young manhood. He seemed able to feel all it meant to her to know that there was a Kind Woman in Heaven, though there were such cruel ones on earth. Old people, who have felt blows and toil and known the world's hand, need, even more than children do, a woman's tenderness. Only a Woman, divine, could know all that a woman could suffer.

Not often, indeed, had Jean Marie Latour come so near to the Fountain of all Pity as in the Lady Chapel that night; the pity that no man born of woman could ever cut himself off from; that was for the murderer on the scaffold, as it was for the dying soldier or the martyr on the rack. The beautiful concept of Mary pierced the priest's heart like a sword.[62]

The text of "December Night" radiates around "Marie," the axis of the Bishop's full name, found in full in the second paragraph here instead of in the novelist's usual truncation to "Father Latour" or "Jean Latour" or "Jean." The "beautiful concept of Mary" is rendered here in symbolically rich signifiers: "Holy Mother/Virgin/Kind Woman in Heaven/Woman, divine/Fountain of all Pity/Lady (of the Chapel)/sword." The mother as a sword piercing the male and female's heart is the Phallic Mother.[63e] In Lacan's terms, she is also here the woman, object and repository of the man's love.[64e]

As Lacan argues elsewhere, male sexuality is a constant, increasingly frenetic and ultimately impotent pursuit of the Other, that realm in which undifferentiated and untrammelled satisfaction of his own desire for the phallus is realized. The Woman/Phallic Mother is the usual experiential object of this pursuit.[65e] Psychoanalytically, Latour's theological "coldness . . . doubt . . . alienation" on the night of the Sada episode is an instance of this impotence; the theological crisis is resolved by maintaining the psychoanalytical crisis. He persists in the pursuit of "The Woman = the Other" by literally raising up Sada and then figuratively raising up himself to the "Woman, divine" in Mary, of whom he gives to the departing Sada "a little silver medal, with a figure of the Virgin": "Ah, he thought, for one who cannot read—or think—image, the physical form of Love." Latour does think, of course; that is, psycho-analytically, he sublimates his erotic impulsion toward the "Fountain of all Pity"—toward the source, toward the Other. A similar sublimation can be found in the fellow Auvergnat whom Latour evokes for his young priests in reflecting on his own garden, Blaise Pascal. In *The Thoughts* Pascal does not evoke the salvific presence of the Mother of Jesus with anything like the force of Cather. It is rather Jesus Himself who becomes that object for Pascal, and his is an androgynous Jesus with features both feminine and masculine. To be sure, psychoanalytic investment in the Other as the woman is similar to Latour's here. Theologically, however, the Image for Pascal is masculine, however feminized. This points to a basic difference between the Catholic sacramentalism of Pascal and that of Latour.

Pascal's theology is alternately patricentric and filicentric. It concentrates on God the Father in most of his public and private writings on either side of the more filicentric *Thoughts* and some of his private writings. Latour's discourse is essentially mariocentric: the divine is a woman—in Lacanian terms, The Woman. To be sure, Latour has absorbed much of Pascal, but, in the familiar centrist thrust of French Catholicism, particularly in its Jesuit expression, he has also edulcorated that thinker's harsher thoughts into an assimilative sacramentalism.[66e] Latour is far less suspicious of images in their potential for an utter immanentism than Pascal. In psychoanalytical terms, the Jansenistic Pascal clings to the Other, but for him it is not the Phallic Mother/The Woman—it is the Phallus/Man. Thus, though one may read into the attraction that Latour feels for the "magnetic" Padre Martinez a homosexual pull, the force of that experiential signifier is itself but a signifier of the French Jesuit Latour's primordial impulsion towards the Phallic Mother. His basic mariocentrism, his deacentrism spares him such phallologocentric commitments. It is not the voice of his God that he hears in Martinez's "beautiful baritone"; instead, he recognizes that baritone as the voice of the male God, Lucifer fallen from the heaven presided over by a queen without consort.

With respect to male voices in Cather, it is striking that this novel is one in which Joseph's tenor is not pejorative. Usually in Cather, tenors are piddling figures, the vocal equivalent of her passive narrator observers and of men in general, particularly lovers and husbands.[67e] Latour is thus better provided in his deacentrism to reject the "power and majesty" of Martinez than Alexandra Bergson is to forsake that "mightiest of all lovers" of her dream. She finally abandons that phallic force: "like no man she knew ... larger ... stronger ... swifter ... yellow like the sunlight ... the smell of ripe cornfields about him." She marries the passive Carl who tells her that he "couldn't even buy one of your cornfields."[68e] Yet, Alexandra's conscious repression of her dream-lover finally links her to Latour: she becomes deacentric as well, her "Queen of Heaven" being herself. In her name she signifies this substitution of the mighty male: she is an Alexandra more worthy to recall Alexander the Great than the hero of Cather's first novel, *Alexander's Bridge* (1911). The heaven over which Alexandra Bergson presides is, of course, fully of this world, a secular realm. With respect to the location of the lost language represented by the central Phallic Mother figure, this suggests that *O Pioneers!* is in the same relation to *Death Comes for the Archbishop* as *A Lost Lady*. In the two Midwest novels this language is located in the secular realm, in the Southwest novel in the religious.[69e] Yet, in all three, the location is that of the Phallic Mother.

That Mother herself is phallocentric. In relation to the three Cather novels I have studied psychoanalytically, this means that neither Alexandra nor Maidy nor the Mother of God is Queen of a heaven here on earth or there in heaven. The "Other" proves to be Øther: "*The* woman" must be written simply "woman." There is no attainment to a realm of undifferentiated, untrammelled desire. That realm does not exist except as a compelling illusion. This compulsion of pursuit is the particular anxiety of the theologically hopeless, the psychically impuissant Jean Marie Latour of "December Night."[70e]

"December Night" parallels, psychoanalytically, the equivocations and compromises of the sacramental theology of the novel. It does so philosophically and linguistically as well. Latour's inability to pray in his dryness of soul on the wet December night suggests a Derridian sense of the irrecuperability of the origin of things, a loss of the divine presence that is a loss of the sense of self present to one's self.[71e] God is lost to Latour. As language, prayer has lost its capacity for him to send messages to God; the Other has proved to be Øther, Mother to be Mother. His decision not to go to the Church because it is cold shows him to have fallen into utter immanentism, into the devil's cold of the cavern in the mountain. The sacramental compact no longer holds for him; the warmth of the Eternal Eucharist's Divine Presence in the tabernacle of the altar no longer constrains the evil of the cold. The devotion to the Blessed Virgin does not come to him as either a primary or an intercessionary figure of access to presence, male or female.

For her part, Cather sets Latour's crisis of language and presence in the familiar legendary mode of the eschatological apparition of the good, Sada's arrival. However, the novelist might have found such deconstructionist perspectives in Pascal's *Thoughts* — a constant awareness of the possibility of deconstructing language and thought from within itself. He follows in this matter one of his usual guides in all questions of doubt and self-doubt, Montaigne.

> Thought.
> All the dignity of man is in thought. But what is thought? How silly [*sotte*] it is!
> Thought is thus a thing admirable and incomparable in its nature. It was necessary that it have strange faults to be despicable [*méprisable*]. But it has such that nothing is more ridiculous. How great it is by its nature, how lowly by its nature, how lowly by its faults.
> The slippage [*écoulement*].
> It is a horrible thing to feel slipping away all that one possesses.[72]

For Pascal this slippage is itself a figure of the possibility of his being cut off from divine presence. His awareness of any human's *présence à soi* (presence to oneself) is his greatest enemy. As one of his most famous thoughts reminds us, the self is hateful. Only divine grace rescues one from this loss of God in Pascal's theology. For a Jansenist the rescue is far less dependent on things of *this* world than it is for Cather's Jesuit in his crises of slippage. For Latour divine grace must come in a figure of this world. That it does come for him and for Pascal, in the latter's case as unmediated infusion, separates both from Derrida. The contemporary French philosopher's deconstruction is radical. "There are no traces by which we can retrack our way back to fundamental Being; Being is itself an idealistic concept, a seeming transcendence that is only a lure of 'reason' (practical), an idea of the universal unanimous community which organizes the idealisatory process thereof. As always, so long as such an idea remains on the horizon, oral law and empiricism join [*s'allient*] to dominate the field."[73] In the face of this "idealisatory process" Derrida remains calmly secular, rejecting the lures of being and divinity or presence of the Other. If the Other is, for Derrida, *at the start* what Lacan shows it to be *at the end* — Øther — the philosopher is more serene than the psychoanalyst in the recognition. For Lacan, as for Pascal and Latour, the recognition that the Mother is Mother is a painful experience, a torment of the soul.

But in late Lacan there is the suggestion of an autonomous if not, in fact, independent feminine sexuality that exceeds and perhaps cancels the phallic paradigm of his earlier thought. This late Lacan provides a possible understanding of Latour's transcendence of his agony.

The mystical is by no means that which is not political. It is something mysterious, which a few people teach us about, and most often women or highly gifted people like Saint John of the Cross — since, when you are male, you don't have to put yourself on the side of VxOx. You can also put yourself on the side of not all. There are men who are just as good as women. It does happen. And who therefore feel just as good. Despite I won't say their phallus, despite what encumbers them on that score, they get the idea, they sense that there must be a *jouissance* which goes beyond. That is what we call a mystic.[74]

In order to realize his mission in this world the Bishop must follow the psychoanalytical law of moving from the son to the mother to find the father (Jean → Marie → Latour). As he prepares to move on to the other world he follows the mystical law of St. John of the Cross and puts himself "on the side" of woman, centering on his middle name Marie. He defers to a "jouissance which goes beyond," the one to which Sada had recalled him in his Pascalian night of fire. In that beyond he recovers, more fully than even his sacramentalism in this world can, the lost language, for it is a language before as well as beyond the calligraphy of his Pascalian garden or of his own fine French hand.

3

Consonance: Diminuendo

"Flavia and Her Artists" (1905)

In her "researches" into the life of the prairie which was to become the cosmopolis of so many of her early stories and early novels, Willa Cather offers what the contemporary French geneticist Albert Jacquard sees as the chief lesson of the workings of human biology: a "eulogy of difference."[1] For Cather that eulogy is due to the multilingual, multicultural demographics of the Nebraska and its avatars in which she sets her prairie novels and stories. The perceptive French Catherian, Michel Gervaud, has written: "Anticipating sociologists and novelists who, one day, would give evidence in their writings of the notion of 'ethnic identity,' Willa Cather had immediately perceived that, in the womb of the American population, the immigrants represented the element of *difference* which, for what concerned her, was indispensable to support the uniformity of her own culture and, later, to nourish her literary creation."[2] Gervaud quotes from Cather's own essay, "Nebraska: The End of the First Cycle" (*The Nation*, 1923), the 1910 census figures showing that three-fourths of the state's population at that time was made up of inhabitants of immigrant origin. This is the statistical and historical ground for the novelist's contention (probably too optimistic, in Gervaud's view) that " 'it is in the great cosmopolitan country known as the Middle West that we may hope to see the hard molds of American provincialism broken up; that we may hope to find talent that will challenge the pale proprieties, the insincere, conventional optimism of our art and thought.' "[3]

Cather's challenge to the convention of American materialism can be heard in the specifically French markings of her first short story, "Peter."

> He had seen all the lovely women of the world there [Prague], all the great singers and great players. He was in the orchestra when Rachel played, and he heard Lizst when the Countess d'Agoult sat in the stage box and threw the master white lilies. Once, a French woman came and played for weeks, he did not remember her name

now. He did not remember her face very well either, for it changed so, was never twice the same. But the beauty of it, and the great hunger men felt at the sight of it, that he remembered. Most of all he remembered her voice. He did not know French, and could not understand a word she said, but it seemed to him she must be talking the music of Chopin. And her voice, he thought he should know that in the other world. The last night she played a play in which a man touched her arm, and she stabbed him. As Peter sat among the smoking gas jets down below the footlights with his fiddle on his knee, he thought he would like to die too, if he could touch her arm once, and have her stab him so. Peter went home to his wife very drunk that night. Even in those days he was a foolish fellow, who cared for nothing but music and pretty faces.[4]

"Rachel" is the great French actress, Elisabeth Rachel Félix (1820–58) and the actress whose name Peter cannot remember is "La Grande Sarah" (Rosine Bernard, 1844–1923) who will play *Hamlet* later in Cather's fiction (*My Mortal Enemy*, 1926). The play is *Tosca* (1887) by the French playwright Victorien Sardou (1831–1908), while the "Countess d'Agoult" is the French writer born Marie de Flavigny (1805–76). In "Peter," we have the earliest premonition in Cather's fiction of the spiritual consonances I traced in part 2.

Rather than see his fiddle sold by his materialistic son, the old man breaks it over his knee and then before shooting himself says: " 'But he shall not sell thee, my fiddle, I can play thee no more, but they shall not part us. We have seen it all together, the French woman and all.' " Paradoxically, in terms of the sacramental linguistics I find in *Death Comes for the Archbishop*, his suicide is a eucharistic transubstantiation of the things or "figures" of this world into the realities of the "other world." He thereby recovers the lost language of the world of his youth, the Old World, a world lost to the New World with its simoniacal sale of the sacramental fiddle. In the New World of America which old Peter piously leaves one speaks English-commerce rather than French-Chopin. The religiously transcendent focus of that challenge through a salvific stress on things French marks as well other stories of the 1890s. For example, in "The Count of Crow's Nest" (1896), the hero, Count de Koch, is a Père Goriot in the setting of a Chicago boardinghouse, where he resides with his frivolous daughter; there, he barely supports them. She constantly urges him to sell for publication some private letters the destitute *émigré* has brought with him to America. The daughter cares for neither her father's sense of honor nor the damage such publication entails for the authors of the letters; she wants the money for her singing career. She thus echoes the son in "Peter." However, in the boardinghouse there also resides an idealistic young American, from whose point of view the story is told. Sympathetic to the Count, he thus echoes Balzac's Eugène de Rastignac in the French writer's famous novel. However, Cather's young man is anything but the ambitious and erotically driven creation of Balzac. Siding with the destitute and honorable Count, he is, rather, an early instance of later priestly young heroes like Jim Burden of *My Antonia* and, even more, Tom Outland of *The Professor's House.* Hierarchs of the past, these characters of the Cather canon have a sacramental sense of relics (the letters in the 1896 story; childhood on the plains and especially Antonia herself in *My Antonia;* Cliff City for Tom).

Cather's French focus is less religious in the French-marked stories she writes soon after returning from the 1902 trip to France. In "Flavia and Her Artists," one of the strongly French-marked stories of *The Troll Garden* (1905), she challenges along more secular lines the "pale proprieties" and "insincere, conventional optimism of our art and thought." Among the secular concerns of this period is one which will increasingly and more overtly preoccupy the novelist in her fictions hereafter: conventional categories of "normal" sexual development as an "adjustment" by the male into "rugged masculinity" and by the female into a "dainty, white, languid bit of a thing." I have quoted from a still earlier story, "Tommy, The Unsentimental" (1896),[5] to indicate that this matter had concerned the writer prior to her travels to France. However, after those travels, the tone of Cather's challenge is without the defensiveness of the earlier story. The later stories have a greater daring and sophistication. They show Cather to be an early, confident, and rigorous student of sexuality, conventional and unconventional, in a very modern vein.

In "Flavia and Her Artists" the indications of unconventional sexuality are quite pronounced. Imogen Willard, the observer and narrator, thinks of the actress Jemima Broadwood as "a nice, clean, pink-and-white boy who has just had his cold bath." Then there is the singer Frau Lichtenfeld: her speaking voice is "baritone," and she is "a woman of immense stature" whom Imogen first sees "in a very short skirt and a broad, flapping sun hat, striding down the hillside at a long, swinging gait."[6] The fact that Imogen Willard is an American home from her studies in philology in Paris is of more than passing subtextual interest for an understanding of later Cather figures who also return from France— for example, Valentine in "Uncle Valentine" and Godfrey St. Peter in *The Professor's House.* Like Claude Wheeler who never returns from France, such characters usually find themselves more at home there than on their native soil. It is clear, however, that, from her earliest stories, Cather adopts the French point of view not only as the cosmopolitan one but, usually, as the most humane one. Imogen is a sympathetic observer of the sartorially and sexually odd artists at Flavia's house even as she is, like some of these artists, the champion of the silly Flavia's beleaguered husband. Given Cather's love of punning with names, we might well see, then, the author of "Flavia and Her Artists" inviting us to "imagine Willa" in "Imogen Willard"—inviting us, thus, to the point of view of Willa Cather returned herself a few years earlier from France.

Home in the States after her philological studies in Paris, Imogen and a number of mannish women and effeminate men have been invited to Flavia's house for an arty weekend. Yet, Imogen is not the specifically French narrative nucleus of the occasion: this is the guest of honor, M. Roux, French writer on the arts and arbiter of taste. At dinner on the eve of Roux's unexpected departure, Flavia and he debate the question of women's capacity for intellectual distinction. In his "Mes Etudes des Femmes" the Frenchman has shown himself hostile on the question. When Flavia challenges him at the dinner, citing " 'Mrs. Browning, George Eliot and your own Mme Dudevant,' " Roux replies: " 'Madame, while the intellect was undeniably present in the performances of these women, it was only the stick of the rocket. Although this woman has eluded me, I have studied her conditions and perturbations as astronomers conjecture the orbits of planets they have never seen. If she exists, she is probably neither an artist nor a woman with a mission, but an obscure personage, with imperative, intellectual needs, who absorbs rather than produces!' " Flavia wonderingly concludes from his tirade that Roux means that such a woman would be one " 'whose first necessity would be to know, whose instincts would be satisfied only with the best, who could draw from others; appreciate, merely?' " The French writer replies "with an untranslatable smile, and a slight inclination of his shoulders, 'Exactly so; you are really remarkable, madam,' he added, in a tone of cold astonishment."[7]

Flavia has been had. If she doesn't know it, her guests and especially her husband, Arthur Hamilton, do. Arthur also learns from a newspaper, as does Imogen whom he had so cherished in her childhood, that, on returning to Paris, Roux had given an interview which the headline summarizes as "Roux on Tuft Hunters; The Advanced American Woman as He Sees Her; Aggressive, Superficial and Insincere." Arthur keeps this derision of his wife to himself. However, at a subsequent dinner, he himself calls Roux a man with no " 'ordered notion of taste,' " to be classed with " 'mountebanks and snake charmers, people indispensable to our civilization, but whose invitations we do not accept.' " Flavia is furious at this outburst. Gallantly refusing to disabuse his wife via the newspaper account, Arthur suffers her anger without reproach. His dismay deeply affects Imogen, however, and she, like Roux, also cuts short her stay at Flavia's; she is too indignant at Flavia's naïveté and even more at her treatment of her husband. He and Miss "Jimmy" Broadwood help Imogen leave, all three maintaining their silence about Roux's duplicity, Arthur's gallantry, and Flavia's naïveté and superficiality.

The story of Flavia is a lesbian judgment of normal notions of sexuality. Its lesbian figures are sympathetic, while one of its two principal figures, the Frenchman Roux, is mocked precisely for his put-down of Flavia's departure from conventional notions of the woman—she is too aggressive for that phallocrat. And in the counteroffensive criticism of Roux himself, the principal male, Flavia's husband Arthur, joins with the lesbian figures. Yet, in an instance of reversal of terms within the phallocratic structure I discussed earlier, Arthur follows those he would lead, particularly the forceful Jemima—even as, in marriage, he had followed more than led his wife. Indeed, in another interpretive frame crucial to the story, one sees that it is less a conventional masculine aggressiveness than something else which leads him to counterattack Roux. If the story of Flavia is a lesbian vent against conventional phallocentrism, it is also an aesthetic vent against the artistically second-rate and their appreciative hangers-on. With his pompous and superficial antifeminism, Roux himself appears in this light. From those terms in which Arthur criticizes Roux, it is clear that on an aesthetic axis he rises to a conventional male aggressiveness. In this respect, Arthur and his lesbian allies are putting down all those uninformed participants at Flavia's dinner table: both performers (the Italian tenor) and appreciators (Flavia included to some extent) are tarred with the brush of Catherian disdain for those without genuine talent or an "ordered sense of taste" that she uses on the young hero of "Paul's Case," also included in *The Troll Garden* but published separately in 1905. Roux is such a pompous figure that he could be seen to cast a dissonant light on France, of course. However, the sympathetic Imogen tempers Roux, a dissonant French light. It is the true light of France that Imogen sheds on the Hamilton household, especially on Arthur, that American household's best representative. The resolution is, thus, of a consonance between the best France has to offer and the best America has to offer.

The lesbian frame in the story of the superficial Flavia and her gallant husband is crucial to the consonance established. As in other stories about socially ambitious and artistically preoccupied women, the husband is in the wife's shadow: he either gallantly accepts her silliness like Arthur Hamilton or finally resists it only when it threatens the well-being of others (e.g., "The Prodigies," 1897). These men are usually gentle, ironic, skeptical, bookish, and ill-at-ease in the signifying chain of heterosexual commitment with its repetitions of intersubjective cruelty. Like Professor St. Peter in *The Professor's House* some twenty years hence (1925), they opt out.

"Eleanor's House"

Cather invites us to the same cosmopolitan and humane point of view in "Eleanor's House" (1907). The narrative strategy of this story is far more complex than that of "Flavia and Her Artists." This tale of a bereaved husband, Harold Forscythe, is told by Harriet Westfield, an old and close friend to whom he comes in nostalgic reminiscence of his dead first wife, Eleanor, and thus in evident infidelity to his second wife, Ethel. Harriet and her husband are living at Arques, on the Normandy Coast near Dieppe, not far from "Fortuney," the house he and Eleanor shared before her death. Harold feels he can confide in Harriet, telling her of his own secret visits to the old house inasmuch as Harriet and Eleanor had been girlhood friends:

> He followed her about in grateful silence while she told him, freely and almost lightly, of her girlhood with Eleanor Sanford; of their life at the convent-school in Paris; of the copy of *Manon Lescaut* which they kept sewed up in a little pine pillow they had brought from Schenectady; of the adroit machinations by which on her fête-day, under the guardianship of an innocent aunt from Albany, Eleanor had managed to convey all her birthday roses to Père-la-Chaise and arrange them under de Musset's willow.[8]

"Eleanor's House" is less the story of a devoted husband than of a devoted girl friend. Harold disappears from Arques—he has not gone to the "absurd little town on the Mediterranean, not far from Hyères," where he and Eleanor once got stranded (very likely the Lavandou where Cather spent such memorable days in 1902).[9e] Instead, he has gone to Fortuney, to "Eleanor's House," as Ethel suspects. She appeals to Harriet to accompany her to find him and bring him back, but Harriet agrees with such apparent misgivings that her husband observes, " 'Ah, so it's to keep her out, and not to help her in, that you're going.' " Harriet replies: " 'I declare to you, I don't know which it is. I'm going for both of them— for her and Eleanor.' "[10] At the house they find Harold immured in Eleanor's old room "which was hung with a heavy curtain. She lifted it, and there they paused, noiselessly. It was just as Harriet remembered it; the tapestries, the prie-Dieu, the Louis Seize furniture—absolutely unchanged, except that her own portrait, by Constant, hung where Harold's used to be. Across the foot of the bed, in a tennis shirt and trousers, lay Harold himself, asleep." Astonished and angered upon waking to find Ethel and Harriet there, Harold argues with his wife for coming. She cries out that Eleanor could not have been " 'so contemptible as you all make her—so jealous!' " And Harold retorts " 'Jealous? Of whom—my God!' "[11] Several weeks later, the Forscythes return to tell the Westfields that they are going to America. Ethel is pregnant, and in the face of this new relationship to his present wife, Harold finally forsakes the first wife, the dead Eleanor. He entrusts the care of "Fortuney" to Harriet. When Harold has left, Harriet and Robert Westfield reflect bittersweetly about Harold's new-found sense of responsibility to Ethel in light of his so long and so intense involvement with the dear Eleanor: " 'Well, we'll have Fortuney, dearest. We'll have all that's left of them. He'll never turn back; I feel such a strength in him now! He'll go on doing it and being finer and finer. And do you know, Robert,' her lips trembled again, but she smiled from her misty eyes, 'if Eleanor knows, I believe she'll be glad; for—oh, my Eleanor!—she loved him beyond anything, beyond even his love.' "[12]

Eleanor has lost Harold to Ethel, and Robert has lost Harriet to Eleanor. Harriet becomes Harold in the psychosexual economy of the story and thus, to use an old expression, "knows what every woman knows"—how helpless and childlike every man is. In psychoanalytical terms, Harold, returned to Ethel, is still caught up in the pursuit of the *jouissance* of the Other, signified for him in the body of Ethel and of the body within the body of Ethel. Harriet has assimilated the phallocentrism of Harold (*he* has become *her* in the narrative troping) and seen it for what it is: a nothing, the Øther in Lacanian terms. Yet, for the women of the final coupling, the sense of nought is not grim. Cather dissolves the phallocentrism of both subjects, male and female, by implicitly and ironically asking: *"où en est le mal?"* (where's the harm of it?). The sub-textual importance of the France in which "Eleanor's House" is located prompts a near-homonym in the French Language which suggests a non-phallocentric consonance: *"où en est le mâle?"* (where's the man?).

Thus, the story represents an early instance of a pattern which will become especially pronounced in Cather's final published novel, *Sapphira and the Slave Girl* (1940): a dénouement to heterosexual striving which issues in a world without men or a world of self-sufficient women among wimpish men like Robert here. However Jamesian in Woodress's view,[13] Cather's early story seems to me to illustrate Lacan's notion that "there is no Other of the Other" and that a "woman is a symptom. The fact that a woman is a symptom can be seen from the structure which I am in the process of explaining to you, namely, that there is no *jouissance* of the Other as such, no guarantee to be met within the *jouissance* of the body of the Other, to ensure that enjoying the Other exists. A manifest instance of the hole, or rather of something whose only support is the *objet a* — but always in a mix-up or confusion."[14] The rejection of phallocentrism in "Eleanor's House" is perhaps personified by Cather in Harold's surname, *Forscythe:* the cutting off not only of the fore(skin) but of the phallus itself. On the other hand, Cather may be punning more phonetically than etymologically: bound to the past of his dead wife at the outset of the story, Harold is more *hindsight* than *foresight.*

4

Dissonance: Crescendo

Shadows on the Rock (1931)

The apothecary lingered on the hilltop long after his severance from the world grew every year harder to bear. It was a strange thing, indeed, that a man of his mild and thoughtful disposition, citybred and most conventional in his habits should be found on a grey rock in the Canadian wilderness. Cap Diamant, where he stood, was merely the highest ledge of that fortified cliff which was "Kébec,"—a triangular headland wedged in by the joining of two rivers, and girdled about by the greater river as an encircling arm. Directly under his feet was the French stronghold,—scattered spires and slated roofs flashing in the rich, autumnal sunlight; the little capital which was just then the subject of so much discussion in Europe, and the goal of so many fantastic dreams.

. . . .

On the opposite shore of the river, just across from the proud rock of Quebec, the black pine forest came down to the water's edge; and on the west behind the town, the forest stretched no living man knew how far. That was the dead, sealed world of the vegetable kingdom, an uncharted continent choked with interlocking trees, living, dead, half-dead, their roots in bogs and swamps, strangling each other in a slow agony that had lasted for centuries. The forest was suffocation, annihilation; there European man was quickly swallowed up in silence, distance, mould, black mud, and the stinging swarms of insect life that bred in it. The only avenue of escape was along the river. The river was the one thing that lived, moved, glittered, changed,—a highway along which men could travel, taste the sun and open air, feel freedom, join their fellows, reach the open sea . . . reach the world, even![1]

On this "fortified cliff which was 'Kébec'" we are far from the "yellow hill among all the green ones," the "rock" at whose aspect Jean Marie Latour could "almost feel the Rhône behind me."[2] *Wedged, girdled, encircling, scattered, dead, sealed, choked, interlocking, dead, half-dead, strangling, slow agony, suffocation, annihilation, swallowed-up, silence, distance, mould, black mud:* in this claustrophobic atmosphere, Euclide Auclair and his "fellow countrymen" think only of getting back to the world via a sea which, as rarely in Cather's fiction for that signifier, is open, a positive signifier. Along the river to the sea and on to the world—to France.

Shadows on the Rock, for which the novelist was awarded the French *Prix Fémina Américain* in 1933, is the most densely French-marked of Cather's fictions. Yet, as these two paragraphs from the early pages of the novel indicate, the markings are primarily atrophic, at best compensatory when they are not outrightly pejorative. The rock-set town reminds the apothecary Auclair of "those little artificial mountains in the churches at home to present a theatric scene of the nativity; cardboard mountains."[3] It is as if he and his emigrated fellow countrymen were actors playing at living in France. Consider especially Auclair and his daughter, Cécile: "as he used to in Paris"[4] and unlike his neighbors, Auclair dines at six in winter and at seven in summer, when the day's work is done, and he regards his dinner "as the thing that kept him a civilized man and a Frenchman."[5] Emigrated when she was only four years old and thus having only a vague recollection of home, his daughter keeps house for her widowed father in the punctilious manner of her mother in the colony before her death. The house is the very model of their house in Paris, thanks to their family's household goods. The colonists "liked to drop in at his house upon the slightest pretext; the interior was like home to the Frenchborn."[6] Cécile herself "wanted to believe that when she herself was lying in this rude Canadian earth, life would go on almost unchanged in this room with its dear (and, to her, beautiful) objects; that the proprieties would be observed, all the little shades of feeling which make the common fine."[7] The Auclairs, père et fille, are emigrants who have not immigrated.

They are, with few exceptions, Northern Frenchmen living in "heavy grey buildings, monasteries and churches, steep-pitched and dormered, with spires and slated roofs, . . . roughly Norman Gothic in effect."[8] In this novel, Cather's French compass of cultural values has been given a half turn, and South is North. The North is in the South, its cold wind withering this "subtle, sensitive, beauty-making Latin race" from within. The "Latin races," that 1902 travel-journal entry ran, "are rotten at heart and must wither before the cold wind of the north." There is more of the rotten than the "subtle, sensitive, beauty-loving" in the novel. To be sure, Euclide Auclair, in keeping with his name (Euclide, the geometer, + "au clair" = in the clear, a bringer of things to clarity), is more subtle than sensitive, and his daughter more sensitive than subtle. Again, there are their friends Father Hector Saint-Cyr, Captain Pondhaven of *Le Faucon* (one of the ships making its annual trip to the Old World), and Pierre Charron the trapper—all no less subtle and sensitive than the Auclairs. However, there are also the far more weighty and influential presences of the "rotten." There is young Bishop Saint Vallier when he is in Quebec; he spends more than half his appointment to the bishopric in courtly intrigue and indulgence in France. There is France itself as it is evoked in the memories of Count Frontenac, Governor of "New France," as the French Colony in North America is called. There is as well a dark image of King Louis XIV since the monarch tolerates in the "Name of Law" the kinds of tortures undergone by poor Bichet, an old man hanged in Paris for petty theft, whose tale Auclair often tells his daughter.

Bichet's story of a rotten old France is matched by an image of rottenness within New France itself: the anguish of Blinker, the wretched old man who runs errands for the Auclairs. Son of an executioner become himself an executioner in France, Blinker has fled to New France haunted by the images of all those he has tortured. The psychosomatic scars of this haunting clear for a time, but suppuration returns when Blinker cannot drive from his mind the memory of a mean mother whom he had executed for the murder of her half-witted son:

> The poor fellow had begun to give off a foul odour, as creatures do under fear or anguish. Auclair watched with amazement the twisted face he saw every day above an armful of wood,—grown as familiar to him as an ugly piece of furniture,—now become altogether strange; it brought to mind terrible weather-worn stone faces on the churches at home,—figures of the tormented in scenes of the Last Judgment. He hastened to measure out a dose of laudanum. After Blinker had gone out of the kitchen door, he made the sign of the cross over his own heart before he blew out the candle and went to his daughter.[9]

Every day...stone faces on the churches at home...figures of the tormented in scenes of the Last Judgment: even the "mild and thoughtful" Auclair has a daily reminder of the New France as the signifier of a rotten Old France.[10e]

These signifiers are not relieved for him by his religion. The apothecary's sign of the cross is not exactly perfunctory, but neither is he a deeply religious man. His Catholicism is itself a "figure" of that "figured" to which his fealty belongs more than to faith or profession or even family: France. When Count Frontenac is dying, Auclair relentlessly refuses to "bleed" the Count against "the urgings of his countrymen and Bishop

Vallier because "the mind, too, has a kind of blood; in common speech we call it hope."[11] Though he is not without heart in the Pascalian sense, Auclair belongs more to the "order of mind." When his heart is moved, as upon the death of the Count, it is a "move" touching his love of the France he sees disappearing in the death of the Count: " 'He belonged to the old order,' " he tells his daughter disconsonately, " 'he cherished those beneath him and rendered his duty to those above him, but flattered nobody, not the King himself. That time has gone by. I do not wish to outlive my time.' " His daughter appeals to him to live on her account: " 'I do not belong to the old time. I have got to live on into a new time; and you are all I have in the world.' " As if his daughter had not spoken, "her father went on sadly: 'The Count and the old Bishop were both men of my own period, the kind we looked up to in my youth. Saint Vallier and Monsieur de Champigny are of a different sort. Had I been able to choose my lot in the world . . . ' "; he continues reflecting on the personal and professional comforts fortune had given him to serve such a man and " 'to be honoured by his confidence.' "[12] The death of the Count seems the "Last Judgment" not only of that exalted official but of the apothecary who served him.

There are no eschatological reassurances in *Shadows on the Rock* like those found theologically in *Death Comes for the Archbishop* and sociologically in *One of Ours*. The sacramental consonances of the Old Catholic World and the New Catholicized World that comfort Jean Latour's life in the Southwest appear all too fleetingly and tentatively in the Northeast of this novel. The "Méridional" Father Hector Saint-Cyr and Captain Pondhaven with his parrot merely visit the Auclairs, bringing them enthusiasm and confidence and beauty only momentarily. Father Hector, from Aix-en-Provence, is "strong and fearless and handsome";[13] Pondhaven, from Saint Malô in western France, is a bluff, adventuring man who brings a live parrot of African rather than West Indian origin with "so many tones of voice" to delight Cécile.[14] As we have seen before in Cather, the parrot is a signifier of the lost language, particularly the more southern its roots (the American tropics in *Death Comes for the Archbishop*, Africa here). But Cécile hears that language only at the dinner party before Pondhaven must return on *Le Faucon* to France. Besides, she prefers the ornament of glass-enclosed artificial fruit she admires on visiting once with the Count—"lovelier than real fruit," for her.[15] She, too, is more of the mind than of the heart, and she is certainly not of the "order of the heart" in the stringent Pascalian sense, where the creature owes the creator love despite the desserts the creator gives the creature. Hers is a more creaturely sense of "charity." In this respect there is much of Maidy Forrester (*A Lost Lady*, 1923) in Cécile, the little "lost lady" of

Cather's fiction. There is also, however, something of Cather's more grim "lost lady," Myra Henshawe of *My Mortal Enemy* (1926).

Like Maidy, Cécile cares for "lost little boys": Jacques, the son of the prostitute, Toinette, is Cécile's Niel Herbert. She takes him under her wing, gets shoes for him through flirtatious dealings with the colony's cobbler, reads to him, brings him into the family for holidays, and intervenes with the awesome Bishop Laval on the child's behalf. The old Bishop is one of Cather's noble Romans. He is a grand, imposing figure with "deep-set, burning eyes" and a "big nose" before whom she is not intimidated but "always felt a kind of majesty in his grimness and poverty."[16] He is the meditative, self-flagellating side of Latour even as Vallier is the adaptive, activist side. This "splitting" of the sacramental personality of Latour is still another signifier of the elegiac mode of *Shadows on the Rock.* When Cécile goes to see him asking him to look after Jacques after she and her father return to France, Laval tells her that he supposes the boy might go to school with the Brothers in Montreal to prepare him for the Seminary. Cécile objects that Jacques is not clever in that way, could never do Latin, and would be unhappy in school. " 'Schools are not made to make boys happy, Cécile, but to teach them to do without happiness,' " the Bishop replies. Blithely passing this Jansenist severity, Cécile answers: " 'When he is older, perhaps, Monseigneur, but he is only seven.' "[17] Not unlike her father when he learns of the death of the Count, the old Bishop falls into a reverie about his own youth, but he does reassure Cécile that he will see what he can do for the boy.

On the other hand, if Cécile, like Maidy Forrester, knows how to care for waifs and to charm majestic old men, she is also, like Myra Henshawe, intolerant of messy uncivilized people. She and Pierre Charron make a trip to the Ile d'Orléans, an island in the St. Laurent River where they stay with the Harnois family. For her, the Harnois (French for "harness") are the Poindexters for Myra. Lying awake on the edge of the large feather bed with its unwashed sheets that she must share with the four unwashed Harnois daughters, Cécile begins "to cry quietly. She thought a great deal about her mother, too, that night; how her mother had always made everything at home beautiful, just as here everything about cooking, eating, sleeping, living, seemed repulsive."[18] The next day she manages to steal away into the nearest wood and makes her way to a clearing:

> a waving green hayfield with a beautiful harp-shaped elm growing in the middle of it. The grass there was much taller than the daisies, so that they looked like white flowers seen through a driving grey-green rain. Cécile ran across the field to that symmetrical tree and lay down in the dark, cloud-shaped shadow it threw on the waving

grass. The tight feeling in her chest relaxed. She felt she had escaped forever from the Harnois and their way of living.[19]

Cécile escapes the harness of the symbolic order to return to the imaginary. In Lacan's terms, she falls into the dream of the *"jouissance* of the Other,"* that realm of infinite pleasure in which the subject, the child, knows the joy (root of Fr. *jouissance*) shared by the father *and* the mother before the subject knows the "lack." She wakes feeling "rested and happy." Instead of going back to the Harnois's (to the "harness") she plans to lunch on "wild strawberries," a signifier of the lusciously erotic realm of the Other she is still in, upon awakening. However, she hears the Harnois girls calling her, " 'Cé-cile, Cé-cile!' rather *mournfully,* and she *remembered* that she *ought* not to cause the family anxiety."[20] Cécile is her clearheaded and "conventional" father's child; she goes back to the order of the symbolic — to memory, to history, to the effacement of both anxiety and the anxious repressed fantasies. There is, after all, only something of Myra Henshawe in her even as there is, after all, not all of Maidy Forrester.

She is neither a God-defier like Myra nor a goddess of the erotic like Maidy. Her religion is warmer than her father's, but it is also a *Catholicisme à travers les vitraux* (stained-glass Catholicism). It is, however, more child-like and certainly less sacrilegious than that of Myra Driscoll Henshawe and her great-uncle John Driscoll. Though adopted by Driscoll, Myra remains, more so than many of Cather's men and women, a spiritual orphan. Her orphanhood is so radical that she seems to have been born of no woman nor to have come from any seed of man. She is a primordial figure, sufficient unto herself, a divinity contesting the "Other" signified by her great-uncle. Like St. Peter's "Kanuck Grandfather" in *The Professor's House* (and, later, Henry Grenfell's grandfather in "Before Breakfast," published posthumously in 1948), Great-Uncle Driscoll figures also as a divinity in Myra's story. Yet, for her he is not the "Founding Father" to whom she pays fealty; rather, he is a rival God, a Zeus defied by Myra-Prometheus, giver of the arts and fire (desire) to humans. We see "Prometheus Bound" in Myra as she stands against the tree on the windswept jut of the Pacific headland on which she dies by her own will, complaining " 'Why must I die like this, alone with my mortal enemy.' "

Her death, like the rest of her story, is told from the viewpoint of Nellie Birdseye. In reprising in a final frame her birdseye point of view, Myra's despair at the loss of her power to love, Nellie emphatically distances herself not only from Myra but also, as so often in Cather, from the erotically driven men and women. As in the final moments of Alfred Hitchcock's *The Birds,* we are thus invited to view the human condition *sub speciae aeternitatis,* the point of view from which Archbishop Latour sees it. Like Latour, Myra echoes Pascal. " 'Religion is different from everything else,' " she tells Father Fay, " 'because in religion seeking is finding.' "[21] Echoes of Pascal's "You would not have looked for me, if you had not found me" (*Mystère de Jésus*). But she subverts this Pascalian wisdom by clinging to her love instead of finding the object of that love in God. Her fate (Myra is possibly from *Moïra*, Greek for "fate") is then to die alone with the "mortal enemy," herself more than Oswald whom she sees as both her lover and her enemy.

For Cécile Auclair God is not a rival God. He is, rather, a "little Lord" in the medieval political sense: "in his gaiety and graciousness and savoir-faire."[22] She loves to hear the nuns of the colony tell stories of the founder of their mission and Father Hector recount the trials of the learned martyr Father Chabanel. (Hector is a Latour-like scholarly contemplative who, learned though he is in European tongues, cannot learn the Indian language even as Latour has difficulty with Spanish and English.) Cécile also loves to read from the *Lives of the Saints* to Jacques. One such occasion is the inclusion of the longest passage in French in Cather fiction: the story of Jesus's appearance to a little French boy not unlike Jacques (two-thirds of p. 85). Comforting legends, stories, and religion in general are supports for Cécile of the conventions to which she returns following her reverie under the symmetrical elm. She will enter still more fully and conventionally into that order by one day marrying Pierre Charron and giving him four sons.

Charron, himself, is perhaps the most positive character of *Shadows on the Rock* in terms of those consonances marking Cather's other novel about the French in North America, *Death Comes for the Archbishop*. "To both Auclair and Madame Auclair, Pierre Charron had seemed the type they had come so far to find; more than anyone else he realized the romantic picture of the free Frenchman of the great forests which they had formed at home on the bank of the Seine. He had the good manners of the Old World, the dash and daring of the New."[23] Unsurprisingly in Cather, he is of *southern* French ancestry. His father was "a soldier of fortune from Languedoc" and, equally unsurprising, he has that "fine bold nose,"[24] the usual Cather signifier of the nobility and majesty of the "subtle, sensitive, beauty-loving Latin races." However, he also has the New World-born's dissatisfaction with the "rottenness" of the French strain of those races.

This dissatisfaction goes beyond the disapproval of Bishop St. Vallier which Charron shares with the Auclairs. Though generally more insouciant and nonchalant than the Auclairs, he has not always been so. As a young man he had been in love with Jeanne Le Ber, the only daughter of the richest merchant of Montreal and known as the recluse since her religious retreat many years before into an upstairs room of the Le Ber house very near to the church. Jeanne was once "warm and ardent, like her complexion gracious in manner, and not at all shy."[25] However, she now lives in abstemiousness, solitude, and devotion, with her only view the church and, at night, the perpetual red light of its altar lamp before the Blessed Sacrament of which she has said: *"I will be that lamp."*[26] Students of Pascal will be struck by the psychic and, to some extent, physical resemblance between Jeanne Le Ber and Jacqueline Pascal, that thinker's younger sister. She too, was a warm, ardent, and gracious young woman who, struck by the pox which marked her lovely complexion, became a recluse at Port Royal. Cather might well have remembered the model from her research for *Death Comes for the Archbishop.*

In renouncing the world in a first vow of five years, then renewed and renewed, Jeanne had also renounced her most ardent and most likely suitor, Pierre. Unable to take the rejection, Pierre tells the Auclairs he has violated the recluse's retreat on two occasions. One early spring morning in the fourth year of her first vow, he accosted Jeanne and her old servant as they were making their way between the garden of the Le Ber house and the church. He was delighted to find that she had not changed: "she did not shrink away from me or reproach me! She was gracious and gentle, as always and at her ease." She unveiled to talk to him, and he noted that she still had some color in her cheeks: " 'not rosy as she used to be, but her face was fresh and soft, like the apple blossoms of the tree where we stood.' "[27] Although kind and glad to see him, she tells him of her decision to renew her vow, meaning she would never see him again. She promises always to pray for him and for his children, when he would have them, and to pray to God that they would meet again in heaven. The second occasion on which he saw the recluse against her own wishes was earlier in the year of the novel. Knowing that Jeanne went into the church to pray before the altar at midnight, he hid himself in the church behind a pillar and had to wait a long time. " 'God's Name, is there any place so cold as churches,' " he says to the Auclairs, reminding the reader of Father Latour's reluctance to go into his cold church on his night of anguish. When he finally does see Jeanne, she is very different: " 'she came in, carrying a candle. She wore a grey gown, and a black scarf on her head, but no veil. The candle shone up into her face. It was like a stone face: it had been through every sorrow.' " Unable this time to approach Jeanne directly, Pierre sobs in spite of himself; Jeanne hears him. Unstartled, she turns toward the sound and, just before leaving the church, says, " 'Poor sinner... poor sinner, whoever you are may God have mercy upon you! And do you pray for me also.' "[28]

Like Cécile in the forest clearing, Jeanne Le Ber has retreated from

this world. She has become that "rich lamp of silver, made in France."
The lamp is a compound signifier not unlike the elm tree: a container
(female signifier) *in* which burns a perpetual flame (male signifier).
In her return to the order of the world, Cécile had identified with the
normative female role of that order. She maternally appeases the anxious
Harnois children who call for her, and she will, eventually, marry Pierre
and become the mother of his four children. In Jeanne's retreat from the
symbolic order, in renunciation of the conventional role of mother, she
returns to the radical phallocentrism of early psychic life. She believes
in—or, more precisely, *wills to be*—the Other, at once the father *and*
mother which is the lamp. Theologically, especially in the Jansenist
theology of these Quebec Catholics, Jeanne is guilty of the worst sin,
pride. She wills to be the divinity, presumes to know Its will. Psychoanalytically, she is also as much "at fault": she believes she is at one with
the Other, that she is the vessel into which the Other has entered so that it
may speak through her to other souls in the symbolic order. Presumably
for Jeanne, these have not yet attained to the Other in their narcissism,
their selfness which is but an empty subterfuge (" 'whoever you are' ") to
conceal or deny the lack. In the cold church near the recluse's retreat
Pierre Charron does not find in Jeanne Le Ber the Sada whom Jean
Marie Latour found in his cold church in New Mexico. The recluse is
neither a figure of the intercessionary Blessed Virgin Mary nor the
Queen of Heaven to whom the King of Heaven seems but a Prince
Consort. The sacramental consonance of *Death Comes for the Archbishop*
has been broken in the case of Jeanne Le Ber in an overdetermination of
one of its terms: the spiritual.

Eventually, it is also broken for Pierre Charron with respect to the
material. As he finishes his story, Pierre tells the Auclairs that " 'all that
is over; one does not love a woman who has been dead for twenty years.' "
He is still anguished by the thought of his childhood " 'playfellow . . .
suffering from cold those bitter nights.' " Moreover, " 'there are all those
early memories; one cannot get another set; one has but those.' Pierre's
voice choked, because something had come out by chance, thus, that he
had never said to himself before."[29] Pierre returns to the order of the
symbolic in its normative workings. He continues his pursuit of the
"object small a," the cause of his desire, by marrying Cécile.

This event takes place in the fifteen-year interval between chapter 6 of
the novel, "The Dying Count," and the epilogue. One might find in the
epilogue another chapter of the novel, an underscoring of the optimistic
fulfillment of the narrative and symbolic thrust of the novel proper. Yet,
in the total structure, novel proper plus epilogue, Pierre's salvific arrival
just after the death of the Count does not close the story. The epilogue

does and its dissonances underscore those of the novel, especially its formal last chapter dominated by the death of the disheartened Count.

Disheartened, not only does the dying Count bequeath the ornament of artificial fruit to Cécile, he also bequeaths his *heart* to France. He tells Auclair that he wants that organ removed and returned for interment in France. Yet, in France he, too, had known deep *psychic* as well as political disfavor. In his dying days, like Professor St. Peter in his "last" summer, Frontenac has a "curious dream." He is a little boy, awakened with a start in the old farm house near Pontoise where he spent the four summers from age four to eight with his nurse, Noémi, whom he loved more than his own mother who was "a cold woman (of) little affection for her own children."[30] The frightened little boy gets up and goes to the slightly opened door leading to the garden: "outside, in the darkness, stood a very tall man in a plumed hat and huge boots—a giant, in fact; the little boy's head did not come up to his boot-tops." Knowing he must keep the stranger out, the boy closes the door, slides the bolt, then goes through the house determined to close the front door. Its heavy iron bolt gives him special difficulty: "it was rusty, and stuck. He felt how small and weak his hands were—of that he was very conscious."[31] He succeeds, but then his fright increases as he thinks of all the other doors and windows through which the stranger might enter. At this point, the Count awakens in fright from his dream of that other frightening awakening.

The Count has had a castration dream: the big boots are the father's phallus, the little boy's "small and weak hands" his own little and imperilled phallus, the house the vagina of the Mother to whom he would give his phallus. The psychic signifiers are familiar. The many-feathered hat of the stranger, his boots, the boy's hands, and their ten fingers are phallic; the doors, windows, and house itself female. The multiplicity of both kinds is phantasmic in the context of the dream, reprising early psychic life in which phallocentrism envisions penetration into the many orifices of the desired mother. The bedroom door with its public garden, the front door with its recall of the mouth, and the back door of the anus are surrogated vaginal entries. The windows evoke ears, eye sockets, nostrils— secondary entries in such a fantasy. In the coldness of the little boy's natural mother there is a resonance of Professor St. Peter's "practical, strong-willed, Methodist mother" in *The Professor's House* (to be discussed later), while "her [other] children," the Count's siblings, in its plurality reminds the reader of the incident of the cherry tree in *One of Ours.* The mother rejects the phallic overtures of the son in token of her own accession to the phallus of the father.

The psychic afterlife of the Count differs radically from that of Claude Wheeler. Claude does not consummate his marriage on his wedding night. One wonders if, throughout the brief time he lived in wedlock with Enid before she left for evangelical work in China and he for France to die in battle, Enid was always "not feeling well" in the same sexually evasive way. However brief his marriage, Claude seems to have found out the truth of the prediction made to him by his then-future father-in-law, Mr. Royce: " 'You'll find out that pretty nearly everything you believe about life—about marriage, especially—is lies."[32] The Count accedes to woman, far less begrudgingly if no more happily. "Not all women had found him so personally distasteful as his wife had done; but not one of his mistresses had felt more than a passing inclination for him."[33] That is, they had not felt the kind of "inclination" Noémi had felt, rich with erotic commitment. (In French, the cognate *inclination* is a euphemistic signifier for the erotic, especially in the seventeenth century in which *Shadows on the Rock* is set—as, for example, in Madame de Lafayette's *La Princesse de Clèves,* 1678). The Count is as alienated from and as dissonant with woman since Noémi as he is in disfavor at the court.

In the Count's dream, the psychic and the political conflate. Noémi (Douai Bible spelling of Naomi) is also the name of the mother-in-law of the Ruth who left her Moabite people to live with her mother-in-law amidst "the alien corn." With the Count's heart finally buried in the Montmort chapel of St. Nicholas des Champs (also near the oldest house in Paris), he will return to the surrogate mother who treated him as a real mother even as the biblical Noémi treated Ruth. He goes back to his dream life. He resolves the oedipal pursuit of the mother in which he at once heeds the father's threat of castration and continues the frenetic pursuit of "The Woman/Mother" by substituting other women, a like signifier. This mythic conflation of the psychic and the political is not without some irony. In returning to Mother/Mother Country, the Count abandons his adopted country and its Moabite people, the Canadian French. There is a psychic and political *raison d'être* for the Count in giving his heart back to France. Much as he continues to pursue the desired Mother he curries the favor of the Phallic Father, the King. He had gained the latter's disfavor precisely by championing the Canadian French. There is also, however, a *dé-raison* in his dying wish, a dissonance with respect to the Canadian French: he separates New World France from Old World France. This breaks the mythic and political compact between the two, so central to the narrative and symbolic consonance of *One of Ours* and *Death Comes for the Archbishop.* The Canadian French begin to become the French Canadians with the Count's dying bequest of his heart. Two and one-half centuries later the French Canadians will have understood this. When General De Gaulle visited them in 1967 to call out to them in his usual home-style address—"Françaises, Français!"

—many of his auditors resented him. They reminded him, as many of them have told me, that his gesture seemed the purest cynicism of *raison d'Etat* after more than two centuries of French indifference to "Le Canada Français."

This psychic and political dissonance of the seeming end of the novel itself informs the real ending provided in the epilogue. As so often in Cather's fictions, the frame sets the narrative and symbolic pattern in which the story itself must be understood. The conventional omniscient, third-person narrator often withdraws from her principal point-of-view of the Auclairs, as in the parenthetical comment I cited above. One striking instance of this withdrawal in the novel is a first frame in the form of an epigraph in French: "Vous me demandez des graines de fleurs de ce pays. Nous en faisons venir de France pour notre jardin, n'èn ayant pas ici de fort rares ni de fort belles. Tout y est sauvage, les fleurs aussi bien que les hommes. (Marie de l'Incarnation LETTRE A UNE DE SES SOEURS, Québec, le 12 août 1653)."[34] Gardens are as rare in *Shadows* as they were numerous in *Death Comes for the Archbishop*. There is too much shadow on the rock of Quebec for gardens like that of Latour. The only one of relative sumptuosity is that of Bishop Vallier, a resonance of that corrupt garden of Fray Balthazar in *Death Comes* which led to that priest's ritual slaying by his exploited Indian parishioners.

In fact, Pierre Charron, husband of Cécile and father of four children, is not the narrative and symbolic cynosure of the epilogue. It is Vallier, of the once flamboyant manner of the rotten Court of Versailles:

> Saint-Vallier was a man of contradictions and they were stamped upon his face. One saw there something slightly hysterical and something uncertain,—though his manner was imperious, and his administration had been arrogant and despotic. Auclair had once remarked to the Count that the new Bishop looked less like a church-man than a courtier. "Or an actor," the Count replied with a shrug. Large almond-shaped eyes under long-growing brown hair and delicate eyebrows, a long, sharp nose—and then the lower part of the face diminished, like the neck of a pear. His mouth was large and well-shaped, but seldom in repose; his chin narrow, receding with a dimple at the end. He had a dark skin and flashing white teeth like an Italian,—indeed, his face recalled the portraits of eccentric Florentine nobles. He was still only forty-four; he had been Bishop of Quebec now twelve years,—and seven of them had been spent in France![35]

This passage provides shades of Frank Ellinger (*A Lost Lady*), of Freytag ("The Affair at Grover Station"), of Padre Martinez and the other ecclesiastical and secular conquistadores of *Death Comes for the Archbishop.* But the hieroglyphics of Saint Vallier's countenance do not show a Manichean power of darkness opposed to the power of light in Latour's uniformly serene and handsome countenance. They show, rather, the phrenological ambivalence Melville portrays in the physiognomy of Claggart: "The face was a notable one; the features all except the chin cleanly cut as those on a Greek medallion; yet the chin, beardless as Tecumseh's, had something of strange protuberant heaviness in its make that recalled the prints of the Rev. Titus Oates, the historic deponent with the clerical drawl in the time of Charles II and the fraud of the alleged Popish Plot."[36] Again, with his sense of grandeur and his ambition, Vallier might have been the ecclesiastical counterpart to the legendary La Salle, the Latour-like adventurer into the lower Mississippi Valley outreaches of New France whom Auclair evokes for his daughter. Vallier too, is divided in his soul as in his countenance. Thus, he undoes the old Bishop's sensible organization of the mission in New France into parishes of movable priests by organizing it into a series of fixed parishes each with its own pastor. Similarly, as the Count is dying, Vallier's crafty eye catches sight of the bequeathed ornament of artificial fruit in Auclair's home, a sign of the apothecary's influence with the Count. Vallier urges Auclair to persuade the Count that he must end the sale of whiskey to the Indians " 'to strengthen the kingdom of God in Septentrional France!' "[37] Auclair refuses and, when Vallier has left, makes note, once again, to his daughter of the new Bishop's "restless eyes."[38]

The Vallier of the epilogue is a much less restless man. He has returned from Europe, including a long "house-arrest" as political prisoner in England, to resume his bishopric. "Every physical trait by which Auclair remembered the handsome and arrogant churchman had disappeared. He would never have recognized, in this heavy, stooped, lame old man going up the hill, the slender and rather dramatic figure he had so often seen mounting the steps of the episcopal palace across the way. The narrow, restless shoulders were fat and bent; the Bishop carried his head like a man broken to the yoke."[39] It is a yoke Vallier has placed about his own neck. In the conversation between Auclair and Vallier which makes up most of the epilogue, we learn that the Bishop will not reside in the Episcopal Palace but at the Hôpital Général. There, he will have " 'un petit appartement which will meet my needs very well' "; there, he will take on the duties of the old chaplain who is soon to retire, an " 'office . . . quite compatible with my other duties.' " When Auclair notes that the duties of a hospital chaplain are "considerable," Vallier replies " 'but very congenial to me.' "[40] In his new humility, Vallier is reconciled to the now dead predecessor, though he acknowledges that he " 'can never hope to be to this people all that my venerable predecessor became, through his devotion and long residence among them.' "[41] The conversation turns to contemporary France and the King, now an old man and for Vallier the symbol that "the old age is dying, but the new one is still hidden." This is a sentiment he had also felt during his captivity in England: " 'the changes in the nations are all those of the old growing older. You have done well to remain here where nothing changes.' "[42]

At this point, Vallier asks about Auclair's daughter. The apothecary reports her marriage to Charron; they are well established with a " 'commodious house in the Upper Town, beyond the Ursuline Convent.' "

> The apothecary's eyes twinkled. "Four sons already, Monseigneur. She is bringing up four little boys, the Canadians of the future."
> "Ah, yes, the Canadians of the future, — the true Canadians."
> There was something in Saint-Vallier's voice as he said this which touched Auclair's heart a note humble and wistful, something sad and defeated. Sometimes a neighbor whom we have disliked a lifetime for his arrogance and conceit lets fall a single commonplace remark that shows us another side, another man, a man uncertain, and puzzled, and in the dark like ourselves.[43]

Vallier's defeated phallocracy cedes to one itself uncertain.

The shadows still fall upon the rock. The very distinction that Vallier draws contrasts with the view of Auclair throughout the novel. The people of Quebec are Frenchmen and Frenchwomen in an overseas colony of the France which Auclair, in particular, preserves in the very way he conducts his life and maintains his home. To be sure, throughout the novel, including the epilogue, Charron and Cécile may have become "true Canadians." Long before she marries, as she and little Jacques watch *Le Faucon* and the other vessels leave, she tells the little boy that she wishes " 'you and I could go very far up the river in Pierre Charron's canoe, and then off into the forests to the Huron country where the martyrs died. I would rather go out there than — .' "[44] However, Auclair has not become one of the "Canadians of the future, — the true Canadians." This perpetual alienation becomes clear in the last paragraph of the novel: "As the apothecary was closing his shop and changing his coat to go up to his daughter's house, he thought over much that his visitor had told him, and he believed that he was indeed fortunate to spend his old age where nothing changed; to watch his grandsons grow up in a country where the death of the King, the probable evils of a long regency, would never touch him."[45] But Auclair cannot very likely expect to survive that long regency (1715–1723). However, what is striking in his reflections is that he is the object of the wilderness protection his grandsons will enjoy. As he did not hear Cécile when she appealed to him on the death of the Count to "outlive his time," so here he does not hear his grandsons protected from those evils; he hears only himself. Nothing has changed for him since first we met him on the rock filled with a sense of severance from the world. His contentment as he prepares to go to his daughter's house for dinner is that the New France is the Old France, the real France. But it is not; Auclair's phallocracy may be preserved, but only in illusion. He lives in Quebec in a reproduction of his house in Paris, and he now shares it with Jacques, become a sailor, when the boy lands at Quebec. He is, we see, still with a little Cécile, someone whom Charron had greeted upon returning the day after the Count's death as " 'petite tête de garçon!' "[46]

The masculinization of a principal female figure for once in Cather bears less on that figure's sexuality than on that of another principal figure, her father. When Bishop Vallier asks if Auclair now lives alone, the apothecary replies:

> "For part of the year. Perhaps you remember a little boy whom my daughter befriended, Jacques Gaux? His mother was a loose woman — she died in your Hôpital Général, some years ago. The boy is now a sailor, and when he is in Quebec, between voyages, he lives with me. He occupies my daughter's little chamber upstairs." Auclair pointed to the cabinet of shells and corals. "He brings me these things back from his voyages; he is in the West India trade. I should like to keep him here all the time, but his father was a sailor — it is natural."[47]

Auclair lives like a Captain Vere whose Billy Budd does not die. Auclair's homoeroticism is not the latent homosexuality of Claude Wheeler. In that part of the year when the boy is gone, like Professor St. Peter, he has relics of his companion in a house where he lives alone, without women. This Canadian Frenchman is more of the "order of the mind" than St. Peter, the erotically driven academic progeny of the French Canadians I shall later consider. Yet, the homosexual troping of Auclair is as clear as that of the Professor and of so many of Cather's mild and conventional father-figures. The apothecary, a widower who lives with a daughter of a boy's mien, is a man who shows no sign in the novel proper of any kind of eroticism, overt or covert, toward women. Auclair has succeeded and will continue to succeed in living in a world without women. When he visits the "commodious house" of Cécile and Pierre Charron he will still be in a world of men — his son-in-law, his grandsons, and his daughter with her "boy's head."

In that house as in the house in which Jacques Gaux is his part-year companion, the companionship will not have the ominous overtones of that of so many of Cather's accompanists. There is little or but muted passion in *Shadows on the Rock*. Its most passionate character, Bishop Vallier, himself finally falls under the shadows on the rock of Quebec. The most balanced character, Euclide Auclair, takes comfort in those shadows against the hard glare of the "probable evils of a long regency" attendant upon the death of the Sun King. In those comforting shadows Auclair will conserve, preserve, and reserve (and re-serve) the stabilities he had known in his home and shop in both Paris and Quebec. These are the stabilities of an unchanging France whose language will be lost in its purity to his grandsons in the inevitable process of linguistic attrition to which all source-languages are subject.

"Québec libre" will be neither French nor Canadian—it will become part of the British Dominion to which New France will yield in 1763. Its citizens will not know the consonance in diversity marking the polyethnic communities on the plains in such novels as *O Pioneers!, My Antonia, One of Ours,* and *Death Comes for the Archbishop.* Severed in tranquility at the end of *Shadows on the Rock* as he was in anguish at its beginning, Auclair will speak a language, French and all its cultural values, that will be increasingly lost to his grandsons. More ominously for him, that language will be lost to the old order of its origin as it passes into the "hidden order" Bishop Vallier adumbrates in his new humility. The French language of consonances between old and new orders, (France's landscapes, faiths, *éthnies,* etc.) is a lost language that only Auclair will speak.

Dissonance is structured into *Shadows on the Rock* in the very "point of view" from which it is mostly observed: that of the autotelic Auclair. As point of view, Auclair is the most stationary of Cather's observers. He does not move about like Jim Burden (*My Antonia*), Nellie Birdseye (*My Mortal Enemy*), or Niel Herbert (*A Lost Lady*). Auclair is city-bred, a Parisian who duplicates his Parisian home and profession in Quebec. That "rock city" is grotesque, a geographically locked and psychically rocked cradle of New France imitating, for Auclair, in particular, the "cradle" of France herself, Paris. The irony in this equation, of course, only underscores the dissonance perceptible in Auclair, the observer centered in the order of the mind. For Cather, as I have noted, Paris was not all of France, and, if any city is its capital for her, it is Avignon, located in the French South of "subtle, sensitive, beauty-loving Latin races." From Paris during her researches for *Shadows* in the summer of 1930 the novelist took only a brief trip to Avignon. Was the trip an interlude from the dissonances of her research? Was her visit there perhaps like Cécile's refuge on the Ile d'Orléans in the novel itself? The island in the St. Lawrence seems homologous with the Ile St. Louis in the

Seine: between two banks, it is a refuge from the city itself. Refuges as well are the intermittent appearances of Méridionaux like Father Hector and Pierre Charron himself. Life in the "Upper Town" at the end of the novel is bound to constrict the independence and nonchalance of a *coureur de bois*. To be sure, the novelist also took a longer interlude at Aix-les-Bains, where she met the equally fabulous "Caro." From there, she travelled into the nearby mountains, following suggestions for the best sight of Mont Blanc from the old lady which proved to be "wholly successful."[48] The traveller's characterization of this part of her trip has more than the ring of the satisfied tourist; it rings of the satisfied researcher. In the majestic reaches of the Alps Cather undoubtedly felt their refreshing contrast with those "cardboard mountains" around the French Canada she was soon to write about in *Shadows on the Rock.*

This French Canada is not Cather's Old France become New France. Beyond Auclair's Kébec illusorily preserved in the image of his beloved Paris lies the cold forbidding wilderness of a country Auclair does not care to know. His own Kébec-as-Paris is but a mock-Paris wedged between rivers (like that other northern city of such ominous meaning for Cather on this continent, Pittsburgh). Across from the city there stands not the "familiar cottonwood" but a forest of pines. These saturnine sentinels do not guard that "Principality of Pines" in which Cather found the Lavandou of 1902 with its "sense of immeasurable possession and immeasurable content." Instead, they oversee "the dead, sealed world of the vegetable kingdom," a veritable realm of the dead. It is this dead France Auclair "undertakes" to preserve like the mummy of Mother Eve whom Tom Outland of *The Professor's House* found in the city of his "lost language." Quebec is a city in which artificial fruit under glass is "much lovelier than real fruit." Like the novel itself, the glass reveals natural consonances that are only illusory.

5

Dissonance: Diminuendo

O Pioneers! (1913)

The young men crowded around Emil to admire his costume and to tell him in a breath everything that had happened since he went away. Emil had more friends up here in the French country than down in Norway Creek. The French and Bohemian boys were spirited and jolly, liked variety, and were as much predisposed to favor anything new as the Scandinavian boys were to reject it. The Norwegian and Swedish lads were much more self-centered, apt to be egotistical and jealous. They were cautious and reserved with Emil because he had been away to college, and were prepared to take him down if he should try to put on airs with them. The French boys liked a bit of swagger, and they were always delighted to hear about anything new: new clothes, new games, new songs, new dances. Now they carried Emil off to show him the club-room they had just fitted up over the post-office, down in the village. They ran down the hill in a drove, all laughing and chattering at once, some in French, some in English.[1e]

This passage, from the pages on the picnic at "French Town," in the section of the novel called "The White Mulberry Tree," obviously resonates with many of the consonances I traced in part 2. Its reflections on the "swagger-loving" French boys and the "egotistical and jealous... Norwegian and Swedish lads" suggest a crack in the polyethnic and polylinguistic oneness in diversity of Cather's Nebraska cited at the beginning of my discussion of her fictions of consonance in diminuendo.[2] Nevertheless, what Gervaud has called her optimism on this account is not too severely compromised by this passage: the reservations about the Nebraskans of Northern-European origin here are carefully qualified ("apt to be egotistical and jealous"). Moreover, set in the joyous, curious, and exuberant tones of the paragraph, these criticisms are further relativized when we remember that we are hearing them from the point of view of the observer-participant of the passage, Emil Bergson. Though somewhat less so than Claude Wheeler, Emil is a rather shy and earnest young man, and, like Claude, he feels more at home in a French ambiance. The French disposition to the new—clothes, games, songs, dances—and the hearty, bilingual chatter put him at ease. In it we have a mutual troping in which the specific languages as such seem but part of the laughter, the swagger, the curiosity, the country itself. All are pictographs of the consonance of this happy moment: Emil has come to the picnic with his sister, Alexandra, knowing he will meet Marie, with whom he has long been in love, though she is now married to Frank Shabata.

Marie is Bohemian. At the picnic she is as well very much a Bohemian in the figurative sense of the word: something of a vagabond and a gypsy, an unconventional person—the sense of the word which can be seen to emerge in the passage I have just quoted from the novel with its linkage of the "French and Bohemian boys" as "spirited and jolly." At the picnic, she wears "a short red skirt of stoutly woven cloth, a white bodice and kirtle, a yellow silk turban wound low over her brown curls, and long coral pendants in her ears."[3] These warm colors, particularly Cather's yellow, make her at once exotic and erotic. The effect is underscored by her fortunetelling:

> The young French priest, Father Duchesne, went first to have his fortune read. Marie took his hand, looked at it, and then began to run off her cards. "I see a long journey across water for you, Father. You will go to a town all cut up by water; built on islands, it seems to be, with rivers and green fields all about. And you will visit an old lady with a white cap and gold hoops in her ears, and you will be very happy there.
>
> "Mais, oui," said the priest, with a melancholy smile. "C'est L'Isle-Adam, chez ma mère. Vous êtes très savante, ma fille." He patted her yellow turban, calling, "Venez donc, mes garcons! Il y a ici une véritable clairvoyante."[4e]

Father Duchesne seems to place the exotic and perhaps the erotic under the sign of heaven. At any rate, he sees no harm in and even delights in the flirtatious Marie's readings of his and others' fortunes at the picnic grounds of the French church, Sainte Agnès, in the "French country."

In her fortunetelling, her exoticism, and her eroticism at the picnic, Marie speaks the lost language of desire to Emil who had lost her to Frank Shabata. At last Emil literally acts out that desire that very night when he and Marie kiss in the dark of the lights she has doused over the picnic grounds—only to bury it again when she withdraws from him in the days after the picnic. On one of these days his best friend, the French

boy, Amédée, dies. The friend's death is itself a signifier of the dissonance between the language of French *joie de vivre* and the language
of industrial expansion and mechanical modernism. Amédée dies from
" 'an awful pain . . . inside' " that he does not tend because he is too busy
using and supervising use of his new farm equipment. As we have seen,
this is one of the dissonances Claude Wheeler of *One of Ours* suffers on
the prairie before going to France; however, Claude repairs his dissonance in the "language" he finds there. Amédée's dissonant death only
prefigures that of Emil and Marie when they finally heed the language
of desire to the full.

In the music sung by another Frenchman at the funeral Mass of
Amédée in the French church Emil had heard that language and determined to heed its message: "He seemed to discover that there was a kind
of rapture in which he could love forever without faltering and without
sin. He looked across the heads of the people at Frank Shabata with calm-
ness. That rapture was for those who could feel it; for people who could
not, it was non-existent. He coveted nothing that was Frank Shabata's.
The spirit he had met in music was his own."[5] As later for Professor
St. Peter, "art and religion . . . come down to the same thing" for Emil.
However, Emil adds a third term to the equation, one which the Professor devalues, as we shall see: physical love. In a conflation familiar to
Americans of every generation—especially of Cather's, I am tempted to
say—the synonym for art in the case of Emil is French. The French voice
in the church, the dancing and other aesthetic aspects of the picnic in
French Town, the very use of the French language—all impel him to
realize in the symbolic order the desire he has repressed for so long. In
possessing Marie he would make up for the lack he had first experienced,
psychoanalytically, in the mother whom he by now has lost in real as well
as psychic fact. It is through if not literally in the language and culture of
France that he will give to the mother, in the person of the like-signifier
who is Marie Shabata, his phallus to make up for the one both prime-
signifier and like-signifier do not have. Unlike Claude Wheeler, the later
Catherian Anglo-Saxon who has long said no to normative phallic commitment and continues to do so even on French soil, on that soil of the
picnic in French Town and the French church Emil says yes. He thinks
he will thereby recover the lost language in which he will enjoy both
untrammelled phallic possession of the mother and return to an Edenic
state in which signifier and signified are one. He will also join a tradition
in which cultural markers are richer and more meaningful than the ones
in which he had grown to manhood and in which he still lives under the
tutelage of his sister.

What he finds instead is death. He and Marie die, gunned down by

her husband. In heeding the signifiers of primal demands, Emil and
Marie find the violent death those signifiers so often court in Cather. As
they lie embraced in death, the French-Bohemian-American consonances
of the picnic finally sound more like the dissonant rumblings of the
underground river of hell to which Bishop Latour had listened in the
cave with Jacinto.

As I suggested earlier, this dissonant experience of a French presence
of America is perhaps an expression of Cather's own "falling out of
love" with a France with which she had thought herself too long and too
deeply in love. After the ecstasies of her own 1902 trip to France, reported
in the travel journal, and a spate of stories celebrating consonances
between France and various lost languages she cherished (art, music,
land, etc.), the writer seems to have looked on France more suspiciously.
The relation between France and "free love"—or, more precisely in
Cather's perspective, "love freed" from psychosexual, social, and religious
conventions—is particularly dissonant in *Alexander's Bridge* (1911) and
O Pioneers! (1913), her first two novels. The French markings of the first
novel are not so pronounced as in *O Pioneers!*, but their subtextual
import is of the same order: literally in a violent river the adulterous
hero of that novel perishes, dragged down to death by the drowning
French-Canadian bridge builders desperately clinging to him. Bartley
Alexander had begun his love affair with the beautiful Hilda Burgoyne
in Paris, where he and Hilda had first known each other as students
before his marriage to Winifred; he continued it adulterously in London,
a city bathed once again in the warm glow of the Paris days. But he dies
in the arms of French-Canadian workers in the rolling waters of a great
Canadian river, not in Hilda's arms in Paris.

Similarly, Marie begins her affair with Emil in "French Town." The
affair ends under the mulberry tree with the violent deaths of Emil and
Marie who had so loved trees: " 'The Bohemians, you know,' " she once
told Emil, " 'were tree worshippers before the missionaries came. Father
says the people in the mountains still do queer things, sometimes—they
believe that trees bring good or bad luck. . . . I'm a good Catholic, but
I think I could get along with caring for trees, if I hadn't anything else.' "[6]
Thus, in Cather's first novel, the tamer of mighty currents who does not
tame the current of his own passion is ultimately tamed by mighty
currents; in her second novel, the lover of trees who could care for them
if she had nothing else dies beneath a tree. In each instance a precedent,
nonhuman force presides over the death of a human overreacher. Indeed,
in Marie's case, given the relation she makes between her religion and
trees as heathen superhuman forces, the mulberry tree seems a very
signifier of the religious faith she implicitly disavows in her comparison.

It is as if she has been punished not only for her adultery but also for her heathenism; her adultery is itself but an expression of that heathenism. She and her lover have misread the sacramental signifiers of the lost language, speaking through if not, in fact, as the mulberry tree.

This dissonant subtext of *O Pioneers!* is, of course, at odds with the consonance of the text of the novel. Emil and Marie do not carry the central message of *O Pioneers!;* Alexandra Bergson does, in her love of the land as in her renunciation of the erotic. Lying in bed the night after finding the murdered Emil and Marie,

> . . . she had again, more vividly than for many years, the old illusion of her girlhood, of being lifted and carried lightly by some one very strong. He was with her a long while this time, and carried her very far, and in his arms she felt free from pain. When he laid her down on her bed again, she opened her eyes, and, for the first time in her life, she saw him, saw him clearly, though the room was dark, and his face was covered. He was standing in the doorway of her room. His white cloak was thrown over his face, and his head was bent a little forward. His shoulders seemed as strong as the foundations of the world. His right arm, bared from the elbow, was dark and gleaming, like bronze, and she knew at once that it was the arm of the mightiest of all lovers. She knew at last for whom it was she had waited, and where he would carry her. That, she told herself, was very well. Then she went to sleep.[7]

She does not, however, "find" this "mightiest of all lovers . . . for whom . . . she had waited," and she is not "carried off" anywhere. Instead, she marries Carl Lindstrum, the mildest of all lovers in the novel. The lover with the "bared . . . dark and gleaming . . . bronze" arm is not, she realizes finally, what she had awaited. " 'You belong to the land,' Carl murmured, 'as you have always said. Now more than ever.' " She agrees with him: " 'How many of the names on the county clerk's plat will be there in fifty years? I might as well try to will the sunset over there to my brother's children. We come and go, but the land is always there. And the people who love it and understand it are the people who own it—for a little while.' " She renounces her dream, she renounces the erotic: " 'I had a dream before I went to Lincoln—but I will tell you about that afterward,' " she tells Carl, " 'after we are married. It will never come true, now, in the way I thought it might.' "[8]

Alexandra Bergson is a truer mythical equivalent to "Alexander the Great" than the great bridge builder, Bartley Alexander of Cather's first novel. She is also faithful to her religion and her faith in the land, as Marie Shabata is not to her Catholicism. Each religion is transcendental, denying the immanences to which Bartley Alexander and Marie gave themselves, foreswearing their own belief in transcendence. Each religion posits a figural agency, a "sacrament," exacting of its adherents a catechetical denial of self, particularly in the realm of the erotic. As in the marriage of Alexandra and Carl, the erotic is itself institutionalized, sacramentalized, contained.[9e] At the logical level, the textual consonances of *O Pioneers!* are as firm as those of *Death Comes for the Archbishop.* At the psychological level, however, the effect is more mixed: in spite of "that exalted serenity that sometimes came to her at moments of deep feeling," as Alexandra tells Carl, her dream " 'will never come true, now, in the way that I thought it might.' " The reader senses that however much of the lost language Alexandra may have recovered, she has not recovered all of it. There is still too much distance between text and subtext in the novel, a distance that marks the dissonant role of *la francité* and the Bohemian in the novel.

"Uncle Valentine" (1925)

I remember my aunt's voice, a tone not quite natural, when she said suddenly, "Valentine, how beautiful the Tuileries gardens are on an afternoon like this — down about the second fountain. The color lasts in the sky so long after dusk comes on, — behind the Eiffel tower."

He was lying on his back. He sat up and looked at her sharply. "Oh, yes!"

"Aren't you going to be a little homesick for it?" she asked bashfully.

"A little. But it's nice to sit sage and lazy on Fox Hill and be a trifle home-sick for far-away places. Even Roland gets homesick for Bavaria in the spring he tells me. He takes a drink or two and recovers. Are you trying to shove me off somewhere?"

She sighed. "Oh, no! NO, indeed; I'm not."

But she had, in some way, broken the magical contentment of the afternoon. The little girls began to seem restless, so we gathered them up and started home.[10]

At the beginning of this century, Fox Hill is a lovely retreat adjoining the estate of Charlotte Waterford, aunt of the narrator, Margaret, in the suburbs of a "City up the river it is scarcely necessary to name."[11e] Valentine, a composer, is the youngest son of the Ramsay family, neighbors of the Waterfords. Home from Paris after a long stay abroad, he has been inspired to write a host of songs; in fact, these are the thirty or so on which his reputation has since rested. We learn as much from Margaret in first frame of the story: a scene in Paris many years after the exchange between Charlotte and Valentine "sage and lazy" on Fox Hill, whose "magical contentment" is "in some way, broken" by Charlotte's recall of the Tuileries gardens. Charlotte's breaking of the spell is a narrative premonition of the breaking of the spell between Valentine's "at homeness" on Fox Hill and his homesickness for Paris. This occurs when the homebound hill-loungers encounter Janet, *née* Oglethorpe, Valentine's former wife and now Mrs. Towne by her second marriage. Janet announces that she has bought the gracious old "Wakeley" house near Fox Hill because " 'it will be nice for Valentine's boy to grow up here where he did, and to be near his Grandfather Ramsay. I want him to know his Ramsay kin.' " Behaving very badly, Valentine tells his ex-wife: " 'He's not my boy, and the less he sees of the Ramsays, the better. You've got him, it's your affair to make an Oglethorpe of him and see that he stays one. What do you want to make the kid miserable for.' "[12]

Broken spells, rejection of sons, family feuds, bad behavior — these are far from the comforting consonances of *One of Ours.* Unlike Claude Wheeler in France, Valentine Ramsay does not find in America continuities of one land in the other. When Janet Oglethorpe Towne buys the Wakeley place, Valentine regards it as a sacrilege. Valentine had been "happily settled in Paris, under Saint-Saëns." There the rich and not especially attractive Janet Oglethorpe had "followed him and married him."[13] But his francophilia is more intrinsic with deeper roots: he is a lover of French wine and excellent speaker of French as well as *amateur* of French literature — especially now in refuge from a dinner party at which Ida Milholland, "the intellectual of the valley" and, as he puts it, " 'that bump of intellect,' " practices " 'her French grammar' " on him.[14] He was the lover in Paris of the passionate, beautiful Louise Ireland, a singer and teacher of voice; for her he had abandoned his wife. He wears Louise's ring, an intaglio of a "three masted ship under full sail" bearing the inscription "in old English letters, *Telle est La Vie.* "[15]

For the francophile Valentine the purchase of the Wakeley place by the rich but culturally poor Oglethorpes/Townes of the New World is a desecration. When the news of the likely sale of the adjoining estate is first announced, he tells Charlotte's husband, Harry: " 'But there are some things one doesn't think of in terms of money. . . . If I'd had bushels of money when I came home last winter, it would never have occurred to me to try to buy Blinker's Hill, any more than the sky over it. I didn't know that the Wakeleys or anybody else owned the creeks, and the forest up toward the Ridge.' "[16] Beneath that sky, in the gardens and the garden lodge of the Ramsay estate as in the drawing rooms of the neighboring and neighborly Waterfords, Valentine has been "making new songs."[17] He has been as happy as Claude in the garden of Olive de Courcy and her handyman Louis. However, the sale of Blinker Hill (the region in which all the estates are located) being a fact, it is only logical that Janet Oglethorpe buy the Wakeley place and begin tearing down the wing of the Wakeley place within a week after purchase. Valentine will linger only a month at the Ramsay place, then hie off to Paris and Louise—only to die there, struck down by a "motor truck, one of the first in Paris."[18] Valentine does not know even the relative consonance between glorious death and site of death known to Claude Wheeler. The composer dies at the hands of those machines Claude had so detested on American soil. These emblems of the mechanical "language" of the modern world have reached into that capital of the world for Claude and his mother: Paris.

During the brief summer in which he composes the thirty American songs, Valentine Ramsay represents a consonance of the two languages of France that were at odds with each other in *One of Ours:* on the one hand, the nonverbal to which Claude responded in the landscapes of the country as well as the songs of Louis whose words he could not understand and, on the other hand, the verbal represented by Madame Joubert, the Fleury family, and, of course, David. Valentine is at once Claude and David. This excellent speaker of French is a lover of gardens *à la française* that inspire him in his art. He is a reader of French literature, especially of a romantic cast: the tale of Tristan and Iseult in French that he offers to read to Margaret.[19] He is a student of Camille Saint-Saëns (1835–1921), whose death occurred at just about the time the "world broke in two" for Cather. Unlike Claude, Valentine is not afraid of women. As he tells the narrator, Margaret, and Harriet, Margaret's favorite cousin, in an outburst that he sees as part of their growing up, he left Janet for a different kind of woman, Louise Ireland:

> "She had certainly run away with desperate men before ... —But behavior, I find, is more or less accidental, Charlotte. Oh, don't look so scared. Your dovelets will have to face facts some day, Aesthetics come back to predestination, if theology doesn't. A woman's behavior may be irreproachable and she herself may be gross—just gross. She may do her duty, and defile everything she touches. And another woman may be erratic, imprudent, self-indulgent if you like, and all the while be—what is it the Bible says? Pure in heart. People are as they are, and that's all there is to live."[20]

Valentine's quip about "aesthetics" and "predestination" echoes that of Professor St. Peter in Cather's novel of the same year as this story, *The Professor's House:* " 'Art and religion (they are the same thing in the end, of course) have given man the only happiness he has ever had.' "[21] The religious connections Valentine makes in contrasting two kinds of women evoke Louise Ireland in the image of Lillith, Adam's legendary first wife, in contrast to the gross Janet Oglethorpe as a manipulative Eve all too readily heeding the call of money and other immanentist lures of the serpent. In the promiscuous Louise we have another Cather "lost lady." Like Maidy Forrester, Louise Ireland is lost to the straightlaced, materialistic world of the grimy "City up the River" and the "wave of industrial expansion that swept down that valley, and roaring mills that belch their black smoke up the heights where those lovely houses used to stand."[22] However, Louise is also like Maidy by living the lost language in so many of its French dialects: music (Maidy's laughter, Louise's songs), good manners, social graciousness, and, especially, erotic energy. In Louise, teacher of song in the capital of France, Valentine had found the lost language in place and art and love.

This finding is lost with Valentine's death. The lost language is to be heard only in his songs, particularly "I know a wall where red roses grow," a recollection of the roses Harry Waterford and Uncle Morton, Valentine's brother, grow on the hillside soon to be ravaged by the industrial expansion. Margaret closes her narration of the story with: "Fox Hill is gone, and our wall is gone. *I know a wall where red roses grow;* youngsters sing it still. The roses of song and the roses of memory, they are the only ones that last."[23] The dissonances between France and America, the contrasts of any of the lost language dialects to any of today's languages are more marked in this *envoi* than in that of *One of Ours.* The observer of this story, the narrator Margaret, does not even share with Harriet the pleasures of Charlotte's house the way the narrator of "Eleanor's House" had.

"Charlotte's House" and all that is associated with an America given three-dimensionality through memories of France exist no longer. Nor does "Bonnie Brae," the Ramsay house on the hillside so aptly named to contain its assortment of odd father and uncles and brother of Valentine. No longer will Valentine write his songs inspired by the Paris-settled Louise Ireland; no longer will his father write his "romance of the French and Indian wars";[24] no longer will Margaret find Valentine reading his "yellow French book" giving the story of one of Wagner's famous operas; no longer will Uncle Roland, Jonathan's brother and Valentine's uncle, play so marvelously upstairs when he is not nipping in disgrace for having tried to seduce the tyrannical Swedish housemaid, Molla Carlsen. The latter's ascendancy through blackmail for that incident already betokened the surrender of the Latinotropic Ramsays to the "cold wind from the north." The fertile womb of the houses in the story, Bonnie Brae and Aunt Charlotte's house, gives birth to the stillborn. This lesson is framed in Louise Ireland's ironic instruction to the young American student in the opening of the story and in Margaret's sense of loss at the end. Let us now turn to another house—perhaps the most famous in Cather's fiction.

The Professor's House (1925)

The Professor had succeeded in making a French Garden in Hamilton.[25]

He had often wondered how she managed to sew with hands that folded and unfolded as rigidly as umbrellas—no light French touch about Augusta.[26]

. . . his practical, strong-willed Methodist mother, his gentle weaned-away Catholic father, the old Kanuck grandfather . . . [27]

St. Peter had met his wife in Paris, when he was but twenty-four, and studying for his doctorate. She too was studying there.[28]

He wore on his head a rubber visor of a kind he always brought home from France in great numbers.[29]

"And now I seem to be tremendously tired. One pays, coming or going. A man has got only just so much in him; when it's gone he slumps. Even the first Napoleon did." They both laughed. That was an old joke—the Professor's darkest secret. At the font he had been christened Napoleon Godfrey St. Peter. There had always been a Napoleon in the family, since a remote grandfather got his discharge from the Grande Armée.[30]

. . . for the present, I don't want anything very stimulating. Paris is too beautiful, and too full of memories."[31]

"Louis," St. Peter spoke with deep feeling, "do you happen to have read a novel of Henry James, *The American?* There's a rather nice scene in it, in which a young Frenchman, hurt in a duel, apologizes for the behavior of his family. I'd like to do something of the sort. I apologize for Rosamond, and for Scott, if he has done such a mean thing."[32]

All the important things in his life, St. Peter sometimes reflected, had been determined by chance. His education in France had been an accident.[33]

The next summer Tom went with the Professor to Old Mexico. They had planned a third summer together, in Paris, but it never came off.[34]

In this ordinary-language recuperation of French markings in the novel I have not culled all such references. However, I trust that these and others I shall adduce in discussing the novel will indicate the subtextual import of *la francité* in this story about an academic of French ancestry who has become famous for his eight-volume study of the Spanish conquistadores in the New World. To be sure, the impact of his Hispanic commitment is as strong as the American and the French in the tricultural valence of his character. In terms of Pascal's famous tripartite depiction of the human condition, St. Peter's Hispanic part may be seen as of the order of the mind, those who are the "curious and the scientists: they have as [their] object the mind"; his American part may be seen as of the order of flesh, those carnal people who "are the rich, Kings: they have as [their] object the body;" his French part may be seen as of the order of the will, those who are the wise "they have as [their] object justice."[35] One must remember, however, that for Pascal, since the Fall, the will has been corrupted (*la volonté corrompue*) and recuperable to its true object of wisdom only through the grace of God. In this light, St. Peter's French will has become deviated, part of a corrupted signifying system; it tropes not towards its real object, God, but towards human objects. In psychoanalytical terms, his French will is the language chosen by his Unconscious to express itself in displacements, elisions, and metonymies, thereby acceding to the objects of desire forbidden by the languages of the two other orders of his human condition.

His family seems to know this. His favorite daughter Kathleen reminisces with him about their deep, shared affection for the dead Tom Outland. Caressing an old Mexican blanket of Tom's in her father's house, she regrets that Tom had not taken the blanket to France because it might have helped him find his lost friend, Rodney Blake: " 'it might have been like the wooden cups that were always revealing *Amis* and *Amile* to each other.' "[36] French culture is the ordinary language between beloved father and favorite daughter, a language of love, the language of a lost love for both of them. As Katherine's husband alone knows, she and Tom had loved each other, even if Tom had left his invention to her sister Rosamond. Like Kathleen, Louis Marsellus, the husband of the other St. Peter daughter, also responds to his father-in-law's basically French nature. Louis tries to speak French, calls St. Peter "*cher* Papa," cultivates French art and culture, engages a French architect for the house he and Rosamond are going to build, and sets up the trip to France from which St. Peter finally withdraws. Planning and executing the trip occupies much of the Hamilton parts of the novel—that is, all but Tom Outland's story. Louis, a Jew, knows of the antisemiti_m he must inevitably face in a community like Hamilton, Michigan, but he senses that he has an ally in the Professor. Rightly so, as the quotation of apology via the Frenchman in James's *The American* shows.

However, the Professor's treatment of Louis might well be regarded as an elegant form of antisemitism. Cather has been criticized for less elegant expressions of that stance in other fictions. However, as A. S. Byatt has noted in her perceptive introduction to the Virago edition of *The Professor's House,* Cather's historical and literary imagination is at work in conceiving Louis. Byatt sees him as a "Louis Napoleon," an heir who cannot carry off the first Napoleon's ideal. He is thus a reprise of the two Marcelluses in one of Cather's favorite works, Virgil's *Aeneid:* "Aeneas in the underworld meets two Marcelluses: one a soldier who has carried off the 'spolia optima,' the spoils of war, and the other Augustus' much-mourned adopted son who married his daughter and died young."[37] Marsellus is Jewish, sensuous, vulgar, generous, and cast in a pageant by St. Peter as Saladin. Byatt does not develop further her interesting intertextual insights. However, on the basis of them, I suggest that in the episode, by casting his other son-in-law, Scott, as Richard Plantagenet, the Professor is depicting the surrender of the peoples of the south to the peoples of the north that had so impressed Cather in her early travels in Provence. Richard Plantagenet is not of the north so obviously as Molla Carlsen is in "Uncle Valentine," nor is Saladin a southerner of the Latin race. Nevertheless, the psychic topography holds to the extent that Richard is a Norman, while Saladin represents some of the qualities of the Latin races that Cather so admired, particularly in their French vestiges.

Louis does carry off the spoils of war: the material fruits of Tom Outland's marvelous invention for the then fledgling aviation industry. This suggests that the learned Cather may also have in mind another Marcellus, the third century B.C. conqueror of Gaul, slayer of a Gallic chief and victor over Hannibal (perhaps a reference born of her love of Flaubert's *Salammbô*). More generally, as a Jew, Louis is one of many in Cather who, superficially, may seem to suffer from the stereotype of Jews as materialistic and rapacious. Yet, in the sociological and psychic economy of her stories, this stereotype is relegated to the point of irrelevancy in the face of the erotic energy of Jews and their capacity, generally, to appreciate in others the lost language. Thus, though he likes Scott, his resolutely Anglo-Saxon son-in-law who has kept Louis out of an exclusive Hamilton club on antisemitic grounds, the Professor prefers his Jewish son-in-law. Beyond the Roman nomenclature he bears, Louis bears another Roman trait approved by Cather: "There was nothing Semitic about his countenance except his nose — that took the lead. It was not at all an unpleasing feature, but it grew out of his face with masterful strength, well rooted, like a vigorous oak-tree growing out of a hillside."[38] From her earliest days in the Roman Midi, we have seen, Cather would admire such French noses. Beyond all his other qualities, in his very name the francophilic Louis must evoke France for St. Peter, forename and surname being capable of a very French onomastic reference: Louis and Marcel.

In his own name, the Professor is obviously French: Napoleon, name of the emperor; Godfrey, name of Godefroi de Bouillon, Duke of Lower Lorraine (1061–1100) and leader in the Crusades; Saint Pierre, which was surely the French orthography of his Kanuck grandfather and, probably, for a while of his father — until, one suspects, the latter met the Professor's Methodist mother. In keeping with his forenames the Professor has much more of the conquistador spirit in the French way than in the Spanish way: he goes on quests not for gold but for spirit. Or he was in that French way, as we learn from his reveries and his dreams of his youth, especially in France: "There was one all Souls' Day when he had gone into Paris by an early train and had a magnificent breakfast on the Rue de Vaugirard — not at Foyot's, he hadn't money enough in those days to put his nose inside the place. After breakfast he went out to walk in the soft rainfall. The sky was of such an intense silvery gray that all the gray stone buildings along the Rue St. Jacques came out in the silver shine stronger than in sunlight."[39] The setting is like the one Claude finds in the environs of the church of St. Ouen in Rouen soon after debarkation. Like Claude, in this legendary light St. Peter encounters a young couple whose condition of mutual love and poverty so moves him that he knowingly overpays for the lovely dahlias he buys from them; he lets them keep the entire five-franc note they had changed, regretting that he had not bought two bunches. He wonders to whom he might give his bouquet, when he sees "the girls of a charity school . . . marshalled by four black-bonneted nuns . . . all looking down, all but one — the pretty one, naturally — and she was looking sidewise, directly at the student and his flowers. Their eyes met, she smiled, and just as he put out his hand with the bouquet, one of the sisters flapped by like a black crow and shut the pretty girl's face from him."[40] Such images of erotic investment abound in St. Peter's reveries, especially as they are of the Thierault boys and, later, of Tom Outland. In those reveries the Professor heeds the romantic signifiers of his two forenames.

He so lives only in reverie now that he is in his fifties, but in reality he lives up to the signifier of his family name: his heart is like stone (*pierre*). This is especially true when he is in the new house he and Lillian have bought with the earnings from his prize-winning study of the Spanish conquistadores. He and Lillian have become profoundly alienated; more precisely, he has become profoundly alienated from her. One of the strains in their relationship lies in his desire to keep working in their old house, indeed so much as practically to live there alone. His wife cannot understand it, especially in view of the modern conveniences of the new house, including a bath. For his daughters, it "should be the most attractive room in the house." He does not agree: "He had spent the happiest years of his youth in a house at Versailles where it distinctly was not, and he had known many charming people who had no bath at all." However, as his wife said: " 'If your country has contributed one thing, at least, to civilization, why not have it?' "[41] In this very conception of civilization Lillian is already enough at odds with her husband; she seems to have been less imprinted with the France in which they had studied and met when young.

However, St. Peter is even more at odds with his daughter, Rosamond. The alienation is apparent enough in their different social and moral values — Rosamond is too much in the social and industrial swing for her father. As the heir to Tom Outland's invention she is as much a taker of the spoils of war as her husband. Her preening before and patronizing of his other and favorite daughter does not help. Yet, there is a more fundamental ground of alienation between the handsome father and the beautiful Rosamond. He has "silky, very black hair . . . tawny skin with gold lights in it, a hawk nose, and hawk-like eyes — brown and gold and green." St. Peter has the stamp of Cather's favored *Méridionnaux* as much as of the Spaniard people saw in him.[42] Rosamond is of the same stamp: "dusky black hair, deep dark eyes, a soft white skin with rich brunette red in her cheeks and lips." Yet, where others found her beautiful, her father found her awkward, remarking to his wife that their daughter had "exactly the same wide femur and flat shoulder-blade of his old slab-sided Kanuck grandfather. For a tree-hewer they were an asset. But St. Peter was very critical. Most people saw only Rosamond's smooth black head and white throat, and the red of her curved lips that was like the duskiness of dark, heavy-scented roses."[43e] Physically, Rosamond is, like St. Peter himself, a signifier of powerful erotic energy, an energy that repels her father. In this large woman he sees the phallic mother even as he sees her in his wife, though more in the latter's personality than physique.

The displeasure the Professor feels before his beautiful daughter and the pleasure he feels in the appearance of her husband are symptomatic. It has been a long time since erotic pleasure has been signified hetero-sexually for St. Peter: he has not only fallen out of love with his wife; he has fallen out of love with women. There are sufficient signs to suggest that he has never been in love with women. He has, to be sure, flirted with that pretty little French schoolgirl, and he has married a beautiful woman whom he met in France. But he flirted with the schoolgirl while he was living at the Thieraults', tutoring their three sons whom he has loved his life long and who inspired his Spanish scholarship. In France he is in flight from his wife and his two little girls — from women. There he turns to Charles Thierault *fils* in particular, knowing that Charles had both much business dealings in Spain and a boat on which the Professor could fulfill his wish to be with that dynamic Frenchman and his crew of Provençal boatmen. Charles is not Gaston, the Thierault son "he loved best," of course.[44] It will not be until Tom Outland, with his French connection (through his desert mentor, the Belgian priest Father Duchene) that he will find a male object in whom to invest his erotic energy so fully once again. Only to lose that object, as he had the first, in a war: Gaston in the Boxer Rebellion, Tom in the First World War.

In both memories and memoriam of that second lost love the Professor lives in his old house, his wife notwithstanding; indeed, he knows that his wife knows. Numerous passages in the novel indicate that Lillian knows she has lost her husband to another man. Most directly, when husband and wife discuss their sons-in-law, he avows he has no taste for the role of "father-in-law," even to Louis:

> "Perhaps," mused his wife, as he rose, "It's because you didn't get the son-in-law you wanted. And yet he was highly coloured, too."
>
> The Professor made no reply to this. Lillian had been fiercely jealous of Tom Outland. As he left the house, he was reflecting that people who are intensely in love when they marry, and who go on being in love, always meet with something which suddenly or gradually makes a difference. Sometimes it is children, or the grubbiness of being poor, sometimes a second infatuation. In their own case it had been, curiously enough, his pupil, Tom Outland.[45]

As St. Peter's history before meeting Tom Outland indicates, the "curiously enough" can only be the Professor's reflection. It is a defense mechanism barely repressing the awareness in St. Peter that Cather's reader reaches by the many evidences, particularly the francocentric ones, the novelist provides.

The evidences of Gaston Thierault *redivivus* that the Professor finds in Tom Outland are numerous. Questioning the young man on his educational background, the Professor asks the national origin of the priest who had taught Tom his impressive Latin and learns that he is a Belgian francophone. Father Duchene figures prominently in "Tom Outland's Story," the story within the story that Cather published separately in the same year as the novel in which it figures. Actually, within the novel, the story of Tom's entry into the Professor's life begins with the Professor's reverie triggered by Scott's observation that "Tom isn't very real to me anymore. Sometimes I think he was just a—glittering idea."[46] From this point on in the first book, "The Family," the story is largely a weaving in

and out of the Professor's and the family's recollections of Tom (pp. 112–76).
Then begins Tom Outland's manuscript about the Cliff City, ending on
page 253 of the novel. One half of the text (142 of 283 pages) thus presents
Tom Outland as part of the life of Professor St. Peter.

The story of Tom Outland and the Professor as a part of the story of
the Professor and his family, particularly his wife, is the text of the novel,
of course. *The Professor's House* is a variation on one of the most familiar
stories in the history of literature: the love triangle. No longer in love
with his wife—perhaps never in love with her as she would have
wished—St. Peter has fallen in love with Tom from the outset:

> The first thing the Professor noticed about the visitor was his manly,
> mature voice—low, calm, experienced, very different from the thin
> ring or the hoarse shouts of boyish voices about the campus. The
> next thing he observed was the strong line of contrast below the
> young man's sandy hair—the very fair forehead which had been
> protected by his hat, and the reddish brown of his face, which had
> evidently been exposed to a stronger sun than the spring sun of
> Hamilton. The boy was fine-looking—tall and presumably well-built,
> though the shoulders of his stiff, heavy coat were so preposterously
> padded that the upper part of him seemed shut up in a case.[47]

Tom has a yellow aura, Cather's frequent signifier of the erotic. That
color suggests, however, another possible signifier for St. Peter: his
Methodist mother. The latter's religious affiliation suggests that his
parents had entered into what the Roman Catholic Church calls a mixed
marriage: one partner Catholic (St. Peter's "weaned away Catholic father"),
one not. Was the Methodist mother of Northern-European stock and, thus,
did she resemble Tom Outland? The text of the novel is not revealing on
this score. However, to the extent that Tom Outland is also of Northern-
European stock and also a non-Catholic, it is possible that in St. Peter's
homosexual troping towards him, Tom is, psychically if not physically, a
signifier for St. Peter in Freud's sense:

> ... future inverts, in the earliest years of their childhood, pass through
> a phase of very intense but short-lived fixation to a woman (usually
> their mothers) and ... after leaving that behind they identify with
> woman, and take themselves as their sexual object. That is to say,
> they proceed from a narcissistic basis and look for a young man who
> resembles themselves and whom they may love as their mother
> loved them."[48]

When Katherine caresses Tom's old Indian blanket and wishes he had
taken it to France so that it might have helped him find his codiscoverer

of the Cliff City, Roddy Blake, her evocation of the twelfth-century *chanson de geste* of Amis and Amile signifies the rediscovery of Tom by the Professor. Wrapped in the blanket in which Tom had wrapped himself, he is both wrapped and rapt in Tom, the Messianic young man, the resurrected God-Man. Like Jesus, Tom seems to be beyond shadows: "St. Peter had noticed that in the stories Tom told the children there were no shadows."[49] Like Jesus, Tom casts out the moneylenders from the temple of his Cliff City—the German peddler, Fechtig (German *fechten: to fence* and, jargon, *to beg*) to whom, while Tom is off to the national capitol in support of the Cliff City, Roddy Blake sells the sacred relics they had found, thus leading Tom to drive Roddy out of the temple as well. Again Jesus-like, he "suffers the little ones [the St. Peter daughters] to come unto me, for they are of the kingdom of heaven." But he cannot suffer the ways of civilization: those ways are not and cannot be his; they are too much of this world for this creature out of this world. He learns this all too well when he goes to the national capital to seek federal support for his Cliff City as a national shrine. He finds no such support there, only ambitious bureaucrats eager to exploit his find for their own careers by tying it in with a forthcoming international archaeological meeting in Paris. No more than they do for Jesus do women figure in "Tom Outland's Story," the manuscript he has left the Professor. However, as I have noted, they do figure in his story as that one-half of the novel beginning with his arrival in Hamilton.

Tom leaves his invention to Rosamond, though he had been in love with Katherine. These relationships suggest that his sexuality is more complex than that of the Professor who is in love with him. Though there is no evidence of Tom's sexual involvement with either daughter, he seems less repelled by those " 'cruel biological necessities' " implied, as St. Peter tells Augusta, by the dress forms she has left in his study in the old house.[50] Nevertheless, in Tom's relationship with Roddy Blake as in the Professor's with Tom and, earlier, the Thierault boys, we have an instance of the primarily homosexual eroticism of the novel. As he had swum in his youth with the Thierault boys, so, during Tom's days in Hamilton, St. Peter goes swimming with Tom and "every Saturday the Professor turned his house over to the cleaning-woman, and he and Tom went to the lake and spent the day in the sail-boat."[51] On such occasions, Tom is the Professor's date. In light of these dates, particularly recalling the Professor's "happiest days in France with the Thieraults," the trip he and Tom were to make to France stands as a projected lovers' voyage.

Thus, Lillian's jealousy is understandable: the Professor has deliberately left her and all women for men. He flees the Phallic Mother, represented by Lillian, Rosamond, and, ontogenetically, his "practical, *strongwilled*

Methodist mother" (emphasis added). His mother had very likely dominated both her husband and her son; her influence undoubtedly had
"weaned" the father away from the Catholic Church. Adverting in all
signifiers, except the explicitly verbal, to this commitment, St. Peter
shows his homosexuality. Gentle, ironic, skeptical, ill-at-ease in the signifying chain of heterosexual commitment with its frenetic repetition of the
intersubjective cruelty of primal demands, he opts out of that commitment.

In middle age he reprises his castration crisis. Now that he is alone in
his old house while the family is in Europe,

> he found he could lie on his sand-spit by the lake for hours and
> watch the seven motionless pines drink up the sun. In the evening,
> after dinner, he could sit idle and watch the stars, with the same
> immobility. He was cultivating a novel mental dissipation—and
> enjoying a new friendship. Tom Outland had not come back again
> through the garden door (as he had so often in his dreams), but
> another boy had; the boy the Professor had long ago left behind him
> in Kansas, in the Solomon Valley—the original, unmodified Godfrey
> St. Peter.[52]

In this reverie of erotic surrender, the operative signifiers are phallic:
sand-spit, motionless pines (seven), Tom Outland, the boy he had been
in that Solomon ("song of," one hears) Valley of his early years.

In this state of mind, St. Peter does not so much plan for as simply
surrender to suicide, to the Nirvana principle of late Freud. The "Professor's House" is a womb. He will let it become his tomb by neglecting
the coal fire with its dangerous fumes, recalling the accident by which
Emile Zola died. In that womb/tomb he forgets the women of his family
and the men of his dreams: "The young St. Peter who was sent to France
to try his luck, had a more active mind than the twin he left behind in the
Solomon Valley. After his adoption into the Thierault household, he
remembered that other boy very rarely, in moments of homesickness.
After he met Lillian Ornsley, St. Peter forgot that boy had ever lived."
But now he remembers his "life with this Kansas boy" and feels that,
"little as there had been of it, [it] was the realest of his lives" and "all the
years between had been accidental and ordered from the outside." Career,
wife, family had been "but a chain of events which had happened to
him." Even "his histories, he was convinced, had no more to do with his
original ego than his daughters had; they were the result of the high
pressure of young manhood," while "the Kansas boy who had come back
to St. Peter this summer was not a scholar." That boy "was not nearly so
cultivated as Tom's cliff-dwellers must have been . . . yet he was terribly
wise," for he had gotten to "the root of the matter. Desire under all

truths. He seemed to know, among other things, that he was solitary and must always be so; he had never married, never been a father." Gone in this Nirvanian perception are all the persons he had loved and who had loved him except his Kanuck grandfather. The Professor's namesake seemed to have come at eighty to the same perceptions in his "own profound, continuous meditation, sometimes chuckling to himself."[53] The grandfather is, psychically, the grand old man, the first Napoleon Godfrey St. Peter, God. Psychically, he is also the Origin, the nonfemale Other whom the Professor finds in the last days of the life he lets pleasantly slip away there in his "*other* house."[54e]

Yet, St. Peter does not die. Instead, Augusta rescues him, bringing him back to life and to the discovery that the other house is an impossible dream; it is the "Øther house" in Lacanian terms. Neither the "Song of Solomon" nor the preentropic sense of repose in the womb/tomb will be his; he will live in love with neither Lillian nor Tom nor with that Kansas boy. Augusta, his companion at the outset of the novel, is his companion at the end of the novel and for the rest of his life. "Augusta was like the taste of bitter herbs; she was the bloomless side of life that he had always run away from,—yet when he had to face it, he found that it wasn't altogether repugnant."[55] Later, while Augusta reads in the room with him, he looks back over his life once again, "trying to see where he had made his mistake." He concludes: "Perhaps the mistake was merely in an attitude of mind. He had never learned to live without delight. And he would have to learn to, just as, in a Prohibition country, he supposed he would have to learn to live without sherry. Theoretically he knew that life is possible, maybe even pleasant, without job, without passionate griefs. But it had never occurred to him that he might have to live like that."[56] Like Alexandra Bergson, St. Peter gives up his dream of the lover with so strong an arm. He will have to give up Tom Outland's hand,[57] the phallic symbol of manhood St. Peter renounces for the erotically neutral ministrations of Augusta.

"No light French touch about Augusta," the Professor had reflected early on in the novel. Nothing of the Latin races in "the sewing woman, niece of his old landlord, a reliable, methodical spinster, a German Catholic and very devout."[58] In the *methodical* here, we see shades of St. Peter's Methodist mother. Although Augusta is Catholic, there is more of late and repentant than early Augustine in her and nothing of the Roman Augustus. This German woman is that "cold wind of the north" before which the "fine, subtle, sensitive and beauty-loving Latin races ... rotten at heart ... must wither."[59] She frames the life in the novel of the Spanish-looking, French-loving, Professor who is as handsome as Mephistopheles[60] and as romanesque in his name as Claude. In his postsuicidal acceptance of Augusta's unimaginative piety and her workaday ministrations she signifies his rejection of such dialects of the lost language as delight, erotic energy, conquest. He had spoken this language primarily in France. Now, however, as he reflects alone in his other house during this summer while the family is abroad and he has only a companion in Augusta, he realizes that like "all the important things in his life, his education in France had been an accident."[61]

The subtext of France and things French is the occasion, Thomistically speaking, of the consonances the Professor had rediscovered in his love for Tom Outland in the text of the novel. That love compensated for the dissonances in the drama of the St. Peter family: his alienation from his wife, his displeasure with his older daughter, his reluctance to live in the new house with its modern plumbing, and so on. But now, with Tom gone forever and the family bound to return, the Professor knows himself bound to live in the false consonances of the family drama. In dismissing his education in France as an accident, he forsakes the real consonances of the subtext, of the couple he had hoped he and Tom would be in that "third summer" they had planned "together, in Paris . . . which had never come off."[62] In the dissonance of the final couple in *The Professor's House*, St. Peter and Augusta, the secular and sexual consonances of *One of Ours* as well as the spiritual and sexual consonances of *Death Comes for the Archbishop* split apart.

"The Old Beauty"

The first night after he had settled himself at the Splendide he became interested in two old English ladies who dined at a table not far from his own. They had been coming here for many years, he felt sure. They had the old manner. They were at ease and reserved. Their dress was conservative. They were neither painted nor plucked, their nails were neither red nor green. One was plump, distinctly plump, indeed, but as she entered the dining-room he had noticed that she was quick in her movements and light on her feet. She was radiantly cheerful and talkative. But it was the other lady who interested him. She had an air of distinction, that unmistakable thing, which told him she had been a personnage. She was tall, had a fine figure and carriage, but either she was much older than her friend, or life had used her more harshly. Something about her eyes and brow teased his memory. Had he once known her, or did she merely recall a type of woman he used to know? No, he felt that he must have met her, at least, long ago, when she was not a stern, gaunt-cheeked old woman with a yellowing complexion. The hotel management informed him that the lady was Madame de Coucy. He had never known anyone of that name.[63]

In "The Old Beauty," written in 1936 and published posthumously,[64e] the observer is "Mr. Henry Seabury, aged fifty-five, American-born, educated in England, and lately returned from a long business career in China."[65] The story begins "one brilliant September morning in 1922."[66] On that morning in the declining summer of 1922 Seabury is very upset by the news that Gabrielle has died in her room at the Hôtel Splendide at Aix-les-Bains where he has spent the past two months. The brilliance of the morning, the very name of the hotel, and the city in which it shines set that key year of Cather's symbolic calendar in a far happier light than in many other evocations of it by the novelist.[67]

It has been a brilliant and splendid summer for Seabury. During it, he has refound Gabrielle, long since divorced from Longstreet and now a widow of one "de Coucy, killed in the war." (Her new married name echoes that of the dignified Olive de Courcy in *One of Ours;* Cather clings fast to her exemplary French women). Seabury asks Mrs. Chetty Allison (Gabrielle's companion and the well-known former "music-hall star," Chetty Beamish) just who was this second husband of whom he has never heard. She replies: " 'I know very little myself, I never met him. They had been friends a long while, I believe. He was killed in action— less than a year after they were married. His name was a disguise for her, even then. She came from Martinique, you remember, and she had no relations in England. Longstreet's people had never liked her. So, you see, she was quite alone.' "[68] Gabrielle, the *Martiniquaise* born of a French mother and an English father, is quite alone and quite sufficient unto herself. As Gabrielle she is pure French. The Frenchness of her second husband is a disguise which, paradoxically, kept her at a distance from the Longstreets, her first husband's family, who had never liked her in her intrinsic Frenchness. It was like her "hard, dry tone" which "was a form of disguise...a protection behind which she addressed people from whom she expected neither recognition nor consideration."[69]

The austere old beauty could not and does not expect recognition or consideration. As Seabury tells the Thompsons, an English family from Devonshire where they had once known Gabrielle, " 'I gather that she is a little antagonistic to the present order,—indifferent, at least. But when she talks about her old friends she is quite herself.' "[70] Through the Thompsons, Seabury has finally recognized the impressive old woman whom he seemed to know since his arrival at Aix-les-Bains. They, too, *are* people who recognize her, of course, and not only by name and face. In France to visit the grave of a son killed in the war, the Thompsons, like

Seabury and Gabrielle herself, recognize the transcendent superiority of the past over the present, of the old over the new. Through the Thompsons Seabury has the chance to meet Gabrielle, to present himself to her as an old friend very much as Cather had presented herself to Madame Franklin-Grout at Aix-les-Bains in the summer of 1930. The parallel of these two chance meetings is underscored by the parallel of the compound English-French last names of the two old beauties. Cather does not parallel her own last name with that of Seabury, of course. Still, in his name we see the two old friends of the two old beauties performing a similar task: they "bury" the two older women "at sea." Now, the sea and deep waters in general are usually, as Slote has noted, ominous images for Cather.[71e] In this story, Slote's insight holds true bivalently. Though it is in the present order in which Gabrielle is "at sea," by burying her in the mountains of her beloved France, Henry *Seabury* gainsays that usually ominous signifier. Like Bishop Latour he shuts up its roiling complaint below the mountain in a most dignified burial. In her last days the old beauty is in the company not only of Chetty, as she calls Mrs. Allison of the "beaming" music-hall good humor, but also of Henry. He, too, had long been willingly out of touch with the present order thanks to his "long business career in China," an ancient civilization whose people are also out of touch with that order.

Gabrielle and Henry had first been friends some two decades before, in New York where he was a young businessman and she a distinguished hostess. At the time, long separated from her jealous husband, she entertained a great many friends, old and young. With respect to these men as with others whom she entertained when she and Longstreet were together, "whether any of them were ever her lovers, no one could say."[72] Knowing Cather women of similar attractiveness, except Maidy Forrester, we assume probably not. The suitors are just a "succession of Great Protectors," like Dr. Archie for Thea Kronberg. It is for his role as a great protector that Gabrielle particularly remembers Henry with gratitude, and he now wants to talk about that protection. However, Gabrielle insists on recalling the night in her New York apartment when Henry, invited, had entered her drawing room and

> beheld something quite terrible. At the far end of the room Gabrielle Longstreet was seated on a little French sofa — not seated, but silently struggling. Behind the sofa stood a stout, dark man leaning over her. His left arm, about her waist, pinioned her against the flowered silk upholstery. His right hand was thrust deep into the low-cut bodice of her dinner gown. In her struggle she had turned a little on her side; her right arm was in the grip of his left hand, and she was

trying to free the other, which was held down by the pressure of his elbow. Neither of those two made a sound. Her face was averted against the blue silk back of the sofa. Young Seabury stood still just long enough to see what the situation really was. Then he stepped across the threshold and said with such coolness as he could command: "Am I too early, Madame Longstreet?"[73]

This is one of the rare scenes of physical sex in Cather. As with the attack on Jim Burden sleeping in Antonia's bed by Wick Cutter, it is a scene of near-rape in which the intended victim is saved by a passive young man.

The scene in *My Antonia* is, of course, double-edged: thinking he will find Antonia in the bed, Cutter rapes a man—the violence is both heterosexual and homosexual. In fleeing that scene, Jim is fleeing his own homosexuality. Typically, his disgust after the event is as much with Antonia as with Cutter. Young Seabury's coolness here is of a piece with Jim's flight from the erotic in general. Later, once the "stout, dark man" has fled, the young man sits with the distraught Gabrielle for a long while as she lies quietly in a "low chair beside the coal grate." Henry thought "he had never seen her when she was more beautiful . . . probably that was because she was helpless and she was young."[74] Later when Gabrielle insists that they have dinner, "the young man caught at the suggestion. If once he could get her mind on the duties of caring for a guest, that might lead to something. He must try to be very hungry."[75] Seabury is both sexually aroused and frightened by his arousal. The something the dinner might lead to is erotic involvement; yet, it also leads away from it, away from the beautiful helplessness of Gabrielle that has aroused Seabury. Seabury had moved away from the arousal on that night some twenty years before, and he does so again on the present occasion. Both on that night and at the Hotel Splendide in 1922 the two old friends talk about the "beast," the "leech" (in Gabrielle's terms) who had attacked her. Seabury tells her in 1922 that " 'the man's accent must have told you that he belonged to a country you did not admire.' "[76] He thus repeats what he had told her after the incident: " 'but that was not an English-speaking man who went from here. He is an immigrant who has made a lot of money. He does not belong.' "[77] The unwanted suitor has traits that echo the antisemitism which Cather scholarship has long noted; most recently, Phyllis Robinson writes: "She romanticized other nationalities and cultures, the Bohemians, the Swedes, the French, but where Jews were concerned, she seemed to have a blind spot. For the Biblical Jews, she had respect and admiration and people she knew, like the Wieners, were certainly not included in her antipathy, but one wonders what they and other Jewish friends who came later made of the obnoxious Jews who populate her stories."[78] The obnoxious Jew is found not only in the novelist's stories but also in the new material she prepared for *Not Under Forty* in 1936 (the same year as "The Old Beauty). In her essay on Sarah Orne Jewett, she asks her reader to

> imagine a young man, or woman, born in New York City, educated at a New York university, violently innoculated with Freud, hurried into journalism, knowing no more about country people (or country folks anywhere) than he has caught from motor trips or observed from summer hotels: what is there for him in *The Country of the Pointed Firs?*
>
> This hypothetical young man is perhaps of foreign descent: German, Jewish, Scandinavian. To him English is merely a means of making himself understood, of communicating his ideas. He may write and speak American English correctly, but only as an American may learn to speak French correctly. It is a surface speech: he clicks the words out as a bank clerk clicks out silver when you ask for change. For him, the language has no emotional roots. How could he find the talk of Maine country people anything but "dialect?" Moreover, the temper of the people which lies behind the language is incomprehensible to him. He can see what these Yankees *have not* (hence an epidemic of "suppressed desire" plays and novels), but what they *have,* their actual preferences and their fixed scale of values, are absolutely dark to him. When he tries to put himself in the Yankee's place, he attempts an impossible solution.[79]

Could we be any further from the consonances of Old World and New World in *Death Comes for the Archbishop,* any further from the *entente plus que cordiale* of the rich polylingual and ethnographic mix of such novels as *O Pioneers!, The Song of the Lark,* and *My Antonia?* In those novels everybody spoke the lost language as if it were a living language. In "The Old Beauty" the lost language of many dialects seems lost forever; it is no longer appropriate to speak of dialects. Gabrielle and Seabury speak an idiolect, the language of "our kind of people," now become, ironically in Cather, the only acceptable code of the lost language, a monolect, in sum. This notion has always been virtual within the concept of lost language, for it has always been precisely *the* lost language Cather's searchers have been seeking. However, in the fictions of consonance, the lost language has many dialects, susceptible of translation into many tongues. A linguistic as well as religious ecumenism characterizes the interlocutors of *Death Comes for the Archbishop.* In both the ordinary-language sense and in the figurative sense speakers of many languages can and do communi-

cate with one another. The multilingual community of that novel is a
"blessed Babel."

However, the language community of "The Old Beauty" is a tower of
Babel, erected by barbarous Americans and "stout, dark men" with
unrecognizable accents into the Alpine empyrean of the last speakers of
the lost language—Gabrielle, Seabury, and the Thompsons. Only two of
its dialects are heard, English and French. In fact, French is more overheard than heard: Gabrielle and Seabury speak *English* in the surround
of *French.* The question of the sheer text is not the issue here. At the level
of text, other fictions with a "French surround" had manifested text in
both the English and the French languages: for example, *O Pioneers!, One
of Ours, Death Comes for the Archbishop,* and, most prominently, *Shadows
on the Rock.* In giving the French language to her English readers
without translation into English, Cather does not indulge in the snob-
bery of an international author. Rather, the assumption is that, even
without knowing French, the reader will perceive the international as
intranational and see English and French as linguistic variants of a "global
village" into which all "speaking beings" are born. The dissonances at the
heart of *Shadows on the Rock* in particular suggest that, with respect
to this intranational ideal of dialectical variants of the lost language,
the novelist is building a dike against the English dominion. She is losing
faith in the linguistic ecumenism of *Death Comes for the Archbishop.*

In "The Old Beauty" the English dominion begins its ascendancy not
only in the "shrill protestations" of American motorists but in the English
that Seabury and Mme. Longstreet speak. In this connection, Gabrielle's
companion is not French, in contrast with the case of so many of Cather's
successful women (Thea Kronberg, for example, or the singer in "Nanette:
An Aside," 1897, and "A Singer's Romance," 1900). Chetty is a former
English music-hall star. In this story there begins, ironically, the atrophy
of the French dominion that will mark *Sapphira and the Slave Girl* in the
person of its limotropic Frenchman, Henry Colbert of Belgian French
origin, as well as in the setting and characters of Cather's last two
published stories, "The Best Years" and "Before Breakfast." For Mme.
Longstreet and Seabury, French and things French surround less the
living and on-going, the lost language refound, than subtextual signifiers of the past. French is only a disguise and a shell protecting the
kernel of the past to which she and Henry cling.

The shell is fragile, in danger of being shattered from within France
itself. When Gabrielle, Chetty, and Seabury take a motor trip into the
nearby mountains to see old monuments, their car has a near-accident
with another. When both cars have stopped, from the other "two women
sprang out and ran up to Seabury with shrill protestations; they were
careful drivers, had run their car twelve thousand miles and never had

an accident, etc. They were Americans; bobbed, hatless, clad in dirty white knickers and sweaters. They addressed each other as 'Marge' and 'Jim'. Seabury's forehead was bleeding; they repeatedly offered to plaster it up for him." Could we be farther from the spirit of Franco-American friendship of the American Expeditionary Force that had brought Claude Wheeler to die in France in grateful return of the assistance France had given the fledgling confederation of American colonies in revolt from Great Britain? Or further from the generosity and tolerance of tomboyish, and possibly lesbian, women in such figures as the heroine of "Tommy, the Unsentimental," Thea Kronberg, and many of those in "Flavia and Her Artists?" The kernel of this serene recapture of lost time is itself but a fragile shell within a fragile shell. Evocations of the past run up hard against fragmenting images of the present. Gabrielle and Seabury dance a "spirited waltz" one night at the hotel: she dances with "attack and style, slightly military, quite right for her tall, straight figure"—a mannish style, but its erotic "attack" is stylized as usual in Cather. The old couple dance less to enjoy themselves than to do something better than the "tired tango" of the modern young dancers they had been looking at with boredom. From this boring, irrelevant, impertinent present Gabrielle's death rescues her: "Gabrielle lay on her back, her eyes closed. The face that had outfaced so many changes of fortune had no longer to muffle itself in fur, to shrink away from curious eyes, or harden itself into scorn. It lay on the pillow regal, calm, victorious, — like an open confession."[80]

Death rather than life in "The Old Beauty" is the occasion of repose, of relief, of release. Death releases Gabrielle from the dissonant present; it re-leases her to and gives her a lasting hold on the past. She need no longer look on that past from the disadvantage of the present as she had earlier in the mountains. There she had looked into a "great open well" at the monastery while Seabury and Chetty left to see other parts of the monastery:

> Mme de Coucy slipped a little mirror from her handbag and threw a sunbeam down into the stone-lined well. That yellow ray seemed to waken the black water at the bottom: little ripples stirred over the surface. She said nothing, but she smiled as she threw the gold plaque over the water and the wet moss of the lower coping. Chetty and Seabury left her there. When he glanced back, just before they disappeared into the labyrinth of buildings, she was still looking down into the well and playing with her little reflector, a faintly contemptuous smile on her lips.[81]

The smile at the play of yellow light on the great open well of the past will return in the last of Cather's published novels to which I now turn.

Sapphira and the Slave Girl (1940)

Sapphira Dodderidge usually acted upon motives which she disclosed to no one. That was her nature. Her friends in her own country could never discover why she had married Henry Colbert. They spoke of her marriage as "a long step down." The Colberts *were termed "immigrants,"* — as were all settlers who *did* not come from the British Isles. Old Gabriel Colbert, the *grandfather,* came from *somewhere in Flanders.* Henry's own father was a plain man, a miller, and he *trained his eldest son* to that occupation. The three young persons were *birds of a very different feather.* They rode with a *fast* fox-*hunting* set. Being shrewd judges of horses, they were welcome in *every man's* stable. They were even (with a shade of contempt and only occasionally) received in good houses; — not the best houses, to be sure. Henry was a *plain,* hardworking, *little-speaking* young man who *stayed at home* and *helped his father.* With his *father* he regularly attended a dissenting church supported by small farmers and artisans. He was certainly *no match for* Captain Dodderidge's *daughter.*[82]

The narrative and symbolic thrust of the story of Henry, Sapphira, and the slave girl, Nancy, is set in the distances established here between the low-born miller and his high-born wife. The terms are familiar to readers of Cather. The symbolic and imaginary fealty of Henry Colbert to the "name of the father" in an original grandfather characterizes Professor St. Peter and still another Henry, Grenfell, of "Beyond Breakfast" (whom I shall discuss later). In the plain grandsons of the plain son of the Belgian French grandfather we see the hold of the first father's rule. The patronymic is richly revealing of the sense Henry Colbert has of himself as a man at once pursued and outcast by God.

Stiff-necked, beardless, buried in his mill most of the time, Henry Colbert has always been a pictograph of noncommunication with others; he has always been "little-speaking." "Staying at home" as a boy, he helped his father and he regularly followed his father's religion, the Lutheran dissent from the dominant Episcopalianism of the high-born Dodderidges as well as from the Roman Catholicism of the majority of his French-speaking ancestors. Sapphira's religion is a very-near variant of the latter and in it, as she reflects later, "all those things" which bothered her husband with his "disadvantage of having been raised a Lutheran . . . had been decided long ago by heads much wiser than Henry's. She had married the only Colbert who had a conscience and she sometimes wished he hadn't quite so much."[83] That the other grandsons of Gabriel Colbert had less conscience is clear in the signifiers of their commitment to a normative phallocentrism: birds, feathers, fast, hunting, every man's stable. In his origins, psychic and linguistic, Henry Colbert is a very different kind of Frenchman from those of Provence whom Cather had so admired on her first visit to France in the beginning of this century. Those were offsprings of the "subtle, sensitive, beauty-loving Latin races." In the cold wind of conscience that blows within him Henry is even more northern than the Norman settlers of *Shadows on the Rock*. He is a descendant of the French apotropaically struggling against the rottenness of the Latin races, the southern roots of his culture.

Sapphira Dodderidge, as her names indicate, is "a wrong match" for him in more than her social position: "*sapphire,* any precious corundum gemstone that is not red, esp. the highly valued transparent blue variety ... C13 *safir,* from Old French, from Latin *sapphirus,* from Greek *sappheiros,* perhaps from Hebrew *sappir,* ultimately perhaps from Sanskrit *sanipriya,* literally: beloved of the planet Saturn, from *sani* Saturn + *pryia* beloved" (*Collins Dictionary*). The wife of the miller has her own hold on a founder in her very name. Saturn is the Latin god, counterpart of the Greek Cronos, one of the Titans, divinity of sowing and of the vine, chased from Olympus by Zeus, and, taking refuge in Italy, the ruler over the Latium of the Golden Age. Little wonder that Sapphira discloses her motives to no one as she sits on the Olympian heights of her first name as firmly as she does on the ridge of her father's name. However, in the time of the novel she sits more in the hard blue light of the most prized stone of the variety of gem her name also signifies. The golden age is behind her in the Chestnut Hill she left in Loudun County with its smug British ancestry to live with the immigrant miller in Back Creek Valley in western Virginia. She has descended neither into the Valley of the Rhône nor that of the Tiber. She has moved backwards, to a very backcreek of a place in which not only the heights of Chestnut Hill but also the lush grandeurs of Tidewater Virginia are as remote as the British Isles from which she claims ethnic and religious ancestry.

As so often in Cather, Henry Colbert and Sapphira Dodderidge Colbert are a mismatched couple. By ancestry, he is a northern francophone tormentedly immersed in his French roots, cut off from his present as much as the French-Canadians in the Kébec of *Shadows on the Rock* from theirs. By ancestry, she is of that Titanic British ancestry which "rules the waves," confident in its past and present conquests and ever on the lookout for new ones. Through this couple, the French/American valence is deflected geographically in this novel as it is in *The Professor's House*. However, the French subtext works as powerfully and in much the same way on the text: the love triangle of Henry, Sapphira, and Nancy, the slave girl of the title.

Nancy has "slender, nimble hands, so flexible that one would say there were no hard bones in them at all: they seemed compressible, like a child's. They were just a shade darker than her face. If her cheeks were pale gold, her hands were what Mrs. Blake called 'old gold.' "[84] Nancy is the Catherian color of desire. This ever-present signifier of desire in the household of the Colberts suggests still another etymological reverberation of Sapphira's name: sapphic, from Sappho, the early sixth-century Greek lyric poet. An aristocrat like Sapphira, the poet is renowned for the lesbian import of fragments of verse, remaining from a fairly extensive canon, which invoke Aphrodite's assistance in the poet's courtship of a beloved girl. In Sapphira Colbert's quarrel with her husband over Nancy there may well be a strong current of lesbian jealousy. However, in Sapphira's courtship of both men and women — even when constrained by illness — her erotic energy is all-embracing: bisexual, polymorphous, androgynous.

The paternity of Nancy is a mystery. "Old Till" is known to be her mother. Was her father the itinerant artist from Baltimore (and originally, Cuba), who had portrayed Henry, Sapphira, and their daughter, Mrs. Rachel Blake? On the other hand, as Henry reflects, "the Colbert men had a bad reputation where women were concerned." There might, then, be something to the rumor that "in spite of her resemblance to the portrait painter from Cuba . . . some people said Guy Colbert was her father, others put it on Jacob. Although Henry was a true Colbert in nature, he had not behaved like one, and he had never been charged with a bastard."[85] The rumor of incest may be stilled within the community, but it is not within Henry himself. He is erotically drawn to his possible niece, and his wife knows it. Sapphira's jealousy is at the root of their quarrel over Nancy "at the breakfast table" on the "morning in March 1856" with which the novel begins. Sapphira wants to sell Nancy. Henry refuses out of abolitionist sentiments whose lack of Biblical warrant, as we learn later, is one of the mysteries of his stern faith that most bothers him. His resistance leads to Sapphira's cruel treatment of Nancy as she later attends her chairridden mistress, ill with advanced dropsy. Sapphira broods on the knowledge that Henry spends so much time, day and night, in his mill on the property. Nancy often visits him there with, as the saucy slave girl Bluebell puts it, " 'bokays' " of " 'vi'lets an' bleedin'-hearts.' "[86] When Henry reflects on the shameless advances his visiting nephew, Martin Colbert, makes to Nancy, his "wrath" turns as much upon himself and his ancestors as upon his nephew:

> His own father he could hold in reverence: he was an honest man, and the woman who shared his laborious and thrifty life was a good woman. But there had been bad blood in the Colberts back on the other side of the water, and it had come to light in his three brothers

and their sons. He knew the family inheritance well enough. He had his share of it. But since his marriage he had never let it get the better of him. He had kept his marriage vows as he would keep any other contract.[87]

After the night of these reflections, he decides to avoid Nancy that morning. "He did not wish to be there when she came to the mill; it would not be the same as yesterday. Something disturbing had come between since then." He feels that Nancy has ceased to be less "like an influence than a person . . . a soft spring breeze; a shy, devoted creature who touched everything so lightly" and who had "divined all his little whims and preferences, and been eager to gratify them . . . for love, from dutiful affection" with "nothing to gain beyond the pleasure of seeing him pleased." In confronting erotic energy within himself Henry recognizes its real terms as Clement Sebastian of *Lucy Gayheart* does not: "now that he must see her as a woman, enticing to man, he shrank from seeing her at all."[88] Henry runs away from his "bad blood," its call of desire. That it is a French blood could not signify a greater dissonance from the sacramental consonances of Eros and Deus (and Dea) blessed by Bishop Latour.

Such consonances do emerge in *Sapphira and the Slave Girl*, but in tellingly contained energies. These are evoked in an "insert-story" which shows this novel with its nineteenth-century setting going back to a past even more ancient than in other Cather novels. In the story of "Old Jezebel" (book 3) the Africa from which the slaves of Back Creek Valley came is evoked with the same contrastive validity as Thea's Panther Canyon (*The Song of the Lark*) and Tom Outland's Cliff City (*The Professor's House*). Here, however, the "ancient civilization" does not have the American-continental root of those two novels with their pursuit of an originary language and culture to gainsay the disappointments of contemporary culture. Moreover, the African continent is not a dead civilization. In the young, fiery, and noble Jezebel on the slaver bringing her to the States, we have one of the most erotically energetic of Cather's "strong women."

She has made a row on the English slaver, the *Albert Horn*. Finally overcome by two guards after biting off one's ball of the thumb, she is tied to a mast and whiplashed. Having had a look at this "female gorilla," the Captain "judged this girl was worth any three of the women, as much as the best of the men. Anatomically, she was remarkable, for an African negress: tall, straight, muscular, long in the legs. The skipper had a kind of respect for a well shaped creature; horse, cow, or woman. And he respected anybody who could take a flogging like that without buckling."[89] The skipper's male-chauvinist overtones might offend many of today's readers; however, his perspective must be assessed within the antebellum conventions that it reflects as well within the aesthetic principle of *vraisemblance*. More cogently, it represents Cather's ironization of her skipper *in the name of her own conception of language*. By setting up "well-shaped" creatures—"horse, cow, or woman" as equivalents, Cather gives us still another of those pictographs which speak the lost language better than any word. However, that the pictograph is *African* and *enslaved* underscores still another and more disturbing irony in Cather: the dissonance between the insert story and the framing story in which it is situated. In that frame, Henry Colbert is, at least in tendency, abolitionist, while Sapphira Colbert is proslavery, though generally kind to her slaves (e.g., she gives "old Jezebel" a fine funeral). Again, the novel will issue in a dénouement of Nancy's emancipation and an epilogue of reconciliation between her and her mistress. Yet the reconciliation is shaped in terms of compromises: Nancy's emancipation is partially due to Henry's "divided self"; Sapphira's jealousy still tinges her final kindness to Nancy and others.

Sapphira's jealousy especially compromises her feelings for her daughter, Mrs. Blake. In Rachel Colbert Blake we have a French marking sharply contrasted to the "bad French blood" of her father. As her mother notes, "Rachel was well-enough looking, in her father's masterful way, but no one could call her pretty. She was reserved to a degree which her mother called sullenness, and she had decided ideas on matters which did not concern women at all." Thus, Sapphira doubts that her daughter would ever "be attractive to young men" and that she could get Rachel married as she had two other daughters. Her doubts are overturned when the "happy, fair-complexioned young Blake, with his warm laugh and mellow voice" asks for the hand of Rachel who, like her Biblical namesake, seemed about to be passed over.[90e]

A member of the Virginia legislature at the time of the marriage, Blake wins a congressional seat that leads him and Rachel to Washington, D.C. There they raise their three children during "the happiest years of her life."[91] The years of happiness are marked in particular by the friendship between the Blakes and "a young French officer who had some post at the French Legation" as well as "a group of Louisiana planters."[92] The Louisiana provenance of the planters suggests still another mark of that French *joie de vivre* of the dinners at the Blakes where Rachel cooked meals after the "instruction of a free mulatto woman from New Orleans." At those dinners, "if she did not appear soon enough after the dessert, the young Frenchman ran down to the kitchen and brought her up on his arm."[93] But the happiness does not last. Michael and Robert die in an epidemic in New Orleans, where Michael had gone on business, leaving many debts and no insurance. Rachel's father pays off his son-in-law's creditors and brings his daughter and his granddaughters to Back Creek to live with him and Sapphira until a new house for them is ready. During the wait Sapphira "grew very fond of Mary and Betty. Mrs. Colbert's relations with her daughter were pleasanter than they had ever been before. To be sure, there were things in the past which she could not forget. Gravest of them was that Rachel had not once invited her mother, then not an invalid but a very active woman, to come to Washington to visit her."[94] Rachel's rationale for not inviting her mother can be divined in the two women's characters.

The mother is erotically open, the daughter erotically closed. The daughter might have feared the competition of her mother in the presence of the French officer, the Louisianans, and especially her husband. Rachel "was conscious of a certain chill in her own nature and was afraid of being insufficient to her pleasure-loving husband. His rich enjoyment of life had an irrestible charm for her."[95] In Washington Rachel heeds the blood of her French heritage by responding to its southern expression. The strain is doubly southern: on the North American continent Louisiana is to Provence as French Canada is to Normandy or Belgium; for Rachel's father this French strain is "bad" in any of its expressions, of course. Henry loves his daughter as her mother does not; moreover, the duties of fatherhood authorize the erotic call a daughter makes upon her father. Again, through her unwomanly advanced ideas on abolition Rachel abets her father's own more hesitant abolitionist sentiments. Thus, she only intensifies the coldness between herself and her mother, especially when these sentiments protect Nancy.

Rachel protects Nancy against Martin Colbert, Henry's nephew through his brother Jacob, one of the candidates for Nancy's paternity. Martin is hardly religious, but his first name as well as his behavior at meals suggest the dinnertable and outhouse erotic indulgences of the Luther who gave his name to the religion of his grandfather and his uncle. He had been invited by Sapphira to Back Creek "before Easter," during that March at the beginning of the novel when Henry and Sapphira quarrel over Nancy. But he arrives in June, earning Sapphira's flirtatious reproach. Nevertheless, she entertains him grandly. The self-indulgent young blade regales his host and hostess with tales of risky carriage rides back at home by Gogarty—not from one of the "best families"—at which some guests from the highfalutin Tidewater "best families" were frightened out of their wits, including a pretty young woman who had broken her nose.[96e] At dinner Martin flashes his bright smile, exceptionally unstained by tobacco but showing a missing tooth. He has lost the tooth in a fight with the brothers of a girl whom he had "fooled." Martin is altogether just the man for Nancy in Sapphira's eyes. The hostess throws him at her, as she planned in inviting him back there "before Easter."

The plan is frustrated by Nancy's fear of Martin, by Rachel, and by "old Sampson," her husband's trusted black hand at the mill. During Martin's stay, prolonged by Sapphira much to Henry's displeasure, Nancy succeeds in resisting Martin while doing chores for him to which Sapphira has assigned her. She cannot sleep well on her accustomed spot on the floor near Sapphira's room, given its easy access to Martin's bedroom. (Earlier in the novel, Sapphira herself could not sleep well for wondering if Nancy had slipped away from her floor bed to join Henry at the mill). When Sapphira sends Nancy out to pick laurel on "holler hill" one morning just before Martin is about to ride out that way, Nancy stops off at Rachel's in fearful dawdling. She tells Rachel that Sapphira had told her " 'to go right before Mr. Martin' " and that Sapphira " 'knowed he was goin' ridin' this mornin.' He had his leggin's on.' " When Rachel says nothing "Nancy burst out: 'Oh, Miz' Blake, he'll surely ride up there an' overtake me in the woods!' "[97] Rachel decides to accompany Nancy on her walk for the flowers. One senses the depth of Sapphira's jealousy in the mission she assigns Nancy: let the girl bring flowers to quite a different kind of Colbert man. The two women do meet Martin, slyly gracious but making no fuss.

This is not the first time Rachel has come to the aid of the oppressed. In her good works as a medical missionary in the Valley she had also defended Casper Flight, " 'as good a boy as ever lived' "[98] from the Keyser boys, bullies who had accused Casper of stealing the communion service from the Bethel church. The Keysers had captured Casper in the woods, as Rachel learns on a visit to the crippled old Mrs. Ringer and her crippled son, Lawndis, christened Leonidas—"the hill people could do queer things with unfamiliar names,"[99] like Cather herself with names of any kind, as she brings out in the note at the end of this novel.[100] Rachel leads the two cripples out into the woods where they confront the three Keysers, led by the biggest bully, Buck, "his sleeves rolled up and his shirt open, showing a thick fleece of red hair on his chest and forearms."[101] Buck is about to whiplash Casper, who is tied to the "chestnut sampling," a signifier of the boy's "goodness." Of Casper, " 'His teacher can't say enough good.' " (And the teacher's word carries weight with Rachel, since the school is run by the preacher, Mr. Fairhead, in whose abolitionist sympathies Rachel finds succor for her own.) Rachel is abetted by Lawndis who shields Casper with his own back, thus living up to the heroism of his baptismal name. At this Thermopylae, Leonidas and Rachel repel the invaders, the real thieves at the church.

Rachel is a young "Mrs. Harris." In this episode in the woods she is also a worthy "countrywoman," through her French blood, of Pierre Charron, the *coureur de bois* of *Shadows on the Rock.* Like him she is no respecter of platitudes and pieties. Ever since she was a girl she has hated all forms of servitude, especially black servitude. At twelve she overheard a conversation between Mr. Cartmell and his daughter, the newly-widowed Mrs. Bywaters and postmistress of Black Creek, with whom Sapphira has "very different opinions on one important subject"—slavery.[102] The postmistress refuses the offer of her father, himself of "abolitionist sentiments," to buy a slave to help her out now that she is a widow. Mrs. Bywaters (in the "bywaters" of the slave-holding region) thus makes her father proud; " 'You are my daughter, Caroline. We'll manage.' "[103] More importantly, the incident resolved Rachel to change a "long smothered feeling" into a "conviction":

> She had never heard the thing said before, never put into words. It was the *owning* that was wrong, the relation itself, no matter how convenient or agreeable it might be for master or servant. She had always known it was wrong. It was the thing that made her unhappy at home, and came between her and her mother. How she hated her mother's voice in sarcastic reprimand to her servants! And she hated it in contemptuous indulgence. Till and Aunt Jezebel were the only blacks to whom her mother never spoke with that scornful leniency.[104]

There is some of Myra Henshawe in Sapphira, as we can see from this passage. On the other hand, there is less in Rachel Blake of the Nellie Birdseye who observes at a distance Myra's commitment to the "injustice" of this world. Rachel has taken some of the Celtic warmth of her husband's nature as well as the fire of her half-French blood to go along with this early political revolt from her mother.

Her accession to that warmth after her long maidenhood can be seen as part of the normal heterosexualization of the subject after the crisis of castration. Yet, the length of that maidenhood and the relative brevity of her marriage also suggest a pattern we have detected in Cather elsewhere. "Normative" sexuality is but a temporary acceptance of the imperatives of phallocentrism. Rachel does not remarry. For example, might not that French officer have been a suitor, or one of the Louisianans? In her long widowhood, as in her long maidenhood, Rachel Colbert Blake stands beyond the symbolic deflections and the phantasmic subterfuges of the primal demands of phallocentrism and phallologocentrism. She becomes, like Mrs. Bywaters, another widow with small children and daughter of a father with sentiments rather than convictions about human servitude, sociopolitical or psychic. In her courageous confrontation of Buck Keyser, of Martin Colbert, and of her mother, Rachel lives up to another namesake, the great French actress of her own time, "Rachel" (Elisabeth Rachel Félix, 1821–58), celebrated especially for her roles in French classical tragedy and the actress whose voice so moves the hero of "Peter" (1892), Cather's first story.[105e] In her loneliness, first as maiden and then as widow, the abolitionist Rachel, defender of men (Casper Flight) and women (Nancy), seems the best example in Cather of that feminine sexuality beyond phallocentrism at which Lacan himself seems to hint in his final writings. I shall return to this aspect of Rachel in considering the novel's epilogue.

The daughter's interventions on behalf of the slavegirl only increase the mother's hostility, only postpone the occasion on which Martin gets Nancy alone. He does so one day when Nancy is picking cherries, perched comfortably up in the cherry tree itself. She hears someone singing: " '*Down by the cane-brake, close by de mill,/Dar lived a yaller gal, her name was Nancy Till.*' "[106] Martin's is the voice of this provocative ditty, learned from Bluebell whose hostility to Nancy is so marked. Thinking to be safe from his gaze in the tree, Nancy remains there, but Martin "came through the wet grass straight toward the cherry trees, his straw hat in hand, singing the old darky song."[107] He has found out from Bluebell where Nancy is. Standing at the foot, he greets Nancy up in the tree: " 'Good morning, Nancy . . . Cherries are ripe, eh? Do you know that song? Can you sing like Bluebell?' " Nancy tells him she can't, that she has " 'no singin' voice.' " Coaxingly, Martin says he doesn't either but sings " 'anyhow. Can't help it on a morning like this. Come now, you're going to give me something, Nancy.' " The girl notes that "his eyes were clear this morning, and jolly. He didn't look wicked." She thinks that maybe he's just in a teasing mood—"she just didn't know how young men behaved over in the racing counties." Martin repeats his question: " 'Aren't you going to give me something on such a pretty day" Let's be friends.' " He holds up his hand "as if to help her down." Nancy doesn't move, "but she laughed a soft darky laugh and dropped a bunch of cherries down to him."[108]

The something that Martin wants is, of course, not the cherries she drops down: " 'I don't want cherries! They're sour, and I want something sweet!' " It is her cherry that he wants, the virginity of which that metaphor is, as in the cherry tree scene in *One of Ours*, an old signifier. Still bantering with her, Martin catches her off guard as she turns to look at a "scarecrow" he says he sees. Martin hops up on the chair she had used to climb into the tree and grasps "her bare ankles, and draws her two legs about his cheeks like a frame." Nancy drops her basket and almost falls out of the tree.

Seldom has a heterosexual embrace, and never with such suggestive focus, been so explicit in Cather (The account of Gabrielle and the stout man comes nearest). Martin rejects her pleas for him to get down, discounting her fear that " 'somebody'll come along, an' you get me into trouble.' " He laughs: " 'Get you into trouble' Just this? This is nothin' but to cure a toothache.' " He means the kind of ache memorialized by his missing tooth and more generally signified by the tooth as a phallic signifier. Nancy goes pale, but in her fright cannot move because he is holding her so hard and he has so "changed in a flash" that she cannot "collect her wits." She entreats him once again to let go, but "Martin framed his face closer and shut his eyes;" he tells her " 'Pretty soon. —This is just nice. — Something smells sweet—like May apples,' " his face coming ever "closer." Nancy screams, " 'Pappy! Oh, Pappy! Come quick!' " Martin steps down at this moment, and Old Jeff comes running around the end of the smokehouse, closely followed by Sampson. She tells the slaves that she had been " 'took giddy like' in the tree," and Sampson gets up on the chair and helps her down, but not without noticing that "there were alredy wet boot tracks on the seat." He leads her away after accepting Martin's lame explanation that he would have helped the girl from the tree if she "had had any sense."[109]

Not only is this the most explicit sexual scene in Cather's fiction, it is also the scene of an attempted rape. As one of the "hired girls" of this novel, Nancy is not Lena Lingard, who actively seeks sex with Jim Burden. She is more the Antonia who chides Jim for " 'kissing me like that. I'll tell your grandmother on you.' "[110] Antonia might well have better told his *grandfather,* Jim being, like St. Peter and Henry Colbert, in the line of the erotically abstemious grandfather. In general, for all her yellow eroticism, Nancy is a "good girl" like Antonia, a sexy creature whose nature and destiny are to be as desexualized in *Sapphira and the Slave Girl* as Antonia in *My Antonia.* When Nancy throws down the cherries, she is not seductively responding to Martin's " 'Come now.' " This phrase is part of conventional male behavior, the assumption that all women are "really dying to have it," the sexual pleasure "come now" invites them to enjoy in mutual orgasm. To be sure, Nancy has a good sense of Martin's desire to have her *come* in that sense, given all the advances he has made during the summer. However, as the rest of the passage makes clear, on this morning of the cherry tree incident, he seems different: his eyes are clear and jolly, his look not wicked; moreover, she just does not know how "young men behaved over in the racing counties." This formulation is at once information from the third-person narrator and the continuation of Nancy's "interior monologue" about Martin's aspect of this particular morning. As she laughs her "soft darky laugh" and drops the "bunch of cherries down," she is neither leading him on nor putting him off. Nancy is responding to his seeming innocence with her own, the one which Henry Colbert also found in her until he learned she was the object of his nephew's lust which triggered his own. Symbolically, Nancy is here the victim of a rape that would have become literal but for her cry for help and its answer by the two slaves.

Saved from rape, Nancy, as Rachel Blake knows, must be removed from Martin's and her mother's reach. Rachel turns to the "underground railroad" with the active help of Preacher Fairhead, whose name personifies his integrity in this and other deeds, and Mrs. Bywaters. Henry provides funds, but he cannot give them directly: he leaves them in his "coat hanging by an open window" so that Rachel can steal her way to the window during the night to remove the money.[111] As usual, Henry is passively helpful.

On the occasion when he makes this surreptitious arrangement with Rachel, Henry objects that sending Nancy to Montreal makes no sense: " 'What would a young girl like her do in a big strange city? An' they talk nothing but French up there, I've heard. You must be gone crazy, Rachel. There she'd come to harm, for certain. A pretty girl like her, she'd be enticed into one of them houses, like as not.' "[112e] We have still another instance of the explicitly pejorative French markings of this novel. For Henry Colbert, the language of his grandfather is the site of "rottenness" in the erotic signification which is his special haunt. After Rachel leaves on this night of conspiratorial planning to which he reluctantly consents, he is reconciled to "Nancy's Flight" (the title of book 7). He broods religiously: "Maybe she would be like the morning star, this child; the last star of night. She was to go out from the dark lethargy of the cared-for and irresponsible; to make her own way in this world where nobody is altogether free, and the best that can happen to you is to walk your own way and be responsible to God only."[113] These are not the convictions of freedom held by his daughter; they are the sentiments of a man whose support of freedom can only be surreptitious. Even then, he is troubled by the awareness that this is a world "where nobody is altogether free" and that "the best that can happen to you is to walk your own way and be responsible to God only." As his search through the Bible had shown him, the ways of God could not be shown to justify abolition.

This Lutheran man of conscience born of French ancestry searches for a clear understanding of God's ways in his favorite author, John Bunyan, but it yields no satisfactory answer. In *A Pilgrim's Progress* he finds the image of Nancy in "Mercy, Christiana's sweet companion."[114] After Sampson has reported to him the incident of the cherry tree, and he has reflected on the large sum of money he withdrew from the bank to try to buy Martin off, he turns to Bunyan's *Holy War.* He opens the book first to "a passage relating to the state of Mansoul after Diabolus had entered and taken up his rule there." The passage is disturbing, full of " 'blast, and a burning instead of beauty.' " He turns to the pages describing the state of Mansoul after she had been retaken and reclaimed by Prince Emmanuel, the Son of God:

> "When the town of Mansoul had thus far rid themselves of their enemies, and of the troublers of their peace, a strict commandment was given out, that yet my Lord Willbewill, should search for, and do his best, to apprehend what Diabolonians were yet alive in Mansoul.... He also apprehended Carnal-sense, and put him in hold; but it came about I cannot tell, but he brake prison and made his escape; yea, and the bold villain will not quit the town, but lurks in the Diabolonian Dens at days, and haunts like a Ghost, honest men's houses at night."[115]

Holy War consoles Henry. "An honest man, who had suffered much, was speaking to him of things about which he could not unbosom himself."[116] Like the "Ghost" of "Carnal-sense" his own "Will(bewill)" cannot "quit" him of the ghost of the French "bad blood" which rises in his reflections on French-speaking Montreal and its "houses" into one of which Nancy will be "enticed . . . like as not." As he finishes that warning to his daughter, "the miller wiped his forehead with his big handerchief. The closed room was getting very hot."[117] The heat comes less from without than from within, from Henry's desire. In Cather's *démeublé* prose we over-hear not only the fear but also the hope of Nancy's enticement "into one of them houses" where he might be one of her "customers." In abetting Rachel's plan for "Nancy's flight" even though for him "it ain't right . . . I can't be a party to making away with your mother's property,"[118] Henry Colbert is relieving his own anguished desire for Nancy. As usual in Cather men, he sends the cause of that desire away, analogizing the flight as an escape "out of Egypt to a better land."[119]

During that flight, Nancy herself would cling to the fable of Sapphira's darkies evoked by Henry. Well into the flight, while they wait anxiously for the emissary from the Pennsylvania Quakers in the next step of the flight, she becomes frightened and pleads with Rachel to let her go back. She doesn't mind " 'Miss Sapphy scoldin' " and " 'ought-a borne better' " her mistress's " 'sufferin!' " She assures Rachel that she " 'kin keep out-a' " Martin's way. However, she submits to Rachel's firm refusal. The Quaker emissary comes and tells her that she will " 'be treated like dey had raised you up from a chile.' " She stands "dumb all the while . . . as if she were drugged, indeed she was, by the bitterest drug of all drugs."[120] Cather does not name or define this drug any further. Is it the drug of freedom, abolishing all servitudes, including the comforts of the "better cared for, better fed and better clothed" conditions of Sapphira's darkies?[121] Or is it the drug of alienation, of separation from those very comforts, of belonging nowhere and to no one? As Nancy stands there, is she benumbed by the shot at freedom that is a shot of freedom, or is she drugged with the sorrow of expulsion from her former servitude? The story of Sapphira and Nancy is rife with examples of ambivalence: Sapphira versus Rachel; Henry's Frenchness versus typical Frenchness in most of Cather's fiction; Lutheran Christianity versus Catholic Christianity; French "bad blood" versus British "best houses"; the Biblical Rachel versus the French actress Rachel; *A Pilgrim's Progress* versus *Holy War;* the mistress's possible sapphic desire for the slave versus heterosexual jealousy of her. Cather's stylistic *démeublement* at this point leaves the answer up in the air as the narrative crackles with the play of its dialectic.

As Rachel leaves the benumbed Nancy, Rachel's parting words are "we shall meet again." They shall, but Nancy will never again see Rachel's little Betty. The child dies during "The Dark Autumn" (book 8), following Nancy's flight, in an epidemic of diphtheria. A presage of this sadness for Rachel might be seen in the tart note from her mother, delivered soon after Nancy's flight: *"Mistress Blake is kindly requested to make no further visits at the Mill House. Sapphira Dodderidge Colbert."*[122] Rachel has momentary regrets not unlike Nancy's about her mother's health: "maybe I ought to have thought and waited."[123] Waiting for her mother's death is the only issue, of course, since Rachel's regrets have to do with the timing of Nancy's emancipation, not the emancipation itself.

Rachel's sadness about her mother is as nothing compared to the sadness at the sickness of her children during the autumn, leading to the death of Betty. That sickness gives rise to a narrative parallel with *Madame Bovary,* perhaps marking Cather's admiration for Flaubert. When Henry Colbert hears that the local physician, Dr. Brush, is attending the children, he is outraged: " 'Why the man's an ignoramus. It may be measles for all he knows. Have you sent to town for my doctor?' "[124] His doctor is Clavenger, and when he does come to attend to the children, he is described as

everything that poor old Brush was not; intelligent, devoted to his profession — and a gentleman. He had come to practice in Frederick County by accident. While he was on the staff of a hospital in Baltimore, he fell in love with a Winchester girl who was visiting in the city. After he found that she would never consent to live anywhere but in her native town, he gave up the promise of a fine city practice and settled in Winchester. A foolish thing to do, but Clavenger was like that.[125]

The rapport between Dr. Brush and Dr. Clavenger recalls that between Dr. Charles Bovary and Dr. La Rivière, the physician who attends Emma Bovary in her dying illness in Flaubert's most famous novel (completed in 1856, the year of *Sapphira and the Slave Girl*'s major episodes of spring, summer, and autumn). Dr. Brush's incidental appearance in the novel makes the resemblance between him and Charles Bovary necessarily notational, but the notes are nonetheless strikingly resonant in their psychological and professional parallels.

The resemblance between Clavenger (a name with French overtones) and La Rivière lies in the transcendent authority each carries as a physician not only in comparison to the "complete ignoramus" so like Emma Bovary's physician-husband but in the intelligence and devotion each shows. Clavenger could have had a "fine city practice" were it not for his "devotion" to the girl from Winchester. Flaubert's great physician is introduced in less ordinary terms, to be sure; he is a far more austere and distant figure, a great source of meaning in the pictograph of his name. "The apparition of a god would not have caused greater emotion," Flaubert writes. The French novelist emphasizes La Rivière's devotion to his profession in more dramatic terms than Cather uses for Clavenger:

> disdainful of medals, of titles and of academies, hospitable, liberal, paternal with the poor and practicing virtue without believing in it, he would have been taken for a saint if the sharpness of his spirit had not made him feared as a demon. His look, more cutting than his scalpel, went straight down into your soul and unravelled every lie behind allegations and modesties. And he went thus, full of this debonair majesty that the awareness of a great talent, of good luck and forty years of hard-working and irreproachable existence gives.[126]

La Rivière presides over the death of Emma Bovary more like a disinterested God than an attending physician.

For all the difference in tone between Flaubert's presentation of La Rivière and Cather's of Clavenger, there is a strong narrative and symbolic reverberation. Clavenger, too, must be summoned from afar, like a god called from his empyrean seat of authority. He attends his patients with less dramatic but no less emphatic authority. He asks few questions of Rachel and Fairhead and "he was deliberate and at ease."[127] Fairhead wants to tell him that he has seen little Mary downstairs the night before, sipping some broth Fairhead had prepared:

> The doctor sat down on the lower step of the hitchblock, leaned against the second step, and *relaxed* into a position of ease, as if he meant to spend the afternoon there *looking at the mountain*. When

David began to tell him what he had seen in the kitchen last night, he listened *attentively,* with his *peculiar expression of thinking directly behind his eyes.* He did *not once interrupt,* but when David ended with: "and I can't believe she is any the worse for it," the doctor gave him a *quizzical smile.*[128]

With no tone of surprise, Clavenger tells Fairhead that they'd best keep the incident "a secret between us, here on Back Creek" and that the child, being hungry, " 'her system began to take up what it needed. That's very simple. What surprises me is that you were struck dumb outside the window and did not go blundering in and take the child's chance away from her.' "[129] In noting his "surprise," Clavenger is not chiding Fairhead, nor is he being ironical or cynical; he is philosophically indifferent and disinterested, assuming the stance of Flaubert's physician. It is not that Clavenger does not "care" about "the child" or "couldn't care less" about Fairhead's wonderment. A physician talking to a minister of God, Clavenger has a more universal view of things than the preacher. In his gaze at the mountain, he is as La Rivière is to his name: one who looks on things from the perspective of great and enduring symbols. This is not to say that the mountain is a "symbol" of God for Clavenger any more than the river is for La Rivière. Quite, if anything, to the contrary. Clavenger is as indifferent to the death of little Betty as he is to the survival of little Mary. He knows the limitations as well as the possibilities of medicine, even as he knows the possibilities of nature (the mountain) as well as limitations of human nature like Fairhead's expected "blundering" and Dr. Brush's medical "ignorance." His professional stance suggests that of the narrator of *Madame Bovary:* "as if the plenitude of the soul did not sometimes overflow by the emptiest of metaphors, could never give the exact measure of its needs, nor of its conceptions, and that human speech is like a cracked cauldron on which we beat melodies to make bears dance, when one wants to move the stars to pity."[130] The "Flaubertian" Dr. Clavenger brings into the novel the sense of Fate, of the mystery of the human condition, of transcendent awe before "Man's Fate."

This note persists in the narrative and character signifiers of the epilogue. "Book IX: Nancy's Return (Epilogue — Twenty-five years later)" is recounted, in its first chapter, by the third-person narrator of the novel up to this point. However, in the second and concluding chapter, a first-person narration begins. The first paragraph of the chapter begins: "It was a brilliant, windy March day. . . . " The second paragraph of the chapter reads: "I had been put into my mother's bed so that I could watch the turnpike, then a macadam road with a blue limestone facing. It ran very near us, between the little yard and the base of the high hills which shut the winter sun from us early."[131] And the beginning of *Sapphira and the Slave Girl* is

Book I

I

The Breakfast Table, 1856.

Henry Colbert, the miller, always breakfasted
with his wife — beyond that he appeared irregularly at
the family table.[132]

Clearly, we have been reading not only a memoir but a memoir within a
frame. The place and date-entry at the head of chapter 1 of the first book
of the novel is like a "journal entry"; it is the "opening frame" of the
novel closed by the epilogue. The narrative device is a familiar one in
Cather, as we know.[133e]

Here, the retrospective effect of the first-person narration in the epilogue implies a first person as the author of the journal entry and as the
narrator of the novel proper. The child in the "mother's bed" waiting for
"Nancy's return" is the grown-up impersonal third-person narrator of
the entire text of the novel. The role of the subjective narrator in the
epilogue is as effaced, however, as that of the objective narrator of the
novel proper. The child seems to be the grandchild of Rachel Blake,
though the latter is called as she is in the novel proper, "Mrs. Blake."
Similarly, the "Mary" (*née* Blake) who would thus be the child's mother
is anonymously referred to as "my mother." I describe the narrator as
child because there is neither nominal nor pronominal clue to the child's
gender; equally indefinite is the identity of the child's parents. Is she or
he, as the case may be, the child of Mary, Rachel Blake's only surviving
child? Is the narrator's reference in the epilogue to Rachel as "Mrs. Blake"
rather than "grandmother," then, formal and deferential — not only a
custom perhaps of the milieu but also an indication of her stately presence
and "presidency" of that milieu? In the child-future narrator of *Sapphira
and the Slave Girl* we have the most effaced and self-effacing of Cather's
first-person narrators.

This effacement and self-effacement preserves in the epilogue the
narrative and symbolic ambivalences of the novel proper. The Nancy
who returns is the Nancy who left. If she was figuratively a "hired girl"
like Antonia at the Mill Farm before the war, in Montreal she has become
more literally a "hired girl." She works there for the family of "Madam"
and "Colonel Kenwood . . . in England for the spring, and that was why
Nancy was able to come home and visit her mother." Henry Colbert need

not have feared for his "Mercy": it is not into one of "them houses" that she has been "enticed," nor is it in the language of his "bad blood" that she lives her days and her nights. "Her husband was the Kenwood's gardener. He was half Scotch and half Indian."[134] There is no more than the mention of the couple's "three children," but, genetically and symbolically, we can expect there will be a still greater blanching in them of Nancy's own "pale gold."

For the child-observer who becomes the first-person narrator and who was sung to sleep with Bluebell's ditty, this blanching is an aspect of Nancy herself.

> Nancy had always been described to me as young, gold-coloured, and "lissome" — that was my father's word.
>
> "Down by de cane-brake, close by de mill, Dar lived a yaller gal" — That was the picture I had carried in my mind. The stranger who came to realize that image was forty-four years old. But though she was no longer lissome, she was other things. She had, I vaguely felt, presence. And there was charm about her voice, though her speech was different from ours on Back Creek. Her words seemed to me too precise, rather cutting in their unfailing distinctness. Whereas, Mrs. Blake used to ask me if she should read to me from my 'hist'ry book" (*Peter Parley's Universal*) Nancy spoke of the his-to-ry of Canada. I didn't like that pronunciation. Even my father said "hist'ry." Wasn't that the right and easy way to say it? Nancy put into many words syllables I had never heard sounded in them before. That repelled me. It didn't seem a friendly way to talk.[135]

In the linguistic alliance here of Mrs. Blake, the child, and her father, one senses the same distancing from the phonetic at its best that Claude Wheeler had expressed and represented in relation to the French language as spoken by David Gerhardt.[136e] Such speech is not friendly and repels speakers of the lost language. In speaking so well not only has Nancy lost her erotic color for the child-observer, she has also lost the language of Back Creek. Nancy speaks the English that her former master spoke: "Henry was born in Loudun County and had grown up in a neighborhood of English settlers. He spoke the language as they did, spoke it clearly and decidedly. This was not, on Back Creek, a friendly way of talking."[137] Though there was no incestuous biological relation between Henry and Nancy, she proves herself to be his symbolic offspring linguistically: the Black White Anglo-Saxon Protestant daughter of a French White Anglo-Saxon Protestant.

During the twenty-five years "hist'ry"/"his-to-ry" between novel proper and epilogue, Henry Colbert, surviving his wife by five years, has died.

"He met his death in the haying season of 1863, when he was working in the fields with a few negroes who begged to stay on at the Mill Farm after the miller had freed all his wife's slaves. The Master was on top of the hayrack, catching the hay as Taylor forked it up to him. He stepped backward too near the edge of the load and fell to the ground, striking his head on the limestone edge."[138] Not surprisingly, the always indecisive Henry had waited for his wife to die before he manumitted her slaves. His own death is a symbolic pictograph of his lifelong confrontation with the conscience that was too much for his wife. He dies from a blow to the head, and his fall backwards from the edge of the yellow grain he was catching was his fall into the abyss of the erotic. His fate is familiar in Cather: the punishment that the author, like a Biblical Jehovah, metes out to all who overreach into the erotic. Yet, one can imagine that his death grieved the community as that of Martin Colbert did not. When Nancy asks what happened to Martin, "Mrs. Blake glanced at her in a way that meant it was a forbidden subject. 'He was killed in the war', she said briefly. 'He'd got to be a captain in the cavalry, and the Colberts made a great to-do about him after he was dead, and put up a monument. But I reckon the neighbourhood was relieved.' "[139] This is hardly the eulogy of a hero. It is the judgment, once again, of heaven and of the author on this erotically driven "forbidden subject" who had been after the Antonia-like Nancy at Mill Farm and in the woods of Back Creek in the summer of 1856. (In fact, Martin had had to content himself with the easily available Bluebell.) Nancy, Mrs. Blake, Aunt Till, the child-future narrator are the principal hosts of the Nancy who returns in the epilogue. Given this company of women, one suspects that the child, too, is female. This is a world without men, presided over by Mrs. Blake.

Rachel Blake may be the best example in Cather fiction of the feminine sexuality beyond phallocentrism hinted at in Lacan's late writings. If so, it must also be noted that "beyond phallocentrism" in Cather's final novel also means "beyond men." This was already implicit in the ancillary, anemic roles she assigns men in her novels and in so many of her stories. In *Sapphira and the Slave Girl* the epilogue suggests that feminine sexuality is not only *beyond* but also literally *without* men. With the Kenwoods in England, might not Nancy's husband also have made the long trip to Back Creek? Could not the gardener have been replaced for such an important trip? Twenty-five years having passed since Nancy's flight into Canada, is it likely that the forty-four-year-old Nancy has such small children that only her husband can look after them? Why, after his enthusiastic rush to meet Nancy as she arrives, is the child-future narrator's father so effaced in the epilogue? The subordination of men in this last chapter of Nancy's story (David Fairhead, so instrumental in her flight, is but briefly mentioned in his role as teacher) raises the question posed by Nicole Ward Jouve at the end of her *Un Homme nommé Zapolski* (a study of the "Yorkshire Ripper" of the late 1970s and the society which produced him): "Is then a true heterosexuality impossible? Crucial question of our period, a question which anguishes me and to which I have no answer."[140] Crucial question as well for the Cather canon in which the only alternative seems to be the world without women of the epilogue to *Shadows on the Rock* or the world without men of the epilogue to *Sapphira and the Slave Girl.*

In the Back Creek Valley of 1881 featured in the epilogue to this 1940 novel, Jouve's anguished question of 1983 seems to be answered in the negative. Indeed, the novel raises directly a related and equally crucial question that emerges less directly in Cather fictions that are either "beyond men" or "beyond women": is sexuality possible? It is not heterosexuality alone that is absented or contained in Cather. As other fictions in the canon show, homosexuality and lesbianism are also absented or contained. Cather's fictions abnegate not only sex but also sexuality, the pleasure of bodies and the Pleasure Principle itself.

This abnegation is perhaps nowhere so strikingly signified as in *My Antonia.* I have already commented on Jim Burden's flight from Wick Cutter when the latter thinks he will find Antonia in her bed but finds Jim instead. More pertinently here with respect to Cather's dénouements in which the sexes are separated from one another, there is the last section of *My Antonia*: "Cuzak's Boys." On this return to see Antonia and Anton many years after the main events of the story, Jim tropes more toward Anton than toward Antonia. This troping is not unlike that in "Eleanor's House" in which characters conflate. Here, the onomastics suggest that Antonia has become Anton. Still more pertinently, for Jim the Cuzak children are primarily boys. The girl-children are very effaced in the narrative even as Antonia has been effaced by, and into, as I suggest, Anton. The very signifier of the earth as womb or mother is masculinized.

> Leo dived behind his mother and grinned out at me. We turned to leave the cave. Antonia and I went up the stairs first, and the children waited. We were standing outside talking, when they all came running up the steps together, big and little, tow heads and gold heads and brown, and flashing little naked legs; a veritable explosion of life out of the dark cave into the sunlight. It made me dizzy for a moment.[142]

Jim Burden is dizzy with the familiar Catherian eroticism of golden colors given off by Leo (lion, the "manliest" of animals and Jim's favorite on this visit) and the other children in this moment of "Cuzak's *Boys*" (my emphasis). It is their phallic energy, symbolized by their "flashing little *naked legs*" (my emphasis), which has dis-Burdened him in this phallocentric and phallologocentric passage. However secular, the eschatological consonances of another dénouement which is a "world without women," that of *Death Comes for the Archbishop,* are rung here. Nevertheless, we remember that the dénouement of *My Antonia* is a part of a manuscript given to us by a first-frame narrator who does not reappear at the end of this novel like the narrator of *Sapphira and the Slave Girl.* Jim will be returning to Mrs. Burden and her artists for long stretches. Are these stretches to be broken only by chance meetings with the first-name narrator, a kind of Imogen Willard of "Flavia and Her Artists"? Will Jim pass on to the narrator new chapters of "My Antonia," the title he had written across his portfolio at the last minute—indeed, changing his original inscription "Antonia" to "*My* Antonia" ("Introduction," no pagination). Will the seemingly missing last frame of these future chapters be ironically provided by the first-frame narrators to imply that the eschatological and psychosexual resolutions due to Jim Burden's recovery of the lost language are still missing?

The very last frame of Cather's published fiction—the epilogue of *Sapphira and the Slave Girl* —offers a bittersweet final image of the consonances Cather sought to restore throughout her canon:

> From the way Till spoke of Mrs. Blake's long visit, hints that she dropped unconsciously, one understood that there was always a certain formality between Mrs. Colbert and her daughter—a reserve on both sides. After tea, for the hour before a supper, the Mistress preferred to be alone in the parlour. There were many snowfalls that winter, on into March. Mrs. Colbert liked to sit and watch the evening light fade over the white fields and the spruce trees across the creek. When Till came in with the lights, she would let her leave only four candles, and they must be set on the tea-table so placed that the candle flames inside were repeated by flames out in the snow-covered lilac arbour. It looked like candles shining in a little playhouse, Till said, and there was the tea-table out there too, all set like for company. When Till peeped in at the door, she would find the Mistress looking out at this little scene; often she was smiling. Till really believed Miss Sapphy saw spirits out there, spirits of the young folks who used to come to Chestnut Hill.
>
> And the Mistress died there, upright in her chair. When the miller came at supper-time and went into the parlour, he found her. The strong heart had been overcome at last. Though her bell was

beside her, she had not rung it. There must have been some moments of pain or struggle, but she had preferred to be alone. Till thought it likely the "fine folks" were waiting outside of her in the arbour, and she went away with them.

"She oughtn't ever to a' come out here," Till often said to me. "She wasn't raised that way. Mrs. Matchem, down at the old place, never got over it that Mrs. Sapphy didn't buy in Chestnut Hill an' live like a lady, 'stead a' leavin' it to run down under the Bushwells, an' herself commin' out here where nobody was anybody much."[141]

There is in the image of the dying Titan, Sapphira Dodderidge Colbert, more of the saturnine than the Saturnalian. She is more the bemused former actress than the amused present spectator of the little play she puts on. She recalls more the dying Myra Henshawe lashed to the tree on the storm-beaten Pacific headland than Thea Kronberg in stag-like erection atop the crag of Panther Canyon or Alexandra Bergson looking triumphantly across her cornfields. There is nothing of the dying Mrs. Harris ("Old Mrs. Harris") nor of the bereaved Mrs. Wheeler turning in their sense of dissonance to the consolations of religion. The play Sapphira looks at is but a reflection of a reflection, a translation into a past from a present in which there is still "a certain formality . . . a reserve on both sides" between daughter and phallocentric mother. Sapphira shows herself still desirously jealous of her husband. She knows he had been drawn to Nancy whom the daughter had protected from the enticed father. The crippled old woman remembers, too, that the father had loved the daughter more than the mother in his half-heeding of French bad blood. As wife and mother, Sapphira would well have wished to see Henry overcome his Lutheran conscience in a full return to her rather than in a half-turn to Nancy.

Till doesn't understand all this, of course; she always was a bit uppity. It is more her regrets at having left Chestnut Hill than Sapphira's that we hear in Till's reflections that close the epilogue and the novel. Sapphira, we remember, "usually acted upon motives which she disclosed to no one"—not to Till, for sure, but not to Rachel or Henry either. To no one but herself, the self with whom she must spend the last March of her life "smiling" in a way that recalls some of Dr. Clavenger's "quizzical smile" but more of Gabrielle Longstreet-de Coucy's "faintly contemptuous smile" as she, too, looks into a reflector of the past illuminated by yellow rays. It is the smile of the indifferent, of those few in Cather who neither rant at the dissonances between past and present nor at the God who allows them to "die alone" with that "mortal enemy" within them. The solipsistic bemusement of the dying Sapphira is, however, not gainsaid by the "regal, calm, victorious" repose of Gabrielle's face in death. Instead, "the strong heart had been overcome at last." In this retrospective closing frame of the closing frame of the novel the kernel of the past is cracked apart by Sapphira's smile. Its fragments come forward to crash against the shell of the framing epilogue, cracking it apart as well.[142e]

6

Resoundings

In the French fictions of Willa Cather which I have examined closely in the preceding pages as occasions of her career-long search for the lost language, I have specified the spiritual, the psychological, and the societal axes along which she has conducted that search. Certain of those fictions have, obviously, conducted the search more on one than on others of these axes, while some have done so in combinations of two or all three axes in different emphases for each. Here, I shall resume in a general and, I trust, in a still more suggestive manner the main lines of Cather's search. To do so, I shall begin with a brief consideration of Cather's last three fictions: the two posthumously published stories, "The Best Years" and "Before Breakfast," and her unfinished and unpublished novel about medieval Avignon, *Hard Punishments*. With this springboard, I shall then reconsider each of the axes of the writer's search for the lost language: the spiritual, the psychological, and the social, enlarging the last to include the political. In this connection, I shall also briefly consider *A Lost Lady* in its implications for the lost language Cather so long and so earnestly sought to recapture.

"The Best Years" and "Before Breakfast"

"The Best Years," the story of Lesley Ferguesson, a young schoolteacher in a remote school on the prairie, is set at the beginning in 1899. It is recorded in the framing story of the one-time County Superintendent of Public Instruction, Evangeline Knightly—a "charming person" of "oval face, small head delicately set . . . hazel eyes, a little blue, a little green, tiny dots of brown" which, "when she laughed, positively glowed with humour . . . in each oval cheek a roguish dimple"—who is considered in the community "an intelligent young woman, but plain—distinctly plain."[1] The Superintendent takes a particular liking to Lesley and the large Ferguesson family: the practical Mrs. Ferguesson; the two little boys and the older brother, Hector, with "the fair pink-cheeked complexion Lesley should have had and didn't";[2] the impractical, talkative, and "thinking" Mr. Ferguesson whose loquacity, like his Populist sentiments, makes him somewhat the butt of his good-humored neighbors. But the idyll of this happy family is broken by Lesley's death from pneumonia contracted when staying with her students through a sudden snow storm soon after Evangeline's visit. The news shatters Evangeline as much as it does the Ferguesson family.

The effect on Mrs. Ferguesson is especially long-lived. Some twenty years after the great blizzard in which Lesley died, Evangeline, now Mrs. Ralph Thorndike living back in her native New England, visits Mrs. Ferguesson in the new house where the more prosperous family now lives. At Mrs. Ferguesson's appeal the talk turns to Lesley. The two women who so loved the young schoolteacher share their happy memories and their sorrow. Mrs. Ferguesson repeatedly regrets the family's new station, longing for the old days, however hard: " 'our best years are when we're working hardest and going right ahead when we can hardly see our way out.' "[3] She indicates that there is a kind of estrangement between her and her ever so busy husband, taken as he is with the modern world. She doesn't like to go out with him in the family car (Evangeline herself has preferred to hire a buggy rather than a car to visit Mrs. Ferguesson): " 'He's had some accidents. When he gets to thinking, he's just as likely to run down a cow as not. He's had to pay for one. You know cows will cross the road right in front of a car. Maybe their grandchildren calves will be more modern-minded.' "[4] Evangeline leaves to visit the old schoolhouse. She does not see Mrs. Ferguesson again, but she writes to her "a long letter from Wiscaset, Maine, which Mrs. Ferguesson sent to her son Hector, marked, " 'To be returned, but first pass on to your brothers.' "[5] So ends "The Best Years."

The letter is probably the story itself, envelope and letter combined—an ingenious variation on Cather's common framing technique. Other aspects of the letter are also familiar: Mr. Ferguesson is a Dillon who has not died; Lesley is a Thea who stays on the prairie; Mrs. Ferguesson is more Mrs. Harris than the Myra or the Sapphira her sprained ankle momentarily makes of her, and she is more Oswald than Myra Henshawe in the sympathy of the Nellie Birdseye-like Evangeline; the plain little girl is boyish in her name (Lesley can be heard as Leslie) even as the manly big brother is girlish in his mien and so on. There is only the barest French marking in the story: Evangeline reverberates with a derived French source, Longfellow's Acadian heroine. In this connection, it is interesting to note that Evangeline Knightly is from Maine and is, possibly, as her first name indicates, partly of Kanuck origin. However, though she goes back to Maine, it is to marry a White Anglo-Saxon Protestant and live on the hither side of French Canada as a Thorndike. Is this a "dike" against the "thorn" of that French branch of those "subtle, sensitive beauty-loving Latin Races"? In any case, become a Thorndike, Evangeline is far from Cather's once-favorite dialect of the lost language—French. This suggests that "The Best Years" is one of the most melancholy of Cather's fictions of dissonance.

In "Before Breakfast" we are beyond the border of French and things French. We are on the thither and northern border of French Canada, with Henry Grenfell on the cliff-side of a remote island off the shore of Nova Scotia. Henry is no Henry Colbert; he is a "gren-fell"—a "fell" ("noun. Northern Brit. *a.* a mountain, hill, or moor. *b.* [*in combination*] fell-walking," with the first syllable of his name possibly "green" but also "grain" [Latin, *granata*]).[6] The whole name thus tells the story of his life: he is from Colorado, the westernmost edge of the land of the grain, and winds up in the land of the fell. There is even less of a French marking, genetically and onomastically, in him than in Evangeline Knightly.

Yet, his story is not without many of the symbolic markings of Cather's other fictions. A middle-aged businessman, he comes to his island retreat to get away from his pretentious, intellectual sons, two of them college professors; in his typically Catherian passionless marriage he gets along well enough with his Flavia-like wife of theatrical and musical interests; for all his impatience with that kind of culture, he *is* a reader—of "Scott and Dickens and Fielding"[7] and Shakespeare. Again, as he "fell-walks" about his island retreat alone, he greets a great old spruce as " 'grandfather' "— a British-Canadian grandfather, of course, not Godfrey St. Peter's "Kanuck" one. He is irritated by the intrusive presence of the geology professor he meets on the boat taking him to the island, although he is somewhat taken by the little-spoken daughter of the academic.

The professor's daughter figures more prominently in the story of Henry Grenfell than he might have suspected on their first meeting. He spends a particularly restless night in a "dryness of soul" not unlike that of the God-bereft Latour. In the morning he rises and goes "to the edge of the spruce wood and out on a bald headland that topped a cliff two hundred feet above the sea." He moves along the cliff trail onto a grassy headland with a beautiful view of "four waterfalls, white as silver, pouring down the perpendicular cliff walls." As he looks on this "splendid sight . . . all his own . . . not even a gull . . . not a living creature," he suddenly spies "a human figure, in a long white bathrobe—and a rubber cap. Then it must be a woman? Queer. No island woman would go bathing at this hour, not even in the warm island ponds." It is a woman: "the geologist's daughter . . . she opened her robe, a grey thing lined with white. Her bathing suit was pink. If a clam stood upright and graciously opened its shell, it would look like that . . . with a quick motion she shed her robe, kicked off her sandals, and took to the water." Grenfell reflects on how "crazy" she is, but he is admiring rather than critical as he makes his way back to the cabin: "everything since he left the cabin had been reassuring, delightful—everything was the same, so was he! The air, or the smell of fir trees—something had sharpened his appetite. He was hungry. As he passed the grandfather tree he waved his hand, but didn't stop. Plucky youth is more bracing than enduring age." When he gets near the cabin he smells the coffee brewed by his "man Friday," William, an islander who helps him but without sharing his cabin. He knows that William has not waited to have his own breakfast: "As he came down the hill Grenfell was chuckling to himself: 'Anyhow, when that first amphibious frog-toad found his waterhole all dried up behind him, and jumped out to hop along till he could find another one—well, he started on a long hop.' "[8] The story ends, with the last published lines of Willa Cather's fiction to date.

We have an upbeat ending to the canon, it would appear, especially to the dirges, fragmenting shells and kernels of the fiction of the thirties. Consonances—particularly of the most distant of all pasts, the "origin of man," and of the present—are restored. In seeing that "nothing has changed," Grenfell is not Euclide Auclair on his Canadian rock at the end of *Shadows on the Rock*. It is not stasis that Grenfell finds in the unchanged Nova Scotian wild; it is the frame of life itself with its change towards growth. In this delight and reassurance the Henry who returns to his cabin has a sense of continuity and consonance between past and present which, however secular, recalls Latour's. On the North Atlantic headland he sees not a Myra Henshawe lashed in dissonance to a storm-whipped tree on the Pacific headland, but a young girl in the bloom of youth. "Fairweather" is her name, and as she takes to the chill waters of the rocky coast she stands for the elements at their fairest. This "comely creature" of breeding, of "delicate preferences" and "lovely eyes, lovely skin, lovely manners" is a "Venus on the half shell" who is herself a shell that cannot be broken by the kernel of dissonances roiling within the sea. Miss Fairweather is consonance restored, the lost language refound in the most ideal way for Willa Cather: pictographically rather than seman-tically. As "The Best Years" may be seen as an utter fiction of dissonance, so "Before Breakfast" may be seen as an utter fiction of consonance.[9e]

Hard Punishments

There is and was to have been *Hard Punishments*, the title, according to Edith Lewis, of Cather's unfinished manuscript of the novel about Avignon during the Papal Exile. The fragment of four handwritten pages (original on deposit in the Alderman Library of the University of Virginia) is too fragmentary for an interpretation of the novel in itself or of the novel in relation to the rest of Cather's canon. That the novelist did not herself destroy what she had completed of the novel before her death, although she ordered its destruction in her will, could suggest that she intended to complete this novel. It is about Pierre, an uncultivated farm boy whose hands have become useless after he had been hung by his thumbs for several hours in punishment for petty thievery, and André, the cultivated nephew of an important official in the Papal Palace, whose tongue has been cut out for blasphemy. Apparently, like David Gerhardt with Claude Wheeler, André takes Pierre under his wing.

It is impossible to say what happens next; we have no full text. What we know of the incomplete text from Lewis suggests that the novel was to have at least been a text of dissonances (cruelties) and a text of consonances (splendours).[10e] Cather may have come to her title in a reminiscence of Dickens's *Hard Times* (1854). Circumstantially, the connection occurs when one notes that Dickens sets his novel in that first half of the nineteenth century in which most of Cather's last published novel, *Sapphira and the Slave Girl,* is set. Again, the hero of the posthumously-published "Before Breakfast" is also a reader of Dickens. Long ago, of course, the novelist had held Dickens at some distance as a novelist very different from the French models she preferred at the time.[11e] The distancing from those models in her fiction of the thirties and forties suggests grounds for a possible return to the Dickens model in this unfinished novel. Of course, Lewis's description of the style of the novel— "'few of her stories have been so completely *démeublé*'"[12]—indicates that she would have relied on a pared-down model of Dickens. Nevertheless, the titles of the two novels, *Hard Times* and *Hard Punishments,* do point to a possible, more intrinsic reverberation. As Dickens attacks in his novel the factualism of the nascent industrial state of the early nineteenth century, so Cather seems, from Lewis's account, to be attacking the factualism of the ensconced literalism of an ecclesiastical state. Both factualisms are scientisms that make for hard times of the kind suffered by Gradgrind's charges and for the hard punishments suffered by Pierre and André for their crimes against the state.

These are familiar Cather motifs and might have been worked out in the familiar narrative and symbolic patterns of Cather's fiction. Pierre, the speaker of a lost language deprived of his hands, his usual means of communication in that language, seems to have been turned into the "stone" that his very name signifies. André seems to have been "unmanned," deprived of his name (Gr. *andros,* "man"), in having lost the very mark

of Man, speech. The names suggest, moreover, possible resolutions familiar in Cather. Pierre will be the rock on whom André will found his
church of a language beyond the phonetic, speech or script. Like the
scriptural Latour with the speechifying Vaillant, Pierre and André will
together make a very pictograph of the lost language recovered. Such a
resolution would be consistent with the Cather of the fictions of consonance.
In those novels and stories she is a later—perhaps the last—moment of
the Emersonian and Thoreauvian faith in the primacy of the pictographic
over the phonetic. In its chiasmatic relation of signifiers, this final pictograph which I project for *Hard Punishments* would perhaps find Cather,
like Jean Marie Latour, waking from the anguish of the fictions of the
thirties and forties "into the morning, into the morning"[13] of restored
sacramentalism.

Yet, in the ordinary language sense, the images of France in the canon
of the first four decades leave only the barest trace in the last decade.
The novelist's eulogy of difference in the fictions of consonance yields
to a sense of difference in the "other" bordering on diffidence towards
the "other" in the dirges of the last decade. As the "Other" proves
finally to be the "Øther" for Lacan, so, for Cather, French seems finally
to prove itself but another signifier of the lost language. She seems
finally to have regarded the pursuit of the lost language as a losing
proposition. The nonverbal, originary reality which all grammars can
only hint at was no longer recuperable, whether in the linguistically
overfurnished mode of a novel like *The Song of the Lark* or in the
démeublé mode of so many of her other fictions. In the withdrawal of the
last decade in particular, she may have felt the impossibility of ever
putting the world back together again after its break "in 1922 or thereabouts." She seems to have despaired of ever restoring the sacramental
linguistics of *Death Comes for the Archbishop*, of ever getting to a past far
enough back to recover the founding image. She gave up writing, did not
finish *Hard Punishments*, the long-projected novel about France when that
country was still not far from its origin in the land.

There is a dissonant note in the very idea that Cather would have set a
story of hard punishments in her beloved Avignon, the capital of France
for her. Perhaps too, then, she could not finish the novel in the face of
that very premise of ambivalence. The shadows on the Valley of the
St. Laurent may have fallen too heavily on the Valley of the Rhône. The
reverberations of Henry Colbert's head as it struck that limestone rock
may have echoed too disturbingly as they reached the handicapped
Pierre and the tongueless André. The novelist thus could not finish the
Hard Punishments on which she had apparently worked since 1941 and
perhaps, according to Lewis, had conceived as early as 1935.

The Spiritual Axis of Cather's Search

The intrinsic and extrinsic ambivalences I point to in the case of *Hard Punishments* seem to me the very emblem of Cather's synchronic dialectic of consonance and dissonance in her entire canon. They seem especially emblematic along the spiritual or religious axis of her search for the lost language. The punishments André and Pierre suffer have been authorized by the ecclesiastical and political authorities of medieval Avignon at the time of the Papal Exile. The handicaps officially inflicted on the two boys are, undoubtedly, among the cruelties Lewis heard in the song of the French guide, and she imagined they would be recreated in Cather's novel. What the splendors would have been, we cannot, of course, know, although they would have undoubtedly appeared in this fiction of Willa Cather. Set in Avignon, they would, perhaps, have been the most magnificent of the many splendors her fictions have given us. Now, it seems to me that, for the most part, Cather scholarship has stressed more the splendors than the cruelties; thus, it also seems to me that a fuller understanding of her art and thought requires a greater emphasis on the cruelties, the hard punishments so many of her sympathetic as well as unsympathetic characters suffer. Through a consideration of this suffering, particularly the suffering of death, I seek to deepen the understanding of the novelist's search for the consonances of the lost language. I think it is a far more troubled search than commonly believed.

Death is a far more frequent and disturbing element in Cather's fiction than the reposeful deaths of Vaillant and Latour or familiar critical emphasis on her work as a paean to life would suggest. Paradoxically, death—the ways and effects of dying—is more vigorous and energetic than the ways and effects of living in many of her works. One can trace this relation from the violent suicide of the hero of the first story, "Peter" (1892), to the sudden death of Dillon, "a young man still," in "Two Friends," and beyond. As Gelfant notes on the suicide of Antonia's father in *My Antonia*, "only the evocative beauty of Cather's language—and the inevitable validation as childhood memory—can romanticize this sordid death and the squalor in which it takes place."[14] For Gelfant, this romanticization is inseparable from the unsexing of Cather's men and women, all fearful of erotic commitment. Gelfant sees women as the chief victims of the violence which eliminates the erotic. Throwing the Russian bride to the wolves in *My Antonia* is "the most graphic representation of Cather's underlying sentiments" for the critic.[15] Yet, the victimization through violent death is the fate of Cather's erotically energetic men or women. To the list of women Gelfant draws up I would add: Emil Bergson, Claude Wheeler, David Gerhardt, Captain Forrester (whose paralysis is

like death), Tom Outland, Fray Balthazar, Frontenac, Dillon—to cite
only some figures in the stories and novels I have discussed.

As important as the violence of the deaths is the accidentality of most
of them. These accidents express a logic of character as well as of moral
perspective. The nature of the accident is in keeping with the *données* of
character; the victim merits death in proportion to his or her accession to
the erotic. Violent death as a punishment from "on high" is especially
characteristic of the dissonant fictions.[16e] In the fictions of consonance
also, however, death has parallel logics. It is usually nonviolent as well as
nonaccidental. For example, there are the natural deaths of Father Vaillant
and Father Latour. As the title of the novel puts it, death here "comes for,"
not "to"; it is in consonance with other natural processes. Natural death
is thus a signifier of approval from "on high" for the character's refusal or
sublimation of the erotic. Even when death is violent in the fictions of consonance (Claude and David in battle in *One of Ours*), it is not accidental.
It is, rather, a part of the design of the familiar Catherian retreat from the
erotic scene of danger. The victim is removed from the scene of the
erotic, relieved of its pressures, heroically translated to a better world—
a world beyond the erotic with its risks of death and loss.

Seldom does this indictment of the erotic not appear in the canon. A
notable exception is *A Lost Lady* (1923). In this novel, a secular analog of
the sacramental linguistics of *Death Comes for the Archbishop* is at work.
A lady lost to and in her sensuality, Maidy Forrester represents a lost
language validated in the novel, linguistically speaking, in a way not
unlike that obtaining between plough/disk and Spanish sword in *My
Antonia*. Maidy *is* the lost language of erotic energy. In his early swash-
buckling and continuing admiration of his wife even in his infirmity, so
too is Captain Forrester. Even in the degraded expression of Maidy's
attachment to Ivy Peters, Cather validates this language. At the party for
Ivy Peters and his cronies near the end of the novel—a sacrilegious
reprise of the first party—her earrings, sacramental "thing of this world"
given her by her husband as figure of the "other world" of erotic energy,
still sparkle. Because Niel represents the buried Spanish sword in this
context he sees them in a bad light. In Maidy and Niel on this occasion,
as throughout the whole novel, one senses a secular expression of the
theological debate about the Eucharist between Catholic and Protestant
opponents at the time of the Reformation. Does that sacrament's validity
depend on the holiness of the act or on the holiness of the agent? In
theological terms, with relation to the priest, in *opero operato* or in *opero
operantis?* In *A Lost Lady* Maidy's *opera operato* triumphs on the occasion
of the party for Peters as much as it does when she is in the state of grace
through marriage to Forrester and to Collins. Yet, however sinful a

"priestess" she be in the eyes of Niel, Maidy Forrester is no more the mistress of Ivy Peters in the conventional sense of mistress than she was the wife of the Captain or will be the wife of Mr. Collins in the conventional sense of wife. She is innocent of such constraints on her erotic power. It is this innocence that is lost in the lady both to Ivy Peters and Niel Herbert, though not to Captain Forrester. The Forresters represent an "age of innocence" in which, indeed, the theological issue of the innocence of either act or agent is not a valid question.[17e]

In the novel, the linkage of death and the erotic emerge in all the force of each energy. In the lovemaking between Maidy Forrester and Frank Ellinger on the snow-covered forest floor, the license Cather gives to the erotic is extraordinary for her. In the scene the couple not only risks discovery of their adultery, but they also risk danger of exposure to the winter cold. The coupling of the fire of passion and the ice of the setting is a striking signifier of the chances that the erotic takes in relation to the dangers of both social and physical death. Yet, even in this rare instance of such risk-taking on the part of two erotically powerful characters, the event is not allowed to express fully the close relation between dying and living. The lovemaking is not foreground but background to Niel Herbert's more typical retreat from the erotic. The risky lovemaking of the adulterers is observed by the disapproving eye of a would-be judge from "on high."[18e] Nevertheless, it is significant and exceptional in the canon that this judge's perspective does not prevail in *A Lost Lady:* Maidy is not punished in the end. Her death in South America, as Ed reports to Niel, is natural. Neither violent nor accidental, yet not under the "sign of the cross" (the deaths of Vaillant and Latour), Maidy's death presents an instance of a consonance with natural processes—a unique instance, in fact, of a secular rather than religious consonance in the canon.

The Psychological Axis of Cather's Search

Death is the signifier of the lack in psychoanalytic terms, of the sense of absence in Derrida's terms. It is this juncture of life or self and death or loss that Cather reduces and evades. This is the hidden theme of Cather's "kingdom of art" whether she is writing about love or language. The passionless marriages of her fictions signify the effort to conceal the primordial sense of loss associated with the threat of castration. The pursuit of a lost language signifies the effort to deny the inherent fugacity (the "escaping tendency" of gases) of language itself. Through such dialectical signifiers Cather seeks to translate—etymologically, to carry over—the lost language: from dead past to living present, from Old World to New, from realism to romance, from the given to the imagined,

from the pictographic to the phonetic. The *démeublé* style which characterizes most of her fiction, especially after "the world split in two in 1922
or thereabouts," represents the belief in this "translatability."

Yet, "as always with language, it is the marriage of limitation with
opportunity"[19] and

> In general, it is assumed that translation proceeds from meaning to
> meaning through the medium of another language or another code.
> Occupied here at the a-semantic origin of meaning, as at the
> unpresentable source or presence, the anasemic translation must
> twist its tongue to speak the non-linguistic conditions of language.
> . . . The "figure" *shell-kernel* ought to be read according to the new
> anasemic and symbolic rule to which however it has introduced us.
> The law that it has given us to read must be *converted* and turned
> back on it. And doing this we will not accede to anything that is
> present, beyond the shell and the figure. Beyond the shell, (there is)
> "non-presence, the kernel and ultimate meaning of all discourse,"
> "the untouched nucleus (l'*intouché nucléiqué*) of non-presence." The
> very "messages" that the text conveys must be reinterpreted with new
> (anasemic and symbolic) "concepts" of sending, emitting, mission,
> or missive.[20]

In the *mots justes,* the Flaubertian ideal, of her *démeublé* style it is this
anasemic process that Cather seeks to arrest: the flight from meaning by
words themselves. Her late work in particular reveals a haunting though
unstated awareness that each *mot juste* is subject to the law that the kernel
is but another shell ad infinitum and that meaning itself is but a signal of
another meaning that is itself only a signal of another meaning, and so on.

Hence, the retreat from words themselves in her fiction, the stress on
the *démeublé,* especially in the work after "1922 or thereabouts." Until
then, she writes as if there is no doubt that beyond words — in fact, before
there were words — there was a reality of "talking pictures." *Death Comes
for the Archbishop* is the supreme example of her life-enhancing faith in
the kinetic and the pictographic over the death-enhancing phonetic.
After "1922 or thereabouts," however, doubt about the phonetic begins to
affect as well the kinetic and the pictographic. The stasis I have traced in
Shadows on the Rock with its time-locked and space-bound French immigrants represents an aesthetic as well as philosophical and psychological
retreat from the mobile and moving immigrants of the earlier, more
famous desert novel. The stillness of *Shadows* settles more and more
upon the subsequent fiction. Though obviously often modeled on earlier
life-enhancing figures of her fiction, the characters of these subsequent
novels and stories become "stills" rather than "moving pictures." They

no longer move about the land like Alexandra Bergson, rise atop mountain crags like Thea Kronberg, ride across deserts and climb mountains like Jean-Marie Latour and Joseph Vaillant. They fall from on high or sink into that pictograph that has almost always been ominous for Cather: deep waters. And with one exception, the beautiful, nostalgic story "The Old Beauty," the deep waters of the Atlantic will no longer be an access to her beloved France—country of the language coming as close as imperfect human language can to the lost language. The pictographs of that "country of the fabulous" become increasingly glum as the deep waters of the Atlantic become an unbridgeable abyss between Old France and the New France Cather had so often made of their American settings.

This abyss between America and France, the splitting of the French/American valence so central to her fictions of consonance, is paralleled in the increasing tendency of the canon to end in "worlds without women" (*Shadows on the Rock*) and "worlds without men" (*Sapphira and the Slave Girl*). In the Cather canon, isolation of the sexes is not the signifier of a fear of sex, the very vehicle of creation, which Gelfant sees in the novelist's predilection for the "reaping hook" and other images of sexual violence. Paradoxically, the isolation maintains desire—*as opposed to its realization.* When sexual difference operates, when there is an exchange of sexual energy of any kind, not only is the circuit of desire broken, but it also is broken violently. For Cather, in terms of René Girard's major thesis in *Violence and the Sacred,* difference leads to violence.[21] In her canon sexual activity leads to murder (*O Pioneers!*), rape or attempted rape (*My Antonia, Sapphira and the Slave Girl*), attempted suicide (*The Professor's House*), drowning (*Alexander's Bridge, Lucy Gayheart*), and other forms of violence foreclosing the detailed realization of desire.

In this light, the novelist's predilection for narrative modes like fairy tale and legend takes on special significance. Her rejection of sequential narrative and Balzacian realism, like her style démeublé, is part of a psychic strategy to maintain desire, to refuse the closures of erotic commitment. The irony could not be greater: celebrated for her sense of the organic—the sights, sounds, smells, and shapes of her beloved landscapes in America and in France—she disengages desire from the detail of desire in its most intense expression: sexual exchange. Fairy tale, legend, and style *démeublé* deflect and sublimate nature's energy in her most persistent natural theme: human love. Increasingly, then, as the canon progresses, a paradoxical stasis affects it as both the danger of erotic commitment and the closure of death itself are dulled in the false repose of half-worlds: a world of women without men, a world of men without women.

Is there no alternative to this intrasexualization in Cather? The religious solution that she offers in the androgynization of Latour in *Death Comes for the Archbishop,* is, paradoxically, itself under the stamp of a world without men of conventional male behavior and commitment at its center. In the place of the paradoxical phallocentrism Cather offers in that novel, the epilogue of *Sapphira and the Slave Girl* posits a vaginocentrism that refutes as strongly as phallocentrism the androgynous sexuality posited by Phyllis Robinson as the outcome of Cather's concern with sexuality. Empirically, androgyny would issue in bisexuality (as I have suggested it may in Sapphira); psychologically and morally, it might issue in the idea that there are neither men nor women—only *individuals.*

This possible and liberating way of looking at Cather's fiction is belied, as I have sought to demonstrate in this book, by the obvious strength of her women and the concomitant weakness of her men, as a rule. In Cather fictions where interaction between women and men is crucial to the outcome of the story, the men are usually wimpish, ineffectual, and unmanly, while the women are usually assertive, aggressive, and manly. In those Cather fictions where either men or women are the principal interactors, the same conventional gender attributes apply, whatever the sexuality of the characters (heterosexual, homosexual, lesbian): usually males are sissies, females tomboys. I say this with both *Death Comes for the Archbishop* and *Sapphira and the Slave Girl* in mind. In the former, the strength of the two priests—especially of Latour, a tower of phallic strength in his very name—is invested everywhere but in sexuality. In *Sapphira and the Slave Girl* the strength of Sapphira-as-cripple and, especially, of Rachel-as-widow is invested finally in things other than and beyond sexuality. Strong as these individuals are in themselves, they may be sexless, but they are not genderless in their attributes. The dénouements of these two novels only express more fully what is evident in the dénouements of so many other Cather fictions: that women (or feminine men) have resolved the problems of the fictional world as the men of that world could not. These strong individuals preside over a world in which sexual investments and their surrogations, of whatever empirical character, are absent from their lives (ultimately, as in the case of Rachel, initially in the case of the two priests). They regard such investments by others in either a condescending way (e.g., Latour towards Dona Isabella) or in a severely judgmental way (e.g., Rachel towards Martin), seeing themselves as vicars of a transcendent order that proscribes investment by themselves and others in the immanentist pleasures of a world lost to the messages of the lost language.

In seeking to get beyond the Reality Principle as she had come to know it—particularly in the modern world after "1922 or thereabouts" —Cather sought to return to earlier worlds, "lost," as Lewis puts it of her friend's unfinished novel, "to us in our times." Yet, in the earlier world of French Canada of the late seventeenth century as in the earlier world of her childhood, the back country of Virginia, she seems to have forsaken not only the Reality Principle but also the Pleasure Principle. By this I mean not only the pleasure of sexual commitments of whatever preference but also of the pleasure of those other dialects of the lost language: spiritual plenitude of the kind found in *Death Comes for the Archbishop;* social and communal fullfillment of the kind found in *My Antonia;* artistic self-realization and cultural distinction of the kind found in *The Song of the Lark* and "Uncle Valentine."

Throughout Cather's canon, as we leave her principal characters in triumph or defeat, their self-sufficiency is profoundly marked by a sense of loneliness and longing. Alexandra Bergson, Thea Kronberg, Claude Wheeler, Napoleon Godfrey St. Peter, Myra Henshawe, Euclide Auclair, Lucy Gayheart, Sapphira Colbert—all live apart from a person and/or place once most dear to them and which they can no longer retrieve. Rare are the characters who escape this loneliness and longing. Archbishop Latour dies in the plenitude of his Pascalian garden, but even he misses his companion, Father Joseph. Marian Forrester dies in South America, apparently as open to life with her new husband as she had been with the Captain, but even this blissful self-sufficiency is framed in the loneliness and longing of Niel as the novel closes. Of course, there is the companionate atmosphere of the women gathered in the epilogue of *Sapphira and the Slave Girl.*

Sharon O'Brien notes that "the fictional portion of the novel ends with Sapphira asking Rachel to spend the winter with her," and the critic, in a biographical perspective linking the child of the epilogue as Cather with Cather's own mother, writes that "the Epilogue thus both ends the novel and, in a way, begins it."[22] The reunion of mothers and daughters (fictional in the novel proper, real in the epilogue by autobiographical extension) thus betokens in both endings for O'Brien a mood of reunion, reconciliation, and recovery of the lost language. Yet, as I have indicated, the mood is far more reserved and melancholic if not, indeed, dour in both endings. If, as O'Brien perceptively notes, Cather's late fiction moves toward a more overtly warm interaction between women and particularly between mothers and daughters, it does so far more hesitatingly than the critic believes. The enduring, demanding ethic of self-abnegation and transcendence of the affective in Cather compromises maternal and other nurturings as surely as it had the sexual in whatever expression.

Like much recent Cather criticism, particularly feminist criticism, O'Brien's work is trenchant and insightful as it releases Cather from the limitations of her traditional casting as the literary patron saint of the

American frontier. This criticism stresses the rich cosmopolitanism of this "child of the prairie" who was open not only to the organic pulsions of the land but also to the organic pulsions of the self in its spiritual, sexual, and socioeconomic longings. It has brought not only Willa Cather out of her lesbian closet, but it has also brought Willa Cather's fiction out of the cloister of suffocating piety about the plains and plain-living into which much traditional criticism had enclosed the novelist. Foregrounding the women of Cather fiction, it has undermined the phallocratic assignment of Cather as little more than a graceful "woman writer." Bailey, Gubar, O'Brien, Rosowski, and Wild, among other recent critics, underscore the imaginative complexity, wide-ranging subtlety, exemplary ethical and practical effectiveness of Cather's women and thus of all women on the land and in the city, in the house and in the office, in the audience and on the stage, in the kitchen and in the bedroom, in the library and at the writer's desk. Cather's women have, thanks to this criticism, finally emerged to full creative citizenship.

Yet, if this criticism breaks with the prudential constrictions of traditional Cather criticism, particularly in its overt address to sexuality, it remains at one with the tradition in its biographical preoccupations. Perceptive and audacious in its concern with revisionist psychoanalysis and contemporary feminism, O'Brien's work, for example, imbeds its interpretation of the fiction in extensively developed sociological and biographical definitions of the "'lesbian writer'" before proceeding to illustrations of the fictional transmutations.[23] Moreover, in both its definitions and its specific illustrations, O'Brien's work corroborates in its concerns, especially lesbianism and the status of the woman writer, key perspectives of mainstream scholarship on the writer. Thus, Cather's lesbianism may have expressed itself very early in life (adoration of her beautiful and austere mother, childhood transvestism, college crushes on female students and teachers, etc.). However, the young writer had to confront her lesbian sexuality in a world that had begun to lose conventional covers of such "friendship between women" an older contemporary like Sarah Orne Jewett could enjoy. O'Brien's review of these features of Cather's personal self is both moving and as detailed as Cather's intense privatization of her own life permits. From this review, O'Brien then demonstrates the increasingly artistic and mature "displacement" onto the fictions of Willa Cather as lesbian writer in categories echoing Woodress, Slote, and others. For example, given the categories of "individual" and "self-limited" Cather herself had used in her harsh criticism of Kate Chopin's *The Awakening,* O'Brien notes the dialectic in Cather's own fiction between the commitment to "sexual needs" and "artistic or intellectual expression." The critic sees Cather's work as "implying that human happiness and achievement must arise from losing the self in something larger, from self-abnegation, not from the self-gratification that the young journalist linked with the pursuit of sexual and romantic fulfillment."[24] In small as in large, O'Brien echoes familiar perspectives of mainstream Cather criticism in the biographical mode. Thus, addressing those who wonder why Willa Cather never married and had children of her own, Woodress calls attention to the writer's deep affection for her immediate family and sees the characters of her fiction as the children who satisfied her maternal instinct.[25] O'Brien's consideration of Willa Cather in relation to the maternal is at once more specific and probing, but even more fixed on the writer's life and roots. O'Brien stresses the frequency of maternal images in the fiction (particularly landscape in *O Pioneers!*) as well as the surrogation of the maternal into artistic creation, with its beautifully paradoxical motif of death linked to regeneration: "The artist may 'die of love' in the process of creation," O'Brien writes, "but he is 'born again.' Cather's romantic apostrophe to the Nebraska soil in the concluding paragraph of *O Pioneers!* also promises rebirth for Alexandra, the novel's artist, after she had faded away into the land."[26]

O'Brien's assessment of the Cather canon as an artistic transmutation of the sexual dilemmas of the writer's life thus continues not only the methodology but also the hagiographic approach to the canon generally characteristic of Cather criticism in the mainstream biographical mode. There is great gain, of course. Upbeat and unabashed in its address to critical problems too often ignored or euphemistically deflected, O'Brien's work advances Cather scholarship on both the well-known novels and the often neglected early stories. Nevertheless, in spite of the breadth and depth of its address, the critic's work tends to subordinate the work to the life and, just as importantly, to downplay problematics which I see as more pervasive in the canon as whole. This is particularly true of Cather as a woman writer at that moment of transition from the Victorian conventions of the second half of the nineteenth century and the nascent liberation of the first quarter of the twentieth. The corrective redescription of Cather fiction by O'Brien and other recent critics has done much to illuminate this transition. Yet, the redescription is as partial and tendentious as the one it seeks to replace. A largely unwitting phallocentric approach has been succeeded by a conscious vaginocentric and feminist one. In each, there are winners and losers, with only the genders changed. Read as an inscription into and subvention of an ideological program, early Cather scholarship gives us the view of an almost unbroken panoply of triumphant characters of whatever gender (Alexandra Bergson, Antonia, Claude Wheeler, Archbishop Latour, Euclide Auclair, Sapphira Colbert, et al.). Read in the same way, a recent program views the canon as a subversive (from the viewpoint of the phallocracy) panoply of solitary and successful women triumphing not only over geographical and sociological circumstances but also over self-doubting and wimpish men.

However, the canon, it seems to me, presents a more complex account, one which might shed as much light on Cather's life as that life might shed on the canon. On the sexual axis, particularly in its feminist implications addressed by recent criticism, the violence to which Cather women and men, committed to unsublimated sexual expression, are subjected has not been sufficiently considered. As I have demonstrated in my reading of various novels and stories, the sublimated expressions of erotic energy in social, political, and religious forms are themselves imbedded in the problematic of language whose importance for Cather I see as prismatically evident in her francotropism. The manly unmanliness of such Cather heroes as Claude Wheeler, the sexual "crossings" (Susan Gubar's perceptive term)[27e] of figures like native-born Frenchmen Archbishop Latour and Euclide Auclair, the schizoid attitude of the writer herself towards the French language as both an access to romance and a rationalistic barrier to the lost language—these and other features of the canon must be more fully explored before attempts are made to link their narrative expression with evidences of Willa Cather's own spirituality and, especially, sexuality (presently acknowledged by O'Brien and others to be problematically scarce).

In examining that sexuality and spirituality through the prism of the French language and culture in which, as O'Brien notes,[28] Cather maintained lifelong interest, I have found a less successful break than O'Brien and others with the phallocentric hegemony under which the writer began and continued to write throughout her life. O'Brien herself acknowledges that the writer did not fully succeed in escaping that hegemony.

> To be sure, Cather never completely freed herself from male constructions of femininity—not a surprising failure in a woman whose youthful imagination was structured so strongly by male writers. Cather's portrayal of erotic and sensual women like Lena Lingard and Marian Forrester particularly reflects male stereotypes; it was more difficult for her to separate female creative power from maleness. Nevertheless, Cather did revise some male stereotypes of women: Antonia Shimerda, viewed by some as an archetypal Earth Mother, is a storyteller who pours her creativity into nurturing.[29]

These and other vaginocentric expressions of an autonomous if not radical feminine sexuality are, indeed, compelling in Cather's fiction. However, they are framed by the novelist herself in a phallocentric and phallocratic structure. In ordinary-language terms, Cather portrays men and women in gender categories of weak/strong, submissive/assertive, domestic/professional, critical/creative, appreciator/artist, and so on. She retains the binary structure which Italian novelist Italo Calvino sees as the very root of literary as well as linguistic activity:

> The storyteller explored the possibilities implied in his own language by combining and changing the permutations of the figures and actions, and of the objects on which these actions could be brought to bear. What emerged were stories, straightforward constructions that always contained correspondences or contraries—sky and earth, fire and water, animals that fly and those that dig burrows; and each figure had its array of attributes and a repertory of its own. The telling of stories allowed certain relationships between the various elements and not others, and things could happen in a certain order and not in others.[30]

Cather, too, retains the order of gender attributes, but in reverse; in the pairs of these attributes I presented above, the novelist, as a rule, assigns the first terms (weak, submissive, domestic, critical, appreciator) to male characters and the second terms (strong, assertive, professional, creative, artist) to women. The very transcendence through "self-abnegation" and the triumph of "artistic and intellectual expression" over "sexual needs" which O'Brien sees as the hallmark of women in particular in the canon is a narrative realization of the linguistic and literary binary pattern I trace here. It shows Cather paradoxically riveted to the phallocentric order with its own binary oppositions concerning male and female social behaviors.

In Lacanian terms, Cather's loyalty to the symbolic order shows her retaining stereotypical surrogations of phallocentric strivings. Cather writes of the "kingdom of art" not as a domain of preoedipal free play of the erotic where one speaks the lost language. In fact, the price Cather exacts of those driven only by the erotic is exclusion from the social order and, often, violent death. Thus, in Cather's fiction, those who do not abnegate the personal self lose both in their own eyes and in the eyes of their creator. Sexuality in Cather seldom becomes both overt and positive. In the major fictions only Marian Forrester comes to mind as an example, and in the canon hers is even rarer in its heterosexuality. Following Ann Ferguesson's lead, O'Brien stresses Cather's own lesbianism as more a matter of self-definition than an overt physical involvement. Indeed, when turning to the fiction, O'Brien finds this lesbian self-definition implicitly applicable not only to woman characters but also to male characters. Same-sex sexuality in Cather's male characters, O'Brien suggests, may be a sign of repressed lesbianism; the homosexual troping of Cather's men, particularly her narrators, is perhaps a cover, a narrative transvesting of the writer's own lesbianism.[31] Yet, the gender attributes of these homosexual males who are really lesbian females leads to a curious logical conclusion. Given Cather's binary pattern of reversing usual gender attributes, these weak, womanish males immediately evoke their contraries in the fictions, the strong, or mannish females. Are these lesbian females not, then, transvestite males—characters dressed like women but psychologically males? However striking and daring Cather's reversal of the gender attributes, its inscription under the phallocentrism continues.

Arguably the most striking image in the novelist's work of this reversal is Thea Kronberg, seen from below by her subservient lover, atop the craggy cliff in erectile sublimity. Again, in both the name and fate of farmer-as-artist Alexandra Bergson (as O'Brien and Rosowski perceptively see her) one can detect the paradoxically phallocratic infrastructure of Willa Cather's imagination. The heroine's first name makes her a worthier bearer of the name of the greatest hero of Greek antiquity than the male bridge-builder who also bore it in *Alexander's Bridge,* while her second name shows her to be a *son* of the mountain (*berg*). Thea's fate is also that of many a successful woman in Cather's fiction: to stand in triumph if not alone then accompanied by a weak male, suitor or husband. In marrying the sensitive but unenergetic Carl, Alexandra abandons her dream of the lover "yellow like the sunlight" who lifted her in his arms and "carried [her] swiftly across the fields."[32] She has, in Cather's familiar reversal of gender roles, become her own male lover, for it is her own strong arms which have done and always will do a man's work. Her female first name, echoing that of Alexander the Great, is, in O'Brien's categories, but a cover for her own phallic prowess. *O Pioneers!* thus foreshadows a pattern to be found throughout the canon: heterosexual interaction issues in dénouements which I have elaborated in this book as worlds without men or worlds without women. Within each of these worlds, phallocracy paradoxically prevails. The worlds without women are peopled by alienated or defeated men, while the worlds without men are peopled by women whose principal characteristic is the enduring strength their menfolk have only rarely or intermittently shown.

Cather's search in her long canon for the lost language does not, like Marcel Proust's in his long "search for lost time," resolve within itself the intractabilities of psychic and social life with which it deals just as seriously. The title under which readers of English know Proust's famous novel, F. Scott-Moncrieff's *Remembrance of Things Past,* seems far more appropriate for the American novelist's canon with one important modification: Remembrance of Things *Lost.* As the title of the final sections, *Le Temps retrouvé,* indicates, what Proust's narrator has lost is rediscovered — time is refound; it is found once again in the end as it had *been in the beginning*. In the Möbius band of Proust's art, from the first event of the novel to the last, the narrator writes not only of but from within a "kingdom of art." The metaphorical sublimations of everyday life, like the metonymic evasions and displacements of imaginative life, are assumed into the kingdom. Cather sees that kingdom through and thus beyond the art of her own writing; Proust sees it as his writing itself.

The panorama of psychosexually driven men and women or artists of whatever sexual orientation is no less grand in Cather than in Proust. However, in her worlds of women without men or men without women, Cather clings to a psychology of a real world in which all are, in spite of their symbolic renunciations, still impelled by the "primal drama." Proust moves beyond such a psychology — beyond psychology itself. In his novel the phallocentrism of psychosexual life as such is underscored, and its frenzy in its "deviate form" is as intense as that Lacan attributes to men in particular in their search for the "Woman." Psychoanalytically, Proust's conviction that his art is beyond such compulsions, even in depicting them, is a sublimation, an illusion — the most literary and sublimest of illusions, perhaps. However, it differs from Cather's sublime illusion about the recuperability through language itself of the lost language. Hers, we might say, is the sublimest of the least literary of illusions: that language is a necessarily imperfect medium translating a perfect reality outside of it.

The Sociopolitical Axis of Cather's Search

As I indicated earlier, Cather's well-known political conservatism is not the conservatism of the *American Century* of her contemporary, publisher Henry Luce. Indeed, Cather's search for the lost language is one which leads her to a seemingly apolitical, if not, in fact, to an antipolitical view. Thus, her fiction is rarely about politics in an obvious sense. Her most political story, "Two Friends," is the most overt illustration of this stance. Because it is also a story about language, I begin here with a brief discussion of it before turning to the larger implication of politics in the novelist's canon-long search for the lost language.

Politics causes the break between the two friends. Dillon is a Democrat and a champion of William Jennings Bryan, Democratic candidate for the presidency in the upcoming election of 1896; Trueman is a Republican. When an eclipse they have watched is over, Trueman starts to talk about it, wondering about distances of the moon, of Venus. Dillon replies brusquely that he doesn't know and doesn't care and that he's more concerned about " 'getting the tramps off the railroad, and manage to run

this town with one fancy house instead of two, and have a Federal
government that is as honest as a good banking business, then it will be
plenty of time to turn our attention to the stars.' " Trueman chuckles,
noting that " 'maybe the stars will throw some light on all that, if we get
the run of them' "; he chides his friend " 'mustn't be a reformer, R. E.
Nothing in it. Life is always what it has been, always will be. No use to
make a fuss.' " He gets up, says " 'Goodnight, R. E.,' " and leaves. The rift
has occurred. Unlike the often impetuous Joseph Vaillant before the
gently chiding Latour, Dillon does not heed his friend. He plunges into
the campaign for Bryan wholeheartedly, hectoring all, including Trueman,
with recalls of Bryan's famous Cross of Gold speech at the Democratic
Convention and its ringing " 'You shall not press this crown of thorns
upon the brow of labour; you shall not crucify mankind upon a cross of
gold!' " The child narrator "thought that magnificent; I thought the
cornfields would show them a thing or two back there."[33] Of course, back
there is where Trueman came from: the East. A currency based on silver
instead of on gold would end the West's domination by Eastern bankers
and industrialists.

As the gold of the moon occults the bright of Venus, so the Republican
McKinley with his gold standard occults the Democrat Bryan and his
silver standard. Politically, Trueman prevails over Dillon. The preva-
lence is not surprising in Cather. Gold is always the color of psychic and
other value for her. Silver, as she says in the essay on Sarah Orne Jéwett I
cited earlier, is a baser metal, the metal of "surface speech" which a bank
clerk "clicks out . . . when you ask for change." It is like the French
language the hypothetical young man of her later essay has learned
without understanding the "emotional roots . . . the temper of the people
which lies behind the language."[34] By the "linguistic gold standard" of
French on which Cather bases the currency of her narrative and symbolic
significations, Dillon is as wrong in his language as he is in his politics.
A Celt, he speaks a currency of some value, but, for all the Romanism of
his head, not the currency of supreme value. That currency is lost to him
because he trades it for the easy money policies of the silver currency of
French learned from the outside not the inside. In terms of Bryan's
Christian trope, it is, ironically, Dillon who is the money lender in the
temple. He must be driven out by Trueman, the Son of the Father, who
thereby restores the temple in "the Name of the Father."

The religious, aesthetic, linguistic, sociopolitical, and psychic conservatism of Cather conflate in the figure of Trueman and his opposition to
Dillon. Trueman's chuckle about the stars at Dillon's political ranting is
sub speciae aeternitatis, the perspective in which Latour sees things. Trueman
hasn't much to say and he never writes letters;[35] he uses telegrams, a

medium for written communication as sparing as his speech. "There was a curious attitude in men of his class at that time, that of being rather above speech, as they were above any kind of fussiness or eagerness."[36] For a short time Dillon is of that class and time. Before his assumption of the silver standard, his own speech is kept within those laconic bounds set by Trueman among those who played the respectable game of cards that went on at his place. " 'Careful of the language around here,' " he would warn those getting out of hand in their talk: "It was never 'your' language, but 'the' language, — though he certainly intended no pleasantry." When Dillon goes out on the stump for Bryan, something happens to his "musical, vibrating voice";[37] it " 'became unnatural'; there was a sting of comeback in it; his new character made him more like other people and took away from his special personal quality."[38] Other people talk too much, in comebacks that respond only to the immediate, to the surface of things. Dillon falls into "phoneticism." It is of little wonder that the little-spoken Trueman withdraws all his money from Dillon's bank to put it in the rival bank across the street. The motives, more than political, are psychic and philosophical; he and Dillon don't talk the same language anymore.

They used to share the lost language. In that language "life is what it always has been, always will be" for human beings. In that language, one gets a purchase on the "eternal verities" of politics, of society, of work, of art. Instead of that language, the politicking Dillon speaks a new language, a French learned in school, an artificial language bereft of the emotional roots of French (or any other language) in its own cultural setting. Dillon's "silvered tongue" is a betrayal of *Trueman,* of the true language of man. As if in a judgment from on high for this betrayal, "before the next Presidential campaign round, Mr. Dillon died (a young man still) very suddenly, of pneumonia."[39] Like that " 'great windbag' " Bryan, whom Dillon supported, his "lungs" give out (Bryan lost the 1896 election as he did in 1900 and 1908). It is as if the Eternal Father shared the political views of Trueman, the surrogate father: "Trueman looked down on anyone who could take the reasoning of the Populist party seriously."[40]

Populists and other left-radicals do not fare well in Cather's fiction. The railroader, Ray Kennedy, a champion of "workers' causes" with socialist-anarchist views, dies in a terrible train accident. Roddy Blake, Tom Outland's friend, is a one-time railroader and a "conscientious reader of newspapers" who "brooded on the great injustices of his time; the hanging of the Anarchists in Chicago, which he could just remember, and the Dreyfus case."[41] Having sold out the Cliff City to the money-lenders, Blake is driven from that temple by the Messianic Tom: " 'you've gone and sold your country's secrets, like Dreyfus,' " Tom tells him.[42] In the reproach one senses as well the charge of "betrayal" by Blake of his own "Anarchist/Populist's" principles. The rejection of these figures by Thea and Tom, like the rejection of Dillon by Trueman, is not without some pain for the rejector. Cather presents Kennedy, Blake, and Dillon sympathetically; all Celts, they speak a language close to the lost language in its closest ordinary-language signifier, French. In the ambiance of a true speaker of the lost language (Thea, Tom, Trueman) they are able, at least for a while, to hear and understand that language.

As I have noted, the political conservatism of the speakers of the lost language is not that of post World War One Republicanism. Cather's conservative politics, like her conservative psychology and religion, is as mythic and fabulous as her art. The modern world which she more and more grumpily rejects in her late work is the world of the machine. "Long ago, before the invention of the motorcar (which has made more changes in the world than the War, which indeed produced the particular kind of war that happened just a hundred years after Waterloo)"—thus begins the story proper of "Two Friends."[43] It was the world, at least until 1932, of a triumphant Republican party. The delight of the narrator-as-child in Bryan's showing the Easterners "a thing or two" is one the author not only of *One of Ours* but also of *Shadows on the Rock* shared in her whippings of the moneylenders.

Indeed, her whipping of them contrasts with her sympathy for the Ray Kennedys, the Rodney Blakes, and the R. E. Dillons of the world. Those Celts are merely benighted in their naive politics and their childlike inefficacy in the "adult" world of nineteenth-century liberal and bourgeois capitalism. The anarchism of these Celts is a part of that heritage of the eighteenth century, the Age of Enlightenment, whose French expression had so influenced American pre-Revolutionary and early Republic thought. Against this French model, Cather's heroes and heroines often choose another French model, that of Napoleon and Empire. The eponymous hero of *The Professor's House* comes to mind in his full name, Napoleon Godfrey St. Peter, but he is not alone. Even the anarchistic Ray Kennedy, the very imperial Thea Kronberg reflects, "had that feeling of empire; as if all the Southwest really belonged to him because he had knocked about over it so much, and knew it, as he said, 'like the blisters of his own hands.' That feeling, she reflected, was the real element of companionship between her and Ray."[44] The oxymoronic import of Ray as an "imperialistic anarchist" indicates that, for Cather, capitalism is a romance in the sense of that term in her early essays on Dumas; it is not an economics and anything but a system for the anti-intellectual novelist.

This is not to say that Cather's romantic and imperialistic anarchy is apolitical. As a writer, hers is an anarchy of the high road, even as Ray Kennedy's and Roddy Blake's is an anarchy of the low road. In Randall's formulation, Cather's "dream of society" is that of "the fellowship of heroes."[45] In terms of Régis Debray's "genealogy of the scribe," through such figures as Thea Kronberg, Tom Outland, and Jim Burden, Cather speaks out of and on behalf of the anarchic (Gr. *an*, "not" + *arkein*, "to rule") freedom of entrepreneurial capitalism. Each of these three Cather figures, exemplary of all her protagonists, is a *clerk*. Jim Burden's teacher of Latin at the University, Gaston Cleric, wanted Jim to become a teacher, too. Cleric's narrative function is to guide Jim to renunciation of Lena and offer instead the example of desire sublimated to art. The teacher's French name (Fr. *clerc* = a cleric, in "Minor Orders" in the medieval Church) points to the larger sociopolitical function of the ecclesiastical rank of *le clerc* defined by Régis Debray:

> More radically, the historical birth of the cleric is that of a collective. The people of God preceded the men of God. This people is anonymous, and men do not raise themselves to churchly dignity except insofar as they inscribe themselves thereto in participating in its obligations and privileges. The word *clerc* comes from Greek *klérikos*, which means *share, heritage*. At the outset, it was applied to the ensemble of the people elected of God as to a single whole; then it became individualized. "The clerics," says Saint Jerome, "are called thus either because they constitute the share that the Lord has reserved to Himself, or because the Lord is Himself their share or heritage." (*Letter LII to Nepotian*) The notion of clerk implies first of all that of participation in an instituted community.[46]

The actions of Thea Kronberg, Tom Outland, and Jim Burden to rediscover lost languages and civilizations are as revealing sociopolitically as they are psychically. They are hieratic actions: if Ray Kennedy and Roddy Blake respect and speak through glyphs (Gk. *gluphe*, "carving") and runes (Old Norse *run*, as Debray points out), Thea and Tom and Jim respect and speak through hieroglyphs (Gk. *hiero*, "holy or divine" + *gluphe*, "carving"). They speak from and through a priestly or clerical function. Thus, Thea insists on precision and punctilio in her reproaches to Jesse Darcy's singing; Tom drives Roddy from the "sacred cliff" for simony (the sin of selling ecclesiastical office); Jim passes the manuscript of his "sacred memoirs" to another "clerc" of the institution of those who *write* rather than *do*. "The pre-eminence of verbal activity over motor activity, and more generally of the symbolic over the technical," Debray observes, "inverts the biological order of factors but orders [ordinates] the fact [status] of the human. It is not by chance that it is the property of all civilizations."[47] Jim Burden's decision not to become a teacher of literature reveals his general reticence before the erotic and its significations. Nevertheless, that he becomes a lawyer also reveals his continuing self-inscription into the clerical corridors of power. It is a self-inscription about which Jim, like Thea and Tom, is uneasy. At a halfway house between the rulers ("divinely instituted kings" or "ministers" elected by the people, as Debray notes) and the ruled, the scribe-cleric is torn in his loyalties to both the ruled and the ruler.

In Cather's canon-long debate about the primacy of the lost and originary language in relation to various phonetic inscriptions (music, law, art of words, plastic art, etc.), one sees this uneasiness—for example, in Jim Burden's manuscript with its fabular prioritization of physical movement in contrast with the distancing from that fable in the first-frame narrator's tone. The lost language is one in which the tensions between power and being, between writing and speaking, between thinking and living are preresolved in a nondialectical Garden of Eden which much of Cather's fiction tries to retrieve. There, according to Debray, "no one wrote . . . ; things offered themselves there at the same time as their signs, in the abundant smile of the moment."[48] Most definitely, Cather does not like the city: Chicago, where the young Thea is accosted by strange men on street corners, or New York, where she becomes a powerful success only at the price of her well-being; Washington, D.C., where Tom tries to persuade the powers-that-be to make a national monument (an unchanging presence) of his Cliff City, more like a natural growth than a man-made structure; New York, where Jim Burden practices law as a clerk of the court from which he flees to the prairie garden of his childhood on trains, the very signifiers of that power and of his anxious guilt about serving it. The train is a phallic penetrator into the garden as Gelfant has noted.[49] As such, it resembles the stylus of the "pen of power" that Jim wields as lawyer for the powerful. Paradoxically, however, the pen is also the instrument by which Jim would deny such power through the unrealistic fables of the Edenic garden of his childhood conceived during his trips aboard the train.

Anxious, guilt-ridden, and ambivalent, Jim Burden and Thea Kronberg and Tom Outland are clerics torn between two languages and caught in the "no-man's land" between convention and imagination. Intellectuals in spite of themselves and of their creator, they live by night in their dreams of the Garden where power is not an issue and by day in the City where power is the only issue. This power is of entrepreneurial capitalism of the mid-to-late nineteenth-century America; it is that of the romantic, imperialist, hieratic anarchy of those Cather calls "dreamers, great-hearted adventurers who were unpractical to the point of magnificence; courteous brotherhood, strong in attack but weak in defense, who could conquer but could not hold"[50]—men like Captain Forrester and

Mr. Trueman of "Two Friends" or the Mathô of Cather's favorite novel by Flaubert, *Salammbô*.

They are men and women whose time is past and whose language is lost, as the Cather of *Obscure Destinies* testifies in an elegiac mood. In this collection she not only pays generic homage to Flaubert with her own set of *"trois contes,"* but she also writes in a Flaubertian mood which gives special French resonance to her late work. The mood becomes almost univocal after her meeting with the great French novelist's niece, for it is the mood of the Flaubert of *L'Education sentimentale.* As she told Mme. Franklin-Grout at that chance meeting, she had recently reread that novel "and felt that I had never risen to its greatness before." In that novel a passive observer looks on the passing parade of the passions and the politics of others as a vanity of vanities. Both the enterprise of bankers, the right, and the naïveté of socialists and anarchists, the left, feel the lash of a personal culture steeped in a wide and an early romanticism. Flaubert's *L'Education sentimentale* of 1869 is as dissonant with *L'Education sentimentale* of 1845 as Cather's *Obscure Destinies* of 1932 is with *O Pioneers!* of 1913.

In "Old Mrs. Harris" from *Obscure Destinies,* Mr. Rosen tells young Vickie Templeton: " 'Listen: a great man once said: "Le but n'est rien; le chemin, c'est tout." That means: The end is nothing, the road is all. Let me write it down for you and give you your first French lesson.' " The name he writes is that of the great French Romantic historian, Jules Michelet.[52] The famous sentence from Michelet echoes Latour's "into the morning, into the morning!" Yet, it is not the young and seeking Vickie who is the heroine of this story; it is "Old Mrs. Harris" who has been mostly ignored in the story — even, finally, by the Vickie whom she has so helped in the young girl's desire to find the funds to attend the university. Old Mrs. Harris dies alone. Having told her story, Cather concludes it:

> Thus, Mrs. Harris slipped out of the Templetons' story; but Victoria and Vickie had still to go on, to follow that long road that leads through things unguessed and unforeseeable. When they are old, they will come closer to Grandma Harris. They will think a great deal about her, and remember things they never noticed. They will regret that they heeded her so little; but they, too, will look into the eager, unseeing eyes of young people and feel themselves alone. They will say to themselves: "I was heartless, because I was young and strong and wanted things so much. But now I know."[52]

This is the voice not of a framing narrator or observer — neither the voice of Mrs. Rosen in the story itself, for example, nor of Nellie Birdseye recording from on high her judgment of the terrible and deserved fate of Myra Henshawe. Neither the secular sympathy of Mrs. Rosen nor the eternal judgment of Heaven is the "point of view" from which we hear these at once consoling and disconsoling reflections. It is the voice of the omniscient and similarly bereft third-person narrator, Willa Cather.

The dissonant final note of "Old Mrs. Harris," will, with rare exception, mark Cather's fictions in the last decade and a half of her life. It is, then, perhaps not surprising that the novelist could not bring herself to persist in the seeking that would have resulted in *Hard Punishments.* "She had wanted for years," Edith Lewis notes, "to write an Avignon story,"[53] perhaps since that day in 1935 at the Papal Palace when she and Lewis had heard that song of "cruelties, splendours, lost and unimaginable to us in our time." At her death, late along her own "long hop" from the Avignon of the travel journal of 1902 to the Avignon of the late fourteenth century in her unfinished novel, Willa Cather seems to have lost the dialect of the lost language she perhaps held most dear in its phonetic as well as its pictographic inscriptions: the language of France.

Notes

SOUNDINGS

1. Quoted by Kates, "Willa Cather's Unfinished Avignon Story" in *Five Stories with an Article by George N. Kates on Miss Cather's Last, Unfinished and Unpublished Avignon Story*, p. 178 (my emphasis).

2e. There are, as well, numerous stories in which singers figure within the canon: "A Singer's Romance" (1900), "The Diamond Mine" (1916), "Uncle Valentine" (1925). In 1935 still another novel concerns a famous singer and his relations with a singer-heroine: *Lucy Gayheart*.

3. Willa Cather, "The Novel *Démeublé*," *Not Under Forty*, p. 52.

4e. "The crisis in the most interesting American works often occurs at those moments when the author tries to externalize the inner consciousness of his hero, tries to insert it, to borrow William James' metaphor, into social and verbal environments that won't sustain it." Richard Poirier, *A World Elsewhere: The Place of Style in American Literature*, p. 14. Earlier, Poirier distinguishes between two environments: "one might be called the provided environment, the other an invented environment" (p. 8). In these terms, Cather may seek to escape the "provided environment" as much as any of the writers Poirier studies; he does not include Cather. However, she would escape by effacing language for the sake of a *reinvented* environment prior to verbal language.

5e. See Bibliography. See also Robert Nelson, "Seeing *Through Words, Seeing Through Words, Seeing Words Through, Seeing Words (as) Through*," *The George Review* 35 (1982): 133–47. In this review of Irwin's book I do not discuss Cather. However, my discussion does anticipate certain aspects of my interpretive strategy here.

6. Willa Cather, "Shakespeare and Hamlet, *"The Kingdom of Art: Willa Cather's First Principles and Critical Statements*, p. 429.

7. See especially Cather's "Writer in Nebraska," KA, pp. 3–29.

8e. "With the writing of *O Pioneers!*, the time came that she could say: 'In this one I hit the home pasture....'" Mildred R. Bennett, "Introduction," *Willa Cather's Collected Short Fiction: 1892–1912*, p. xiii. Bennett reports that the remark was "inscribed by Willa Cather in the copy of *O Pioneers!* belonging to her friend Carrie Miner Sherwood."

9. Willa Cather, *The World and the Parish: Willa Cather's Articles and Reviews: 1893–1902*, II, p. 944.

10. WP, II, 921.
11. WP, II, 891.
12. WP, II, 921.
13. KA, fn. 6, p. 37. My emphasis.
14. WP, II, 928.
15. WP, II, 952.
16. WP, II, 946.
17. "Willa Cather's Unfinished Avignon Story" in *Five Stories with an Article by George N. Kates on Miss Cather's Last, Unfinished and Unpublished Avignon Story,* p. 211.
18. "A Chance Meeting" in NF, p. 24. My emphasis.
19. Brown and Edel, *Willa Cather: A Critical Biography,* p. 211.
20. WP, II, 948–49.
21. OD, p. 81.
22. OD, pp. 194–95.
23. WP, II, 951.
24. NF, pp. 15–16.
25. WP, II, 583–85. My emphasis.
26. Robert Nelson, "French Classicism: The Crisis of the Baroque," *L'Esprit Créateur* 11 (1971): 269–86; and Nelson, "Molière and Racine: The Bipolarity of French Classicism," *Essays in French Literature,* No. 8 (1971): 11–28.
27. WP, I, 335, under a pseudonym of French resonance, "Helen Delay."
28. KA, p. 325.
29. NF, p. 24.
30. NF, p. 17.
31. NF, p. v.
32. SSG, p. 295.

CONSONANCE: CRESCENDO

1. OO, p. 22.
2. OO, p. 7.
3e. The reader may wish to return to my earlier etymological probing of Claude's name, above, p. 19.
4. OO, p. 17.
5. OO, p. 18.
6. OO, pp. 26–27.
7. OO, pp. 27–28.
8e. "On the basis of this assertion of a phallic phase (the term appears in 1924) common to two sexes, Freud is able to give his well-known description of how the Oedipus complex in the boy is brought to an end by the crucial experience of seeing the female genitals; the threats against masturbation made earlier by the mother have a deferred effect. From then on, acceptance of the possibility of castration puts an end to the Oedipus complex, as narcissistic interest in the penis gets the better of libidinal investment in parental objects. Phallic organization breaks down on the threat of castration. But at the same

moment the Oedipus complex is not only repressed, it is literally destroyed, and object cathexes are abandoned, and rapidly replaced by identification (in particular with the father: the formation of the super-ego)." Jacques Lacan, "The Phallic Phase and the Subjective Import of the Castration Complex" in *Feminine Sexuality: Jacques Lacan and the "Ecole Freudienne,"* edited by Juliet Mitchell and Jacqueline Rose, p. 101. Hereafter, references to this volume will be shortened to Mitchell-Rose.

9. John J. Murphy, "The Widening Gyre" in *Five Essays on Willa Cather: The Merrimack Symposium,* p. 58.

10. OO, p. 551. In the French setting of this conversation, one is reminded that "Claude" can be a masculine or feminine name in French.

11. OO, p. 408.

12. OO, p. 432. My emphasis.

13. OO, pp. 409–10.

14. OO, pp. 436–37.

15. Lacan, "God and the Jouissance of Woman," Mitchell-Rose, p. 142.

16. Murphy, "The Widening Gyre," p. 60.

17e. Having noted the crucial importance of the "no to the Phallic function," Lacan goes on: "That is the conclusion of the analytic experience. It does not stop him from desiring the woman in any number of ways, even when the condition is not fulfilled. Not only does he desire her but he does all kinds of things to her which bear a remarkable resemblance to love." Mitchell-Rose, p. 143.

18. OO, p. 391.

19. OO, p. 61.

20. OO, p. 172.

21. OO, p. 319.

22. OO, p. 399.

23. OO, pp. 431–32.

24. OO, p. 411.

25. OO, p. 356.

26e. One is reminded here of the young Cather's charge that, though it is the language of "sympathetic criticism," the French language has the "fatal attribute of perfection." See above, p. 13.

27. OO, p. 415.

28. OO, p. 392.

29. OO, p. 458.

30. OO, p. 263.

31. OO, pp. 458–59.

32. OO, pp. 207–8.

33. DCA, pp. 303–4.

34. DCA, pp. 313–14.

35. DCA, p. 97.

36. CF, pp. 137–46.

37. CF, pp. 187–97.

38. CF, p. 145.

39. DCA, pp. 57–58.

40. DCA, pp. 287–88.
41. DCA, p. 100.
42. DCA, p. 152.
43. DCA, p. 141.
44. DCA, pp. 147–52.
45. DCA, p. 171.
46. DCA, p. 109.
47. DCA, p. 170.
48. DCA, p. 169, p. 10.
49. DCA, p. 179.
50. In *The Nation.* I shall turn more fully to this essay in 3 here.
51. DCA, pp. 273–75.
52. DCA, p. 217.
53. DCA, p. 218.
54. DCA, p. 222.
55. DCA, p. 256.
56. Phyllis Robinson, *Willa: The Life of Willa Cather,* p. 159.
57. DCA, p. 254.
58. DCA, p. 325.
59. DCA, pp. 239–40.
60. DCA, p. 243.
61. DCA, p. 245.
62. DCA, pp. 246–47.

63e. "At a more primordial level, the mother is for both sexes considered as provided with a phallus, that is, a phallic mother." Lacan, "The Meaning of the Phallus," Mitchell-Rose, p. 76.

64e. "It is the man—by which I mean he who finds himself male without knowing what to do about it, for all that he is a speaking being—who takes on the woman, or who can believe that he takes her on, since on this question convictions, those that I referred to last time as convictions, are not wanting. Except that what he takes on is the cause of his desire, the cause I have designated as the *objet a.* That is the act of love. To make love, as the term indicates, is poetry. The act of love is the polymorphous perversion of the male, in the case of the speaking being. There is nothing more emphatic or more strict as far as Freudian discourse is concerned." Lacan, "God and the Jouissance of Woman," Mitchell-Rose, p. 142. In "convictions" Lacan is playing on the French word *con,* the female genitals.

65e. "The result is a centrifugal tendency of the genital drive in the sexual life of man which makes impotence much harder for him to bear, at the same time as the *Verdrängung* [repression] inherent to desire is greater." "The Meaning of the Phallus," Mitchell-Rose, pp. 84–85.

66e. Latour's affection for Pascal is ironic; Latour is a member of the Society of Jesus, the Jesuits, Pascal's great adversaries and objects of his brilliant invective in *Les Lettres provinciales.*

67e. Contrast, on the other hand, Martinez's great baritone voice in its very

maleness. However, along the Mario-centric lines I develop here, the very maleness of this voice suggests that maleness is Luciferian.

68e. OP, p. 122. I anticipate here certain lines of my discussion of *O Pioneers!*
as a novel of dissonance in diminuendo.

69e. Taking the "novels of the plains" as a springboard, Rosowski sets Catherian
tropes of "family" and "other," "growth" and "death," the "finite" and the "infinite"
in the larger framework of the "public self" and the "personal self." Through this
larger framework the critic discerns "the pattern of Willa Cather's novels" as what
might be called a Hegelian striving towards resolution of the two "selves." "The
Pattern of Willa Cather's Novels," *Western American Literature* 15 (Winter 1981):
243–63. Elsewhere, Rosowski sensitively explores, both sociologically and psychologically, the problems posed for a woman writer in the effort to resolve the
dialectic of the two selves. "Willa Cather's Women," *Studies in American Fiction* 9
(Autumn 1981): 261–65.

70e. "The fact remains, however, that the enigma is there, in that whatever
the sex of the subject, the only conceivable pleasure in his or her image depends
on finding in that image or thinking that he or she finds there (which means if
only in the mind) something withdrawn from sight which answers or corresponds
to what we have called the monadic phallus. Narcissism is henceforth a 'phallo
narcissim,' which means, and the expression has no other meaning, that the
subject loves himself or herself as a phallus, in the two senses that grammarians
give to that phrase." Moustafa Safouan, "La Sexualité féminine dans la doctrine
freudienne," Mitchell-Rose, p. 125.

71e. "Just as there is no Being or essence of *the* woman or of sexual difference,
there is no essence of *es gibt* in the *es gibt Sein,* of the giving and the gift of Being.
This 'just as' without conjuncture. There is no gift of being starting with which
something like a determinate gift (of the subjects, of the body, of the sex and other
similar things—woman will thus not have been my subject) lets itself be prehended
or put in opposition." Jacques Derrida, *Eperons: Les Styles de Nietzsche,* my translation of the French text in the University of Chicago Press edition, p. 120.

72. Blaise Pascal, *Pensées,* fr. 626 in the Sellier edition. My translation.

73. Jacques Derrida, *La Vérité en peinture,* p. 132. My translation.

74. Lacan, "God and the Jouissance of Woman," Mitchell-Rose, pp. 146–47.

CONSONANCE: DIMINUENDO

1. Albert Jacquard, *Eloge de la différence.*

2. Michel Gervaud, "Un Regard autre" (originally entitled "Les Américains
et les autres"), *Actes du GRENA* (Groupe de Recherches et d'Etudes Nord-
américaines), p. 70.

3. Loc. cit.

4. CF, p. 542.

5. CF, p. 476.

6. CF, pp. 150–51.

7. CF, p. 159.

8. CF, pp. 101–2.
9e. See my quotation from Cather's travel journal of 1902, above, pp. 6–7.
10. CF, p. 107.
11. CF, p. 108.
12. CF, pp. 110–11.
13. James Woodress, *Willa Cather: Her Life and Art,* p. 125.
14. Lacan, "Seminar of January 21, 1975," Mitchell-Rose, p. 168.

DISSONANCE: CRESCENDO

1. SR, pp. 5–6.
2. DCA, pp. 273–74.
3. SR, pp. 4–5.
4. SR, p. 10.
5. SR, p. 17.
6. SR, p. 22.
7. SR, p. 25.
8. SR, p. 6.
9. SR, pp. 162–63.
10e. Cather may be remembering here the effects on her of her first sight of Bartholomé's monumental sculpture of the Last Judgment during her journey to France in 1902. See above, p. 8.
11. SR, p. 257.
12. SR, p. 261.
13. SR, p. 147.
14. SR, p. 222.
15. SR, p. 60.
16. SR, p. 231.
17. SR, p. 232.
18. SR, p. 192.
19. SR, p. 193.
20. SR, pp. 193–94. My emphasis.
21. MME, pp. 95, 94.
22. SR, p. 66.
23. SR, p. 172.
24. SR, p. 172.
25. SR, p. 130.
26. SR, p. 130. Cather's emphasis.
27. SR, p. 179.
28. SR, pp. 182–83.
29. SR, p. 181.
30. SR, p. 245.
31. SR, p. 245.
32. OO, p. 150.

33. SR, p. 246.
34. "You ask me for seed of the flowers of this country. We have them brought from France for our garden, having none here very rare or very beautiful. Everything is wild here, flowers as well as people." My translation.
35. SR, p. 121.
36. Herman Melville, *Billy Budd, Sailor,* pp. 40–41.
37. SR, p. 256.
38. SR, p. 258.
39. SR, p. 270.
40. SR, p. 274.
41. SR, p. 274.
42. SR, p. 27.
43. SR, pp. 278–79.
44. SR, p. 234. My emphasis.
45. SR, pp. 279–80.
46. SR, p. 264.
47. SR, p. 278.
48. "A Chance Meeting," NF, p. 13.
49. OO, pp. 339–40.

DISSONANCE: DIMINUENDO

1e. OP, pp. 214–15. I have used the 1913 edition. In citation, I shall note inclusions Cather excised in subsequent revision for republication of the novel.
2. See above, p. 54.
3. OP, p. 216.
4e. OP, pp. 219–20. This passage has been considerably revised in subsequent republication of the novel. Most notably for my purposes here, the passage in French does not appear.
5. OP, p. 255.
6. OP, pp. 152–53.
7. OP, pp. 282–83.
8. OP, pp. 307–8.
9e. Jennifer Bailey considers the status of an "unattached woman" like Alexandra Bergson, prior to her marriage to Carl, in Cather's fictions, particularly in the prairie novels, in light of the dialectic of "garden" versus "house." Bailey releases Alexandra as well as other Cather heroines from the traditional feminine domesticity of the house in stressing their extension of the usually secondary and attached garden into that domain usually reserved for men: the farm. The critic thus confirms the similar insight found in much recent Cather criticism, particularly that of Rosowski and O'Brien: the Catherian project shows women acceding to and succeeding in domains usually reserved for men. Obviously, as my consideration of Alexandra's nostalgic renunciation of her dream indicates, I believe that this reversal of gender prerogatives in Cather's fictions raises as

many issues as it resolves. I shall consider these issues extensively later here. See Jennifer Bailey, "The Dangers of Femininity in Willa Cather's Fiction," *Journal of American Studies* 16 (December 1982): 392–406.

10. Willa Cather, *"Uncle Valentine" and Other Stories: Willa Cather's Uncollected Short Fiction,* pp. 34–35.

11e. UV, p. 4. The city is, of course, Pittsburgh.

12. UV, pp. 35–36.

13. UV, p. 7.

14. UV, p. 18.

15. UV, p. 15.

16. UV, p. 33.

17. UV, p. 31.

18. UV, p. 19.

19. UV, p. 19.

20. UV, p. 14.

21. PH, p. 69.

22. UV, p. 38.

23. UV, p. 38.

24. UV, p. 22.

25. PH, p. 14.

26. PH, p. 23.

27. PH, p. 30.

28. PH, p. 49.

29. PH, p. 71.

30. PH, p. 163.

31. PH, p. 164.

32. PH, pp. 169–70.

33. PH, p. 257.

34. PH, p. 259.

35. Pascal, *Pensées,* fr. 761, Sellier edition. My translation.

36. PH, p. 131.

37. PH, "Introduction," no pagination.

38. PH, p. 43.

39. PH, p. 102.

40. PH, p. 104.

41. PH, p. 12.

42. PH, pp. 12–13.

43e. PH, pp. 36–37. Red lips and lips in general are a frequent signifier of erotic power and lure in Cather. The geological formation through which Latour enters the infernal cavern is described as "Stone Lips" (DCA, p. 146). In "The Affair at Grover Station" (1900), Freymark, jealous slayer of Larry O'Toole for the love of Miss Masterson, has "a pair of the most impudent red lips that closed over white, irregular teeth" (CF, p. 342). In Rosamond's having chosen a Jew as her husband one might again see Cather's antisemitism as founded not only on the stereotype of Jewish materialism in the conventional sense but in the philosophical sense of materialism-immantentism-secularism. On the other hand, however much that liking reveals a homosexual impulsion due to Louis's masculine sensuousness, St. Peter's liking his Jewish son-in-law mutes the antisemitism. However, for a different view of antisemitism in *The Professor's House,* particularly as expressed by the Professor himself, see Paul Comeau, *"The Professor's House* and Anatole France," *Critical Essays on Willa Cather,* ed. John J. Murphy, pp. 217–27. More generally, Comeau's article is an incisive tracing of narrative and thematic debt in the novel by Cather to Anatole France's 1897 satire, *Le Mannequin d'osier.*

44. PH, p. 105.

45. PH, p. 49.

46. PH, p. 111.

47. PH, pp. 112–13.

48. Sigmund Freud, "Three Essays on Sexuality," *Standard Edition,* Vol. 7, p. 145, note 1.

49. PH, p. 123.

50. PH, p. 21.

51. PH, p. 176. Though less explicit in its sexual implications than I suggest, Barbara Wild stresses the friendship between St. Peter and Tom in her "The Thing Not Named in *The Professor's House,*" *Western American Literature* 12 (Winter 1978): 263–74.

52. PH, p. 263.

53. PH, pp. 264–66.

54e. PH, p. 77. My emphasis. Here, I spring off the full text: "my other-house garden."

55. PH, p. 281. St. Peter's assessment of Augusta may be seen of a piece with the phallocratic way in which men perceive women in Cather's fictions traced by Margaret Doane, "In Defense of Lillian St. Peter: Men's Perception of Women in *The Professor's House,*" *Western American Literature* 17 (Winter 1984): 299–302.

56. PH, p. 282.

57. PH, p. 21 and elsewhere.

58. PH, p. 16.

59. From Cather's 1902 travel journal. See part 1, "Willa Cather and France."

60. PH, p. 13.

61. PH, p. 43.

62. PH, p. 102.

63. OB, p. 4.

64e. Now considered one of Cather's finest stories by many readers, "The Old Beauty" was begrudgingly accepted by the editor of *The Woman's Home Companion,* although she did not like it too much. Cather asked to have it returned. The other two stories in the volume are also published posthumously: "The Best Years" and "Before Breakfast." I shall comment on them later here.

65. OB, pp. 3–4.

66. OB, p. 3.

67. This was the year "or thereabouts in which the world broke in two" for Cather.

68. OB, p. 42.
69. OB, p. 33.
70. OB, p. 37.

71e. Ominous sea-images also occur in an early story, "On the Gull's Road: The Ambassador's Story" (1908), and the novels *Alexander's Bridge* and *Lucy Gayheart.* In such fictions, the sea and deep waters are pictographs of the dissonant search for the "lost language." They stand in sharp contrast to what Slote perceptively calls the "pull of the land" in the canon. KA, p. 107.

72. OB, p. 23.
73. OB, pp. 52–53.
74. OB, p. 54.
75. OB, p. 55.
76. OB, p. 49.
77. OB, p. 56.
78. Robinson, *Willa,* p. 48.
79. NF, pp. 93–94.
80. OB, pp. 65–66, 70.
81. OB, p. 64.
82. SSG, pp. 22–23. My emphasis.
83. SSG, p. 108.
84. SSG, p. 18.
85. SSG, p. 66.
86. SSG, pp. 191–92.
87. SSG, pp. 191–92.
88. SSG, pp. 192–93.
89. SSG, pp. 93–94.

90e. SSG, p. 132. The "masterful" good looks of father and daughter echo the beauty of the women of Arles celebrated by the Cather of the 1902 travel journal. See above, p. 11.

91. SSG, p. 131.
92. SSG, p. 139.
93. SSG, p. 140.
94. SSG, p. 144.
95. SSG, p. 142.

96e. This "mutilation" might be added to those noted widely in Cather by Blanche H. Gelfant, "The Forgotten Reaping Hook: Sex in *My Antonia,"American Literature* 43 (March 1971): 60–82. I shall comment more fully on Gelfant's thesis later.

97. SSG, p. 168.
98. SSG, p. 124.
99. SSG, p. 123.
100. See above, p. 20.
101. SSG, p. 71.
102. SSG, p. 137.
103. SSG, p. 137.

104. SSG, p. 137. Cather's emphasis.
105e. See above, p. 55.
106. SSG, p. 178. Cather's emphasis.
107. SSG, p. 178.
108. SSG, p. 179.
109. SSG, pp. 179–82.
110. MA, p. 224.
111. SSG, p. 228.
112e. SSG, p. 226. Henry here shows himself to be one of those Americans for whom, as I noted earlier, the French are a little too taken with the erotic. See above, p. 20.
113. SSG, p. 229.
114. SSG, p. 67.
115. SSG, p. 115.
116. SSG, p. 115.
117. SSG, p. 126.
118. SSG, p. 227.
119. SSG, p. 229.
120. SSG, p. 238–39.
121. SSG, p. 229.
122. SSG, p. 245. Cather's emphasis.
123. SSG, p. 248.
124. SSG, p. 254.
125. SSG, p. 259.
126. Gustave Flaubert, *Madame Bovary: moeurs de province,* p. 297. My translation.
127. SSG, p. 262.
128. SSG, pp. 263–64. My emphasis.
129. SSG, p. 264.
130. *Madame Bovary: moeurs de province,* p. 179. My transation.
131. SSG, p. 279.
132. SSG, p. 3.
133e. See my discussion in part 3 of this aspect of *Shadows on the Rock,* for example.
134. SSG, p. 285.
135. SSG, p. 284.
136e. See above, p. 31.
137. SSG, p. 5.
138. SSG, p. 291.
139. SSG, p. 290.
140. Nicole Ward Jouve, *Un Homme nommé Zapolski,* p. 387. My translation.
141. SSG, pp. 293–95.
142e. Sharon O'Brien sees the final days of Sapphira in less dissonant terms, stressing in particular what she sees as the restored, mutually nurturing relationship between mother and daughter in the final pages of the novel. I shall comment on the relationship between Sapphira and Rachel in a more extended consideration of O'Brien's views on sexuality in Cather later here.

RESOUNDINGS

1. OB, pp. 75–77.
2. OB, p. 99.
3. OB, pp. 136.
4. OB, pp. 137–38.
5. OB, p. 138.
6. *Collins Dictionary of the English Language.*
7. OB, p. 148.
8. OB, pp. 161–66.

9e. Thus, E. K. Brown sees the story as "a kind of *De senuctute* in fictional form, an admission that 'Plucky youth is more bracing than enduring age,' but at the same time an assertion that however old one may be, life doesn't really change: if old age brings its trials and life has its difficulties, the process of living is still a challenge and a delight." Brown and Edel, *Willa Cather: A Critical Biography,* p. 246. Woodress begins his commentary on the story by stressing its bleakness, but the young woman's appearance at the end leads him to conclude " 'life will go on.' That girl on the beach, like the first creatures that crawled out of the primeval seas, will endure. Willa Cather would have applauded William Faulkner's Nobel Prize speech in 1950, in which he said that not only would man endure but that he would prevail. Grenfell also thinks as he walks back to his cabin: 'Plucky youth is more embracing than enduring age.' " Woodress, *Willa Cather: Her Life and Art,* p. 268.

10e. In the parentheses here I return to the categories of Edith Lewis with which I began this book. See part 1, "Cather and Language."

11e. "The fact remains that Balzac, like Dickens and Scott, has a strong appeal for the great multitudes of humanity who have no feeling for any form of art, and who read him only in poor translations. This is overwhelming evidence of the vital force in him, which no rough handling can diminish. Also it implies the lack in him of certain qualities which matter to only a few people, but matter very much. The time in one's life when one first began to sense the things that Flaubert stood for, to admire (almost against one's will) that peculiar integrity of language and vision, that coldness which, in him, is somehow noble—that is a pleasant chapter of one's life to remember, and Madame Franklin-Grout had brought it back within arm's length of me that night." Cather, "A Chance Meeting," NF, p. 25.

12. Kates, "Willa Cather's Unfinished Avignon Story," *Five Stories,* p. 210.
13. DCA, p. 314.
14. Gelfant, "The Forgotten Reaping Hook," p. 81.
15. Ibid.

16e. In addition to the many such figures I have cited, I would recall here the singers Clement Sebastian and his student, the heroine of *Lucy Gayheart:* both die violently by drowning. As in *Alexander's Bridge* watery depths are paradoxical signifiers of the "on high" which each character's illicit surrender to the erotic merits: Lucy for her adulterous relationship to Clement, and he for that relationship but also for his ill-concealed homosexual pull towards his accompanist, James Mockford.

17e. Unlike the heroine of Edith Wharton's *The Age of Innocence* (1923), Cather's "lost lady" rather enjoys the retreat from America in which she ends. Wharton's Countess seems entrapped in her Parisian apartment as the novel ends, while Maidy drives around her South American city in the "fine French car" her new husband has given her. LL, p. 176.

18e. Because he does not understand this "innocence," Niel cuts the wires during Maidy's frantic phone conversation with the unfaithful Ellinger. In doing so, Niel is short-circuiting his own erotic impulses toward the "lost lady" and cutting himself off from the "lost language" of desire Maidy and Frank speak on this and other occasions. For an incisive consideration of Niel Herbert's complex relation to Maidy see Kathleen Nichols, "The Celibate Male in *A Lost Lady:* The Unreliable Center of Consciousness" in *Critical Essays on Willa Cather*, ed. John J. Murphy, pp. 186–97.

19. Jacques Derrida, "ME—Psychoanalysis: An Introduction to the Translation of 'The Shell and the Kernel' by Nicholas Abraham," reprinted in *Diacritics* 9 (March 1979), 6.

20. Ibid., p. 10.

21. See Bibliography.

22. O'Brien, "Mothers, Daughters, and the 'Art Necessity': Willa Cather and the Creative Process," *American Novelists Reconsidered: Essays in Feminist Criticism*, pp. 294, 295.

23. See, for example, Sharon O'Brien, "'The Thing Not Named': Willa Cather as Lesbian Writer," *Signs* 9 (Summer 1984): 576–99.

24. Sharon O'Brien, "The Unity of Willa Cather's Two-Part Pastoral: Passion in *O Pioneers!,*" *Studies in American Fiction* 6 (Autumn 1978): 158.

25. Woodress, *Willa Cather: Her Life and Art,* p. 86.

26. O'Brien, "The Unity of Willa Cather's Two-Part Pastoral," p. 168.

27e. Susan Gubar, "Blessings in Disguise: Cross-Dressing as Re-dressing in Female Modernists," *The Massachusetts Review* 22 (Autumn 1981): 477–507. Gubar's article is a wide-ranging survey of transvestism and other "tomboyish" behaviors by women in modern art and literature. Of Cather she writes that the novelist "seems far more aware that male dress could alienate her from conventionally female roles and activities. Indeed, this complex realization that she dramatized through her clothing in her youth was profound enough to inform not only the themes but even the structure of her mature fiction" (p. 485). Gubar does not detail this "informing" process in this article.

28. O'Brien, "'The Thing Not Named,'" pp. 588–89.

29. Ibid., p. 596.

30. Italo Calvino, "Readers, Writers, and Literary Machines," *New York Times Book Review,* September 7, 1986, p. 1.

31. O'Brien, "'The Thing Not Named,'" p. 596.

32. OP, p. 206.

33. OD, p. 224.

34. See above, p. 102.

35. OD, p. 228.

36. OD, p. 205.
37. OD, p. 195.
38. OD, p. 223.
39. OD, p. 229.
40. OD, p. 226.
41. PH, p. 187.
42. PH, p. 243.
43. OD, p. 194.
44. SL, p. 220.
45. John H. Randall, *The Landscape and the Looking Glass: Willa Cather's Search for Value,* p. 371.
46. Régis Debray, *Le Scribe: genèse du politique,* p. 42. My translation.
47. Ibid., p. 33. My translation.
48. Ibid., p. 23. My translation.
49. Gelfant, "The Forgotten Reaping Hook," p. 64.
50. LL, p. 106.
51. OD, pp. 158–59.
52. OD, p. 190.
53. Cited in Kates, "Willa Cather's Unfinished Avignon Story," *Five Stories,* p. 177.

Bibliography

WORKS OF WILLA CATHER

Alexander's Bridge. Introduction by Bernice Slote. Lincoln and London: University of Nebraska Press, 1977.

Death Comes for the Archbishop. Drawings and designs of Harold Von Schmidt. New York: Alfred A. Knopf, 1940.

Five Stories with an Article by George N. Kates on Miss Cather's Last, Unfinished and Unpublished Avignon Story. New York: Vintage Books, 1956.

The Kingdom of Art: Willa Cather's First Principles and Critical Statements, 1893–1896. Selected and edited with two essays and a commentary by Bernice Slote. Lincoln: University of Nebraska Press, 1966.

A Lost Lady. Introduction by A. S. Byatt. London: Virago, 1980.

Lucy Gayheart. New York: Vintage Books, 1962.

My Antonia. Preface by A. S. Byatt. London: Virago, 1980.

My Mortal Enemy. Introduction by Marcus Klein. New York: Vintage Books, 1954.

Not Under Forty. New York: Alfred A. Knopf, 1936.

Obscure Destinies. New York: Vintage Books, 1974.

The Old Beauty and Others. New York: Vintage Books, 1976.

One of Ours. New York: Alfred A. Knopf, 1922.

O Pioneers! Sentry Paperbound ed. Boston: Houghton Mifflin Company, n.d.

The Professor's House. New Introduction by A. S. Byatt. London: Virago, 1982.

Sapphira and the Slave Girl. New York: Alfred A. Knopf, 1940.

Shadows on the Rock. New York: Alfred A. Knopf, 1946.

The Song of the Lark. 1915. Reprint. Lincoln and London: University of Nebraska Press, 1978.

"Uncle Valentine" and Other Stories: Willa Cather's Uncollected Short Fiction 1915–1929. Edited with an introduction by Bernice Slote. Lincoln: University of Nebraska Press, 1973.

Willa Cather's Collected Short Fiction 1892–1912. Rev. ed. Edited by Virginia Faulkner. Introduction by Mildred R. Bennett. Lincoln and London: University of Nebraska Press, 1970.

The World and the Parish: Willa Cather's Articles and Reviews, 1893–1902, I and II. Selected and edited with a commentary by William M. Curtin. Lincoln: University of Nebraska Press, 1970.

Youth and the Bright Medusa. New York: Vintage Books, 1975.

OTHER WORKS CONSULTED

Bailey, Jennifer. "The Dangers of Femininity in Willa Cather's Fiction," *Journal of American Studies* 16 (December 1982): 392–406.

Bennett, Mildred R. *The World of Willa Cather.* New Edition with Notes and Index. Lincoln/London: University of Nebraska Press, 1961.

Brown, E. K., and Leon Edel. *Willa Cather: A Critical Biography.* Completed by Leon Edel. New York: Avon Books, 1980.

Calvino, Italo. "Readers, Writers, and Literary Machines," *New York Times Book Review,* Sept. 7, 1986, pp. 1, 30–31.

Collins Dictionary of the English Language. Reprinted and updated. London and Glasgow: Collins, 1982.

Comeau, Paul. "*The Professor's House* and Anatole France." In *Critical Essays on Willa Cather,* ed. John J. Murphy, 217–27. Boston: G. K. Hall & Co., 1984.

Debray, Régis. *Le Scribe: genèse du politique.* Paris: Bernard Grasset, 1980.

Derrida, Jacques. *La Vérité en peinture.* Paris: Flammarion, 1978.

——. "ME—Psychoanalysis: An Introduction to the Translation of 'The Shell and the Kernel' by Nicholas Abraham." *Diacritics* 9 (March 1979): 4–12.

——. *Spurs: Nietzsche's Styles/Eperons: Les Styles de Nietzsche.* Introduction by Stefano Agosti. English Translation by Barbara Harlow. Drawings by François Loubrieu. Chicago and London: The University of Chicago Press, 1978.

Dickens, Charles. *Hard Times for These Times.* Edited with an introduction by David Craig. Harmondsworth: Penguin Books, 1969.

Doane, Margaret. "In Defense of Lillian St. Peter: Men's Perceptions of Women in *The Professor's House.*" *Western American Literature* 17 (Winter 1984): 299–302.

Flaubert, Gustave. *Madame Bovary: moeurs de province.* Edition de Ed. Maynal: Editions Garnier Frères, 1961.

——. *Trois Contes: Un Coeur simple, La Légende de Saint Julien L'Hospitalier, Hérodias.* Chronologie et préface par Jacques Suffel. Paris: Garnier-Flammarion, 1965.

Freud, Sigmund. *The Complete Psychological Works of Sigmund Freud.* Vol. 7, *Three Essays on Sexuality.* Translated and edited by James Strachey in collaboration with Anna Freud *et al.* London: The Hogarth Press and the Institute of Psychoanalysis, 1953–1974.

Gelfant, Blanche H. "The Forgotten Reaping Hook: Sex in *My Antonia.*" *American Literature* 43(March 1971): 60–82.

Gervaud, Michel. "Un Regard autre." (Originally published as "Les Américains et les autres.") In *Actes du GRENA* (Groupe de Recherches et d'Etudes Nord-américaines). Aix-en-Provence: Publications de l'Université de Provence, 1982. 65–81.

Girard, René. *Violence and the Sacred.* 1972. Reprint. Translated by Patrick Gregory. Baltimore: The Johns Hopkins University Press, 1977.

Gubar, Susan. "Blessings in Disguise: Cross-Dressing as Re-dressing in Female Modernists." *The Massachusetts Review* 22 (Autumn 1981): 477–507.

Irwin, John T. *American Hieroglyphics: The Image of the Egyptian Hieroglyphs in the American Renaissance.* New Haven: Yale University Press, 1980.

Jacquard, Albert. *Eloge de la différence: la génétique et les hommes.* Paris: Editions de Seuil, 1978.

Jouve, Nicole Ward. *Un Homme nommé Zapolski.* Paris: Des Femmes, 1983.

Lacan, Jacques. *Feminine Sexuality: Jacques Lacan and the "Ecole Freudienne."* Ed. Juliet Mitchell and Jacqueline Rose. Translated by Jacqueline Rose. London and Basingstoke: The MacMillan Press Ltd., 1982.

Melville, Herman. *Billy Budd, Sailor: An Inside Narrative.* Ed. Milton R. Stern. Indianapolis: The Bobbs-Merrill Company, Inc., 1975.

Murphy, John J. "Willa Cather: The Widening Gyre." In *Five Essays on Willa Cather: The Merrimack Symposium.* Edited with a Preface by John J. Murphy, 51–74. North Andover, Mass.: Merrimack College, 1974.

Nelson, Robert J. "French Classicism: The Crisis of the Baroque." *L'Esprit Créateur* 11(1971): 269–86.

———. "Molière and Racine: The Bipolarity of French Classicism." *Essays in French Literature* No. 8 (1971): 11–28.

———. *Pascal: Adversary and Advocate.* Cambridge: Harvard University Press, 1981.

———. "Seeing *Through* Words, *Seeing* Through Words, *Seeing Words Through, Seeing Words (as Through)*." Essay-Review of Irwin. *The Georgia Review* 35 (1982): 133–47.

Nichols, Kathleen. "The Celibate Male in *A Lost Lady:* The Unreliable Center of Consciousness." In *Critical Essays on Willa Cather.* Ed. John J. Murphy, 186–97. Boston: G. K. Hall & Co., 1984.

O'Brien, Sharon. "The Unity of Willa Cather's Two-Part Pastoral: Passion in *O Pioneers!*" *Studies in American Fiction* 6(Autumn 1978): 157–72.

———. "Mothers, Daughters, and the 'Art Necessity': Willa Cather and the Creative Process." In *American Novelists Revisited: Essays in Feminist Criticism.* Ed. Fritz Fleischmann, 265–98. Boston: G. K. Hall & Co., 1982.

———. "'The Thing Not Named': Willa Cather as Lesbian Writer." *Signs* 9 (Summer 1984): 576–99.

Pascal, Blaise. *Pensées—Nouvelle Edition établie pour la première fois d'après la copie de référence de Gilberte Pascal.* Ed. Philippe Sellier. Paris: Mercure de France, 1976.

Poirier, Richard. *A World Elsewhere: The Place of Style in American Literature.* New York: Oxford University Press, 1966.

Randall, John H., III. *The Landscape and the Looking Glass: Willa Cather's Search for Value.* Boston: Houghton & Mifflin Company, 1960.

Robinson, Phyllis C. *Willa: The Life of Willa Cather.* New York: Holt, Rinehart, and Winston, 1983.

Rosowski, Susan J. "Willa Cather's Women." *Studies in American Fiction* 9 (Autumn 1981): 261–75.

———. "The Pattern of Willa Cather's Novels." *Western American Literature* 15(Winter 1981): 243–63.

Todorov, Tzvetan. *La Conquête de l'Amérique: la question de l'autre.* Paris: Editions de Seuil, 1982.

Wild, Barbara. "'The Thing Not Named' in *The Professor's House.*" *Western American Literature* 12 (Winter 1978): 263–74.

Woodress, James. *Willa Cather: Her Life and Art.* Lincoln: University of Nebraska Press, 1975.

Index

A Note on the Author

Robert J. Nelson is a graduate (1949) of Columbia College at Columbia University where he also received his M.A. (1950) and Ph.D. (1955). He has written a number of books and articles on French and comparative literature. His *Play Within a Play: The Dramatist's Conception of His Art, Shakespeare to Anouilh* (Yale, 1958) was published while he held a Morse Fellowship from Yale for research on his *Corneille: His Heroes and Their Worlds* (Pennsylvania, 1963). His *Immanence and Transcendence: The Theater of Jean Rotrou* (Ohio State, 1969) emerged from research during his year as a Guggenheim Fellow (1965) and his *Pascal: Adversary and Advocate* (Harvard, 1981) from research during his appointment as an Associate at the Center for Advanced Studies at the University of Illinois (1975). He has taught at Columbia, Yale, the University of Michigan at Ann Arbor, the University of Pennsylvania and as visiting professor at New York University, Stanford, and the University of Reading (England). He is presently professor of French at the University of Illinois at Urbana-Champaign, where he has also served as professor of Comparative Literature. He resides in Urbana during the academic year and in the Village de Joucas (Vaucluse) in summer.